THE LADDER OF HIGH DESIGNS

Structure and Interpretation of
the French Lyric Sequence

THE LADDER OF HIGH DESIGNS

Structure and Interpretation of the French Lyric Sequence

Edited by Doranne Fenoaltea
and David Lee Rubin

University Press of Virginia
Charlottesville and London

THE UNIVERSITY PRESS OF VIRGINIA

First published 1991

Library of Congress Cataloging-in-Publication Data

The Ladder of high designs : structure and interpretation of the French lyric sequence / edited by Doranne Fenoaltea and David Lee Rubin.

p. cm.

Includes bibliographical references and index.

ISBN 0-8139-1271-7 (cloth)

1. French poetry—History and criticism. 2. Lyric poetry—History and criticism. 3. Sequels (Literature) 4. Poetry—Editing. 5. Intertextuality. 6. Literary form. I. Fenoaltea, Doranne. II. Rubin, David Lee.

PQ405.L33 1991

841'.0409—dc20 90-48039

CIP

Printed in the United States of America

Contents

Doranne Fenoaltea

Preface

A book of poems is both a unity and a multiplicity. It is at once an entity, a body of work brought together, and a collection composed most typically of a number of individual poems, not necessarily—and even not usually—written with a view to the book, at least in the form in which it finally appears. The composition of a book of poems follows the composition of the individual poems, which have their own origin and meaning. At the same time, the grouping of poems with other poems is not insignificant; the form and content of the collection affects, to some degree, the resonances of the individual poems. The book is a work in its own right, and as such, it too has significance for the reader. It is the complex and subtle interplay between poems and collection that has engaged the attention of the writers of the essays included in this volume. The questions they address—How does the perception of the individual lyric relate to the perception of the collection? And how does the form of the collection affect the resonances of the poems that compose it?—are a means to understanding how choice, arrangement, and form come to be part of a poet's or a work's design. The issues involved are important and extraordinarily complex, involving as they do considerations of intratextualities and reading practice, but they have received remarkably little critical attention. When discussed at all, the disposition of collections has been considered largely in the broad terms of genre, theme, and narrative or developmental logic or chronology, while the potential significance of principles of arrangement and the effect of context and arrangement on meaning and interpretation have often gone, if not unrecognized, then at least largely unexamined.

The interpretation of individual poetic texts as part of an ordered body of work, the value to be accorded to context, and the implications or significance of arrangement are nonetheless of fundamental theoretical and methodological importance. Critical presuppositions concerning the nature and function of poetic collections are far from neutral, for they affect in a variety of ways the perception of the work and of the poems. The issues are delicate, because they raise—inter alia—questions of primacy (of critical focus, although not necessarily of importance), of polysemy (to what extent a poem can legitimately be interpreted differently as an independent utterance and as part of the collection), and of intentionality. Attention to the relation between texts and contexts strongly suggests that poems often exist in an uneasy and somewhat ambiguous relation to the collection, and that the tension between the autonomy of the poem and the collection in which it participates can profoundly affect the individual lyric.

From the poet's point of view, questions of inclusion, exclusion, and arrangement are essential to the process of composing a work, and a large number of issues, both artistic and practical, may affect the ultimate form. For the reader, questions arise concerning the source of perceived patterns and the importance to be accorded them for interpretation. It is precisely here that interesting critical problems surface—e.g., defining the equilibrium between the poems and the collection, the nature of the poem's participation in the work and the degree of meaning dependent on that participation, as well as the balance to be struck between (often implicit) poetic intention and readers' perceptions.

Factors affecting the arrangement of poetic works are of many sorts, and there are potentially as many patterns or arrangements as there are collections of poems. Arrangement may be simple or complex, obvious or hidden, it may be (consciously) intended or not, systematic or disrupted in various ways. Different organizing principles may be at work in a single collection. Personal, traditional, generic, ideological, and historical considerations and even "extraneous" factors such as deadlines, size constraints, and publishers' demands inevitably affect to varying degrees the ultimate result. The relation between parts and whole, the kinds of form perceived as available to the poet and those retrievable by (and meaningful to) the reader, are, in part, historically and culturally determined. While we know that poems are bound to some degree by such conventions, we recognize less clearly that collections may be as well.

Precisely because of the complexity of these issues, methodological considerations must be kept clearly in mind in approaching them. For instance, the source of the collection, as established, is significant: poet, editor, and anthologist all compile in valid and significant ways, but their aims, and thus the implications of the constituted work, will vary. Furthermore, critics may seek to elucidate the poet's intention or they may take a reader-centered approach, but their posture will affect the questions asked and the implications of the answers. It may be possible, and indeed desirable, as has been recently suggested,[1] to formulate a poetics of collections, but the question is a vast one, and it will require careful distinctions and clear methodology.

Petrarch, whose Italian love poetry is fundamental to modern Western poetry, was well aware of the basic problem of achieving *concordia discors* by forging unity out of multiplicity, by suggesting the order underlying varied elements, and by seeking the harmony of independent utterances, even where each continues to maintain, even insist on, its autonomy. Thus, he called his *canzoniere* (song book) of love poems *rime sparse,* and he returned again and again to the question of the ordering of the lyrics. The poets of ancient Rome grouped poems by genre and also structured their collections symmetrically, using techniques of ring composition. Japanese haiku collections, compiled by anthologizers, make use of highly codified schemes of patterning, not readily discernible to the uninformed reader.[2]

The essays in this volume are devoted to studies of French poetic collections organized by poets, rather than by editors or compilers.[3] As their general focus, the authors aim to show how aspects of arrangement in a book of poems give rise to significance at the level of the work. The works discussed are in themselves varied and reveal a variety of types of arrangement, and the analyses, taking different approaches, are related by a concern with the means by which a body of discrete and sometimes heterogeneous poems coalesces into a whole, a work that incorporates and transcends the notion of collection to generate meaning. They suggest ways in which the interplay between the separate utterances, which are the poems, and the notion of the whole, which is the work, creates productive tensions. They explore how poets resolve the problem of creating a work from a varied poetic production without subordinating the essence of their production, the lyric utterance, to the arrangement that they adopt.

Because the essays included here deal with a variety of works from the Middle Ages to the present, historical concepts of order and coherence emerge as essential elements of changing form: poetic collections appear to respond both to earlier forms and to a current sense of order or disorder, continuity or discontinuity. That this should be so is hardly surprising; what is more so, is the apparent lack of interest, in criticism, on the effects of such decisions, be they conscious or not, on the constituted works and on the sense that we make of them. We find, for example, that the strategies employed to relate the poems often reflect the poet's response to other works in ways not unlike the better-recognized forms of intertextualities. Solutions that earlier poets appear to have found when forming a lyric collection thus furnish a basis for later poets' attempts to do the same. The conclusions reached in these essays also appear to suggest that preceding solutions not only serve as models but also furnish a basis on which later poets build. Whether they follow similar lines or strike out in new, but not entirely unrelated, directions, intertextualities appear to play a significant role in the choices adopted for the arrangement of the work, as they do in the elaboration of individual poems. It may be that crises and rebellions manifest themselves at the level of the collection as well as at the level of expression.

These essays further suggest that the concept of the collection is affected by broader historical and cultural issues, such as the concept of identity and the related notion of the authority of the individual voice, the sense of the moral implications of poetic form, even the view of the structure of the world. Thus, as views of the shape of the universe and the laws that govern it have evolved, so has the concept of form, and as Aristotelian theories of coherence have been supplanted, the ways in which coherence is achieved or negated has been reexamined. The organizing devices examined in these essays often suggest, indirectly but in extremely probing ways, an implicitly self-reflexive attitude to the issue of the poet's role as a lyric voice. This is form in the most fundamental sense, and these essays show poets sensitive in various ways to the implications of their work as it seeks to express a vision that reflects but transcends that of the individual speaker who is its source and is in harmony with its circumstances, broadly conceived.

Kevin Brownlee's essay on Machaut's *Remede de Fortune* and Sylvia Huot's on Villon's *Testament* are both concerned with the lyric anthology incorporated in a narrative work. The variety of the lyric elements of the work disrupt the narrative, while the narrative furnishes the means of integrating the exemplary expressions of the fixed forms. Brownlee shows how the text works toward affirmation of the poet's role as the authoritative voice that integrates experience and song, at a period in which the notion of individual consciousness was still problematic. Similarly, Huot addresses the question of the functional role and status of the nineteen rondeaux and ballades incorporated into the *Testament*. Where Machaut's work appears to have constituted poetic identity, Villon's explores the complex question of its variants and dissolution, revealed through the arrangement of the lyrics themselves and the terms of their incorporation in the narrative.

In discussing Marot's "Certaines oeuvres qu'il feit en la prison," published as a group in 1534 and later dispersed in the *Oeuvres* of 1538, George Joseph shows the poet playing arrangement against narrative expectations. Where the earlier works of Machaut and Villon grounded the lyrics in the (narrative) voice of the protagonist, Marot's poems work against the implied narrative grounding, and indeed, as Joseph shows, deny the possibility of plotting a certain historical or quasi-historical context for the poems, while continuing to allow for an interpretation of the poet's situation. The dispersal of the poems in the *Oeuvres* of 1538 destroys all pretense of chronology, giving rise to a generic and non-narrative disposition in which the oeuvre effectively supplants the experience.

In his first published work, the 1550 *Odes*, Ronsard turned less to his immediate predecessors than to the ancients, choosing to form books of poems devoted to a specific genre, the ode, cultivated by Pindar and Horace, but also assured of the primacy of the poetic voice (which Marot had attained) and the possibility of denying narrative logic. Unlike the works previously considered, the *Odes* as a group do not depend on narrative; in place of that device, Doranne Fenoaltea suggests, the poet adopts an ancient and Renaissance concept of architectonic form, with its hierarchy and principles of order, thus affirming, in a way rather different from that of his French predecessors, the poet's power over the variety of experience.

By probing in depth the metaphoric patterns of Saint-Amant's four seasonal sonnets, Catherine Ingold uncovers shared fundamental metaphoric and thematic patterns, and similar structural and developmental devices. This fundamentally rhetorical unifying structure occurs in a climate in which poetry has defined its territory, and it provides the means of going beyond the superficial relationship implied by the seasonal themes. The structure draws the poems together, grounding them in a metaphoric system and related developmental devices that not only give them coherence but also define their place in the independent world of poetic form.

In an essay that points to possibilities beyond the organization by themes or devices used by La Fontaine's predecessors, David Lee Rubin argues that in the *Fables*, the poet used the basis of poetic rhetoric to work permutations and combinations of generic elements (formal, technical, and stylistic), as well as themes, to establish, deviate from, and return to a norm that stabilizes and provides a reference point for the entire sequence.

In the more modern context first defined here by *Les Fleurs du mal*, the question of form becomes fraught with uncertainties, and difficulties arise in part from the rejection of classical notions of composition and form. But as these outmoded views are displaced, the question of form does not, as one might think, disappear. Rather, it appears to enter the process of composition and arrangement in a somewhat more dynamic way.

In considering the arrangement of Baudelaire's 1857 and 1861 versions of *Les Fleurs du mal*, John Porter Houston draws on the contemporary artistic and philosophical concept of organic form to examine how, through effects of sequence, juxtaposition, and cross-referencing, each work attains perfection of form. In neither version can the form of the work be tied to any predetermined type of formal coherence; it is a part of an ongoing and changing process, in which the form is determined by the evolving poetic consciousness from which it springs. As a result, achieving a sense of form requires great agility and openness of response on the reader's part. The reader's role becomes essential and problematic.

Sandra Daniel takes as her topic the issue of coherence in Mallarmé's *Hérodïade*, an issue on which critical thought has been sharply divided. Her argument stems from considerations of the book (and Mallarmé's preoccupation with *Le Livre*) and the reader: *Hérodïade* is presented as an experimental text in reading process, which furnishes the source of textual coherence as well as the means by which the act of reading itself recreates the book and thus generates meaning. The coherence of *Hérodïade* is thus achieved by the reader who, by gradually displacing the place of reading and the interpretation of signs, becomes free from his conditioning to read in a new and liberated way.

For Suzanne Nash, Apollinaire's *Alcools* similarly finds its coherence in process: the poet's changing view of modern art and its relation to the past—both in its artifacts and in its view of the artist and poet—gives rise to a work paradoxically centered in a process of destruction and disintegration. Thus, *Alcools* subverts the notion of the work, dissolving it even as it uses conventional poetic topoi and forms, and Nash argues that *Alcools* records the poet's efforts to detach himself from the past by sacrificing it, by giving the poems the status of *brocante* (bric-a-brac). While certain themes, the recurrence of forms and formal procedures, and the framing provided by the initial and final poems help focus the collection, it never coalesces into any static or reassuring "unity."

That the temptation of perfect aesthetic forms, the creation of an ideal world within the confines of the book, nonetheless continues to tempt the poet is demonstrated in Sarah Lawall's closing study of Bonnefoy's *Pierre écrite*. Here, the issue implicit in collections from *Les Fleurs du mal* appears to have been confronted directly, as part of the poet's ontological concerns. However, the notion of unity—central to Bonnefoy's poetic enterprise—can be located only in the problematic relation between the poetic consciousness and an ultimately deferred reality. For perfect aesthetically pleasing form, with its attendant moral implications, alluded to only to be denied, the poet substitutes a gradual unfolding of personal and cultural associations, never achieving final form.

While the poems themselves are the source of the collection and its essential worth, the frame that includes them is not without significance and value. We note, for example, that the implications of arrangement extend to philosophical and moral as well as to artistic and literary concerns. Arrangement in the premodern period appears tied to efforts to bring together and to give coherence to the disparate pieces that are to constitute the collections by relatively strong means: narrative, formal and symmetrical, generic. In the modern poets, on the other hand, a more problematic sense of coherence comes from the formulating vision, be it the poet's or the reader's, and the works reflect a sense of the changing, fluctuating world of our understanding.

This is but one conclusion, not surprising perhaps, but to date insufficiently investigated. Readers will find that the studies in this volume mark a number of tentative signposts for future travelers along this relatively unmarked path. We hope that they will find it an area worthy of further exploration, a means of seeing how harmony and greater meaning, *concordia discors*, arises from the organization of a collection of poems into a poetic work.

Notes

1. See Neil Fraistat, Introduction to *Poems in Their Place: The Intertextuality and Order of Poetic Collections*, ed. N. Fraistat (Chapel Hill: University of North Carolina Press, 1986). See also M. L. Rosenthal and Sally Gall, *The Modern Poetic Sequence* (New York: Oxford University Press, 1983).

2. Earl Miner, "Some Issues for Study of Integrated Collections," in Fraistat, ed., *Poems in Their Place*, pp. 18–43.

3. These essays focus on works in which the poet's role in arranging the poems appears uncontestable. It is necessary at the same time to realize that readers' perceptions of the implications of arrangement are precisely that: poets do not say, generally, why they adopted a specific order; neither, of course, do they generally say why their poems take the form they do nor what they "mean." It is also useful to remember that more than one principle of organization may be at work: for example, thematic, generic, sequential, developmental, and symmetrical principles can enter the disposition of a work to varying degrees.

THE LADDER OF HIGH DESIGNS

Structure and Interpretation of
the French Lyric Sequence

Kevin Brownlee

1. Guillaume de Machaut's *Remede de Fortune:* The Lyric Anthology as Narrative Progression

Guillaume de Machaut's *Remede de Fortune* (Fortune's cure) (written before 1349, possibly as early as 1342) constitutes a new stage in the development of the lyric anthology in late medieval French literature, at the same time that it provides a privileged locus for investigating Machaut's reformulation of the lyric mode. Presented simultaneously as an art of love (*ars amandi*) and an art of poetry (ars poetica), this first-person narrative poem contains a series of eight intercalated lyric pieces, one superlative example of each of the major fixed forms of the fourteenth century, arranged in order of decreasing difficulty.[1]

The present essay seeks, first, to examine the complex, dialogic relationship between lyric and narrative, song and story, that serves as one of the *Remede de Fortune*'s key structuring elements.[2] I propose to treat each of the dit's lyric set pieces in sequence—the seven with musical accompaniment as well as the single nonmusical example—in order to examine how and to what effect they are marked, within the body of the narrative verse, as a different kind of poetic discourse: as lyric, as song. At the same time, the way in which these intercalated lyrics may be said to function narratively will be investigated in some detail.[3] I will thus be particularly concerned with the frame that serves simultaneously to differentiate the intercalated lyric from and to integrate it into its narrative context. In each case a double framing—both onomastic and temporal—is at issue: on the one hand, the individual lyric set piece is introduced and followed by a specific generic designation; on the other, it is carefully set into the ongoing narrative temporality as a discrete event, i.e., as a performance.

Second, a consideration of the *Remede de Fortune*'s programmatic thematization of the process of lyric composition will reveal what is posited as a new conception of the relationship between love experience, inspiration, and song. Indeed, an expanded lyric configuration is seen to emerge in which a radical distinction is established between various components of a formerly unified lyric ego. For in the course of the dit the first-person voice of the narrator-protagonist is increasingly differentiated from that of what I shall call Machaut-*poète,*[4] author of the *Remede de Fortune* as a whole and of the œuvre in which the *Remede de Fortune* participates. The relationship of the first-person Machaut-*poète* (in dramatic contradistinction to the first-person Machaut-narrator-protagonist) to his lyric subject matter adumbrates—for the first time, I believe, in French literature—that of the "modern" author to his "book."[5]

Throughout the *Remede de Fortune* the narrator-protagonist is the devoted lover of a lady, and he recounts the development of his love in what constitutes the story line of the dit.[6] The first stage of this love experience involves a period in which the narrator serves his lady long and well, but secretly, since her presence always causes him to lose countenance. The narrator's courtly love service seems to be synonymous with poetic activity, for an important, indeed crucial, aspect of the narrator's identity as lover is his self-presentation as love poet. This self-presentation involves what might be called a standard lyric configuration: love experience at once generates and authenticates song, which, reciprocally, guarantees the validity of the love experience as such. "Inspiration" simply identifies the unidirectional transformation of love experience into lyric poetry:

> Et pour ce que n'estoie mie
> Tousdis en un point, m'estudie
> Mis en faire chansons et lays,
> Baladez, rondeaus, virelays,
> Et chans, selonc mon sentement,
> Amoureus et non autrement;
> Car qui de sentement ne fait,
> Son oeuvre et son chant contrefait. . . .
> Et mes cuers moult s'i deduisoit
> Quant ma dame a ce me duisoit
> Qu'a sa löeange et a s'onnour
> Me faisoit chanter pour s'amour.
> (ll. 401–8, 419–22)[7]

> And since I was not always in one mood, I learned to compose *chansons* and *lays, balades, rondeaux, virelays,* and songs, according to my feelings, about love and nothing else; because he who does not compose according to his feelings falsifies his work and his song. . . . And my heart took great pleasure when my lady led me to sing a song in her praise and honor, for love of her.

The extensive use of generic terminology here is the first indication of the special status of lyric song in the *Remede de Fortune*. At the same time it is an important preparatory signal with regard to the organization of the dit as a whole: all of the lyric forms mentioned here will in fact be incorporated into, imbedded in, the narrative verse of the *Remede de Fortune*. It is worth noting, however, that the order in which they are listed here does not correspond to the order in which they will appear in the unfolding of the dit.

The first appearance of a specific lyric poem occurs almost immediately after the narrator's general self-presentation as lyric poet, as he introduces the *lay* "Qui n'aroit autre deport" (ll. 431–680) (He who has no other pleasure), whose thematic content serves to epitomize his amorous condition at the time of writing: Although the lover-protagonist considers the state of loving (and writing love poetry) to be its own reward, he still wants his lady to know of his love, but fears a possible refusal so much that he does not dare to declare his feelings to her.

It is significant that the term *lay* carefully frames the intercalated poem: "Fis je ce dit qu'on claimme *lay*" (l. 430) ("I composed this piece that is called a *lay*"); "Einssi me fist ma dame faire / Ce *lay* qu'oÿ m'avez retraire" (ll. 681–82) ("Thus my lady inspired me to compose this *lay* you've heard me recite")—emphasis added. On the one hand, the *Remede*'s first lyric set piece is thus identified by explicit references to its generic identity, which differentiates it discursively from the surrounding narrative verse. On the other hand, the tense structure of this frame suggests a conflation of two temporalities: the time in which the *lay* was composed and the time in which it was performed. What results is the privileging of the intercalated lyric as a narrative event—i.e., as a diegetic performance[8]—while at the same time Machaut-*poète* signals his awareness of its status as an independent discursive entity, perceived as such by the *vous* (l. 682) designating the extradiegetic audience.

On another level, the striking technical excellence of the *lay*,[9] the most demanding of the fourteenth-century fixed forms, may be seen as an indication of the presence of Machaut the *poète* in the very text of the dit. The sense of this presence is intensified when the *lay* is considered in light of the didactic Prologue and the sequence in which Amours and the lady are presented as teachers: a lyric poem has been, as it were, generated from doctrine through the artistry of the *poète*.

Finally, on the level of the plot, this lyric poem functions to advance the narrative in which it is embedded. The lady discovers the *lay*, has the poet-narrator read it to her, then asks him the name of the author. It is noteworthy that the verb *lire* is repeatedly used to *describe* (indirectly) this presentation of the *lay* by the protagonist to his lady:

> . . . en sa presence cilz lays vint . . .
> Qu'elle me commanda au *lire*.

> Si ne li osay escondire,
> Ains li *lui* tout de chief en chief.
> (ll. 690, 693–95; emphasis added)
>
> [this *lay* came into her presence . . . and she ordered me to *read* it. I dared not refuse her, but rather *read* it from beginning to end].

The net effect is to distance the inscribed performance (in the presence of the diegetic lady) from the enunciating subject. Ironically, this suggested separation of the *je* of the performer from the *je* of the lover-protagonist is false within the context of the plot.[10]

Unable either to admit that he wrote it (since this would involve confessing his love) or to lie to his lady, the narrator is overcome with fear and embarrassment and cannot speak a word. Without taking leave he flees her presence (l. 752), sighing and weeping. Melancholy and lost in thought, the narrator wanders aimlessly until he arrives at a *plaisance,* the Park of Hesdin,[11] in which the largest single narrative segment (ll. 802–3043) of the *Remede de Fortune* takes place.

The second intercalated song follows an initial, gloomy assessment of the development of his love affair by the narrator. It is introduced by an explicit and highly stylized account of the process of transformation of "experience" into lyric poetry:

> Et en ce penser ou j'estoie
> Je m'avisai que je feroie
> De Fortune et de mes doulours,
> De mes pensers et de mes plours,
> .I. dit qu'on appelle complainte,
> Ou il averoit rime mainte,
> Qui seroit de tristre matiere.
> Si commenchay en tel maniere.
> (ll. 897–904)
>
> And while I was in this mood, I decided to compose about Fortune and my sorrows, my thoughts and my griefs, a piece called a *complainte,* in which there would be many rhymes and a sad subject. So I began in this manner.

Poetic activity is thus thematized in a way that highlights (as had the introduction to the *lay,* discussed above) the specifically lyric framework of the poetry in question—it is presented, within the context of the story line, as generated by the narrator-protagonist's personal love experience. Yet the evident artificiality of this process serves to reduce the first-person narrator-protagonist to the status of a literary device. By implication, the intercalated lyric *complainte* derives from the "experience," not of the narrator, but of the *poète*. And, as we shall see, this "experience" is to a very large and very visible degree a literary one. At the same time, the diegetic temporality of the *complainte*—its status as narrative event—involves conflating the time of composition with the time of performance. Within the plot line of the *Remede* a visibly fictitious simultaneity thus obtains that is operative for all eight of the dit's intercalated lyrics.

The *complainte* itself, "Tieus rit au main qui au soir pleure" (ll. 905–1480) (He laughs in the morning who weeps in the evening), is by far the longest of the *Remede de Fortune*'s songs and may be divided along thematic lines into two sections. The first (ll. 905–1208) deals with Fortune and opens with a long discourse on the nature of Fortune in general (ll. 905–1192), presented in a clerkly didactic tone. The arbitrariness and inconstancy of Fortune are described in detail, by means of standard medieval thematic and imagerial topoi, and Boethius is cited explicitly as auctor (l. 982). Next the image of the statue from Nebuchadnezzar's dream (Daniel 2:31–35) is presented as an emblem of Fortune (ll. 1001–96), further strengthening the clerkly character of the diction. Significantly, this passage involves an "interpretation" of the dream that is quite different from that found in Daniel[12] and thus constitutes, in effect, a reworking of biblical material by Machaut for his own poetic purposes. The way in which this literary process (the explicit transformation of a biblical subtext) is made to call attention to itself as such highlights the presence of the *poète* behind the *complainte* and the dit of which it is part. Further traces of the presence of the *poète* figure abound in the very verbal organization of the *complainte*. As the emotional tone becomes more intense, so does the rhetorical patterning of the language used to characterize Fortune. Extensive use is made first of anaphora and oxymoron (ll. 1129–52), then of antithesis and paradox (ll. 1161–76) in a series of topoi, which culminates in that of "the omnipotence of Fortune," which is brought to a close by means of chess imagery reminiscent of Jean de Meun and Rutebeuf:

> Mais partout ou elle [Fortune] s'embat,
> De ses gieus tellement s'esbat
> Qu'en vainquant dit: "Eschech et mat!"
> De fiere vois.
>
> (ll. 1189–92)

> But everywhere [Fortune] wanders she gets such pleasure
> from her tricks that in victory she exclaims proudly:
> "Checkmate!"

It is only at this point in the *complainte* (ll. 1193–1208) that the clerkly discourse on Fortune in general is related to the particular situation of the narrator. From clerkly we pass to courtly diction, from an impersonal (almost auctor) stance to a personal one, from "didactic" to "lyric" (though, it must be stressed, this lyric moment is both contained within the musico-poetic unity of the *complainte* and integrated into the unfolding narrative of the dit as a whole).

Immediately following this lyricization of the discourse on Fortune comes the second (and final) section of the *complainte* (ll. 1209–1480), which deals with Amours. This section opens with a continuation of the lyric mode that will predominate throughout the remainder of the intercalated poem:

> Amours, Amours, ce m'as tu fait,
> Qui m'as fait faire le mesfait
> Qui toute ma joye desfait!
> (ll. 1209–11)
>
> Love! Love! You've done this to me, you who made me commit the offense that is destroying all my joy!

This lyric complaint is, however, based on, generated from, the narrative situation of the narrator-protagonist established before his entry into the *plaisance*. Thus, after stating that he will die if, as a consequence of his *mesfait* ("offense"), he is deprived of the presence of his lady, the narrator proceeds to accuse Amours of treating him unfairly. He has performed loyally in the service of Amours and has been poorly rewarded (ll. 1353–68). A meditation on his present unhappy state, void of *esperance* ("hope") (ll. 1369–1419), is followed by a gloomy reflection on the future (ll. 1420–40) and a reiteration of the unfortunate fact that his lady remains unaware of his love and suffering (ll. 1441–64). The *complainte* concludes with a final exclamation against the cruelty of Fortune and Amours, coupled with a restatement of the lover's devotion.

The second half of the narrative frame for the *Remede de Fortune*'s longest intercalated lyric is proportionally elaborate:

> Et quant a par moy debatus
> Me fu assés et combatus,
> Et fait ma plainte et ma clamour
> De Fortune amere et d'Amour. . . .
> Estoie je cheüs en transe.
> (ll. 1481–84; 1493)
>
> And when I had sufficiently debated and struggled alone, and had made my lament and cry about bitter Fortune and Love. . . . I'd fallen into a trance.

Again, there is a conflation of the time of the *complainte*'s composition and the time of its performance: At the level of plot, they are presented as a single narrative event. The first half of the *complainte*'s onomastic frame (esp.

ll. 901–3) stresses its status as composition, while the second half of the frame (ll. 1483–84) stresses its status as diegetic performance.

The act of performing the *complainte* has the immediate narrative consequence of inducing a trance in the exhausted performer. The broader narrative function of the *complainte* involves the preparation for the sudden appearance of a miraculous, but unnamed, *bele dame* (l. 1503) ("beautiful lady"), who immediately begins to comfort the lovesick narrator. The construct of a complaint on the inconstancies of Fortune followed by the appearance of a superhuman female figure who brings consolation recalls, of course, the opening scene of *The Consolation of Philosophy*.[13] The visibly literary construction of this narrative situation heightens the presence of the *poète* in his text and differentiates him from the narrator. At the same time, it invites us to read the entire central section of the dit as a reworking of Boethius. Even before she is named, the lady in the *Remede de Fortune* thus appears as, in some sense, a transformation of Lady Philosophy.[14]

The *bele dame*'s progressive consolation of the narrator involves a detailed defense of Amours against the accusations made in the narrator's *complainte*. A playful kind of textual self-consciousness is involved here as the *bele dame* is implicitly presented as a "reader" responding to the narrator's intercalated lyric poem. In addition, the formal opposition between lyric and narrative verse is stressed at the same time that the two are integrated into, contained by, the larger generic structure of the dit. Both of these suggestions are developed as the lady argues (ll. 1701 ff.) that Amours has in fact granted the request made earlier in the narrator's *lay* that his love be discreetly revealed to his lady. The visible signs of Ovidian lovesickness combined with the inability to speak openly of his feelings have demonstrated that the narrator is a *loial amant* ("loyal lover").[15] In conclusion the as-yet-unnamed lady tells the narrator that the only sign of the true lover that he lacks is "Esperance." She then promises to give her help and take him under her protection. As if to guarantee her promise (and her power), the lady proposes to sing a *chant roial:*

> Mes pour toy un petit deduire
> Et pour tes mauls a joie duire,
> Tel vueil dire un chant nouvellet;
> Car chose plaist qui nouvelle est.
> (ll. 1973–76)
>
> But to distract you a little and bring your sorrows to joy, I want to sing you a new song, because new things are always pleasing.

The narrator now briefly intervenes (ll. 1977–84) stressing his position within the story line as audience and reemphasizing the fact that the lyric piece to follow is a *chant nouvel* (l. 1984) ("new song"). Interestingly, the lady's song has the effect of deepening the trance of the lover-protagonist into sleep:

> Lors d'une voys clere et serie,
> Douce, sainne, en tel melodie
> Commença son chant delez mi,
> C'un petitet m'i endormi;
> Mes ne fu pas si fermement
> Que n'entendisse proprement
> Qu'ainssi commença par revel
> Joliement son chant nouvel.
> (ll. 1977–84)

> Then at my side in a sweet, harmonious voice—clear and rich—she began her song with such a melody that I soon fell asleep; but not so deeply that I didn't accurately hear how her new song began beautifully and gaily.

The lady's *chant roial,* "Joye, plaisance, et douce nourreture" (ll. 1985–2032) (Joy, pleasure, and sweet sustenance) is the third of the *Remede de Fortune*'s intercalated lyrics. As was the case with the first two, its thematic content is directly related to the ongoing narrative progression in which it is contained: true lovers are joyous and content with their condition; they should not ask for more; Amours rewards his own. Again, the *chant roial* is explicitly framed by the narrative verse in which it is embedded: "Et quant elle ot son chant finé, / Vers moy a son chief encliné" (l. 2033) ("And when she had finished her song, she nodded her head in my direction").

The simultaneous opposition and interrelation between lyric and narrative (heightened in retrospect by the ironic reading of the *chant roial* suggested at the very end of the dit) signals the presence of the *poète* figure. This presence is intensified by the fact that, for the first time in the course of the *Remede de Fortune*, a character other than the first-person narrator-protagonist (i.e., the *bele dame*) has expressed herself, within the context of the story line, by means of an intercalated lyric poem (which the text repeatedly calls attention to as such). The narrator is thereby differentiated from the *poète,* whose identity as the global author who has composed *all* the intercalated lyrics becomes increasingly visible in the very poetic organization of the dit. Both the (first-person) narrator and the (third-person) *bele dame* in their capacity as lyric poets are thus reduced to the status of fictional constructs emanating from and contained in, or by, the *poète*. The relationship *poète*/text is implicitly presented as underlying a sophisticated narrative configuration in which characters are depicted as poets. The increased distance between narrator and *poète* has important implications for the depiction of poetic inspiration in the dit. An opposition seems to be suggested between the highly conventionalized process by which lyric poems are generated out of the narrator's love experience, on the one hand, and the more all-inclusive, more literary, but lyric-based, process of poetic inspiration and composition of the *poète,* on the other. The stance of lyric poet thus seems to be presented as contained by the *poète*'s "larger" identity.[16]

After she finishes her song, the *bele dame* bends down over the narrator and speaks to him encouragingly (ll. 2039–93). It is important to note, however, that she begins by asking his reaction to her song (ll. 2041–46) and then explicitly praises it herself: "Se ce n'estoit pour moy vanter, / Je diroie de mon chanter / Que c'est bien dit" (ll. 2047–49) ("Were I not to flatter myself, I'd say that my song was well sung"). This represents, on the part of Machaut the *poète,* a playful insistence on the intercalated lyric as such, and on his own identity as its author. At the same time, this reference to her *chant roial* by Esperance constitutes the final element of what is, in effect, a double frame: The song is introduced first by Esperance (ll. 1973–76), then by the protagonist (ll. 1977–84); its conclusion is noted first by the protagonist (ll. 2033), then, by Esperance (ll. 2047–49). This chiastic double frame, I suggest, emphasizes the *chant roial*'s double genesis: Machaut the author and Esperance the character. In this way also, the *chant roial* is further distanced from the dit's first-person protagonist. Part of this process involves, in addition, an emphasis in the frame on this intercalated lyric's diegetic status as performance: it is designated exclusively by the term *chant* (or *chanter* as a substantive) (ll. 1975, 1979, 1984, 2033, 2048), while Esperance utilizes the verb *dire* (implying performance rather than composition) to refer to her presentation of the *chant roial.* As we shall see, among the *Remede*'s seven lyrics set to music, it is only the two songs assigned to Esperance whose frames do not contain the verb *faire* (implying composition rather than performance).

The fourth intercalated song of the *Remede de Fortune* occurs after the *bele dame* has revealed her identity as Esperance (l. 2286) and is about to leave the newly instructed and comforted narrator. She reaffirms her promise to help Amant wherever he needs her, advising him to put aside his timidity and pursue his beloved. Before disappearing, Esperance announces her intention to sing a second lyric poem, giving Amant instructions on how to "use" it:

> Mais ainçoys de ma clere voys
> Te diray une balladelle,
> De chant et de ditté nouvelle,
> Laquelle tu emporteras
> Et en alant la chanteras,
> Afin que tes cuers s'i deduise
> S'il a pensee qui li nuise.
> (ll. 2850–56)

> But first I'll sing you a *balladelle* in my limpid voice, with new words and music, which you'll carry off with you, singing it to cheer up your heart as you go along, if it's troubled by any concern.

This intercalated lyric is thus explicitly differentiated from the narrative progression at the same time as it is thematically integrated into the unfolding story line. This textually self-conscious presentation again heightens the presence of the *poète* as author figure. It is compounded by the frame effect of l. 2893: "Quant elle ot finé sa ballade" ("When she had finished her *ballade*"), which also reemphasizes the status of Esperance's diegetic performance as a narrative event. For the second and final time in the *Remede*'s seven intercalated lyrics set to music, the verb *dire*(/*pardire*) (ll. 2851, 2905) is used to the exclusion of *faire* in order to designate the third-person character's more performative relation to her song.

The *balladelle,* "En amer a douce vie" (ll. 2857–92, a duplex ballade) (To be in love is a sweet and happy life), gives Amant such pleasure that he immediately begins to learn both the melody and the words by heart:

> Mais se li dous chans me plaisoit,
> Tel joie le dit me faisoit
> Que ne savoie au quel entendre.
> Si mis moult grant paine a l'aprendre,
> Et la soz en si poy d'espasse
> Qu'ains qu'elle partist de la place,
> Ne que toute l'eüst pardit,
> Je la soz par chant et par dit.
> Et pour ce que ne l'oubliasse,
> Failloit il que la recordasse.
> (ll. 2899–2908)

> But if the sweet music pleased me, the words brought me more joy than anyone could conceive. So I made a great effort to learn it, and memorized it so quickly that before she'd left the place or had even finished singing it, I knew both the words and the music. And so that I'd not forget it, I had to imprint it upon my memory.

While Amant is absorbed in this activity, Esperance vanishes (l. 2919).

The fifth lyric set piece is sung by Amant when, after having successfully memorized both the *balladelle* and the general advice of Esperance, he begins to walk toward the *guichet* ("wicket") by which he had entered the garden, now feeling much stronger and more self-assured. For the first time he becomes aware of the joyous birdsongs to which he had been deaf before the visit of Esperance. This sequence (ll. 2981–92), with Amant delighted by birdsong only on his way *out* of the garden, seems to involve a reversal of the narrative construct found at the beginning of the dream in the *Roman de la Rose*. Again, the stress on the *Rose* as subtext and the process of transformation of a literary model serves to highlight the presence of the *poète* in the text of the *Remede de Fortune*. Further, the courtly convention of birdsong as a metaphor for lyric poetry (also elaborately exploited in the *Rose*) is artfully developed. On hearing (and being moved by) the birdsong, Amant becomes a bird (i.e., a lyric poet) himself:

> Si m'abeli tant leur douls chans,
> Qu'ainçoys qu'il fust soleil couchans
> Je me senti a volenté
> De cuer, de corps, et de santé,
> Tant pour la douce remembrance
> Que j'avoie en Bonne Esperance,
> Comme de ce que je pensoie
> Que briefment ma dame verroie.
> Et pour ce qu'estoie au retour
> De veoir son tres noble atour,
> Tantost fis en dit et en chant
> Ce ci que presentement chant.
> (ll. 3001–12)

> But now their sweet singing so delighted me that before sunset I felt restored in heart, body, and health, as much for the sweet memory I had of Good Hope as for the thought that soon I'd see my lady. And since I was on my way back to see her very noble self again, I composed at once the words and music I shall now sing.

The sweet songs of the birds lead him to think that he will soon see his lady, which in turn leads him to sing the *balade* "Dame, de qui toute ma joie vient" (ll. 3013–36) (Lady, from whom all my joy comes). Again, the explicit presentation of a conventionalized lyric inspiration and poetic production differentiates the poet-protagonist from the *poète*. Similarly, as with the other intercalated lyrics of the *Remede de Fortune*, the *balade*'s formal separation from its narrative verse setting is emphasized at the same time as it is thematically integrated into the story line: its primary motif being the lover's hope (*espoir*) of seeing his beloved.

Further, the narrative progression is reinstituted in a way that serves both to frame the intercalated lyric and to set it into the ongoing sequence of narrative temporality: "Ainssi fis mon chant et finay" (l. 3037) ("Thus I composed and sang my song"). Interestingly, this second half of the *balade*'s frame completes its presentation as the only one of the *Remede*'s intercalated lyrics not to have a precise generic or terminological designation. I would like to suggest somewhat speculatively that this is because it shares the generic identity of the song that immediately precedes it: the (duplex) *balade* of Esperance. Thus, from the perspective of the reader of the dit as a whole, it is "unnecessary" to identify the *balade* as form for a second time. To the extent that this interpretation is valid, the reader's perspective is, of course, emphasized as such, at the very moment when the first-person protagonist reassumes his role as singer of the *Remede*'s lyric set pieces. In this connection, the frame for Amant's *balade* stresses the distinction between composing and performing. A double set of first-person verbs both introduces and follows the *balade: faire* (ll. 3011, 3037) emphasizes the composition of the lyric; *chanter* (l. 3012) and *finir* (l. 3037) emphasize its performance.

Having left the garden, Amant's journey continues until he spies his lady's castle from afar. At this point, there occurs the only intercalated lyric set piece in the *Remede de Fortune* that is not set to music: the *prière* "Amours, je te lo et graci" (ll. 3205–3348) (Love, I praise and thank you).[17] This *prière* is spoken by Amant as he kneels in the direction of his lady's chateau, and begins with an affirmation of devotion to the service of Amours, couched in quasi-religious terms. Amant then asks forgiveness for having earlier complained of love's pains, thus presenting the *prière* as, in part, a palinode to the *complainte* in a way that suggests a structuring function for the lyric set pieces. There follows an elaborate (and elaborately rhetorical) expression of praise of Esperance and gratitude to her for having saved Amant from the torments of love. The correspondence between an increased density of linguistic patterning and a lyric intensity of emotion may be viewed as a sign of the *poète*. The *prière* concludes with Amant requesting help in his next meeting with the lady.

The frame for the *Remede*'s only nonmusical lyric presents its diegetic performance as coterminous with its composition:

> Encommenchai ceste prïere,
> En eulz [= Amours and Espoir] merciant humblement
> De leurs biens tout premierement. . . .
> Et quant j'eus finé mon depri . . .
>
> (ll. 3202–4, 3349)

> I began this prayer, first of all thanking them (= Love and Hope) humbly for their blessings. . . . And when I had finished my prayer . . .

The seventh intercalated lyric (the sixth set to music) is the only one explicitly motivated by the request of Amant's beloved and is immediately performed for her, in her presence. The textual position of the song thus makes the reader and the lady here (and only here in the *Remede de Fortune*) coincide as receivers. An elaborately conventional courtly setting provides the narrative (and semiotic) context for Amant's most successful performance as poet-lover. Having left the walled garden of Esperance, he comes upon an elegant and noble company dancing in a charming park. The scene is, of course, reminiscent of the dance (*querole*) of Deduit's troop in the *Rose*, and its literary genesis stresses the presence of the *poète* and the fictionality of the narrator. As Amant sees his lady among the dancers (l. 3381), he begins to feel helpless and afraid, but remembers Esperance and her advice. He approaches the group and is recognized by his lady, who invites him to join. After having danced for a brief time, Amant is requested by his beloved to sing:

> Je li respondi sans demour:
> "Ma dame, vo commandement
> Vueil faire; mais petitement
> Me sçai de chanter entremettre.
> Mes c'est chose qu'il couvient estre,
> Puis qu'il vous plaist." Lors sans delay
> Encommenchay ce virelay
> Que on claimme chançon balladee;
> Ainssi doit elle estre clamee.
> (ll. 3442–50)

> I replied without hesitation: "My lady, I want to do your bidding, but I know very little about singing. Yet since it pleases you I have no choice." Then without delay I began this *virelay,* which is called a *chanson balladée;* this is what it should be named.

This introduction to the intercalated lyric conflates the first-person voice of Amant the narrator-protagonist and the first-person voice of the *poète,* concerned with matters of poetic terminology (ll. 3448–50).[18] The first of these voices is associated with performance (*encommenchay,* l. 3448); the second, with composition.

The *virelay* "Dame, a vous sans retollir" (ll. 3451–96) (Lady, to you without reservation) that follows is an impeccably courtly declaration of love and devotion. Significantly, the second half of its frame emphasizes exclusively its status quo performance as part of the narrative:

> Aprés ma chançon commença
> Une dame qui la dança . . .
> Si prist a chanter sans demeure:
> "Dieus, quant venra li temps et l'eure
> Que je voie ce que j'aim si?"
> Et sa chançon fina ainsi.
> Quant finé l'ot, ma dame dist:

"C'est bien et joliëment dit,
Mais il est temps de nous retraire."
(ll. 3497–98, 3501–7)

After my song a lady, who had been dancing there . . . began at once to sing: "Dear God, when will the time and hour come that I may see the one I love?" And she finished her song with this refrain. When she'd finished it, my lady said: "That's nicely sung, but now it's time for us to return."

The performance of Amant's *virelay* is thus carefully presented as, narratively speaking, one in a series of past events. There is, however, an important contrast between it and the lyric performance by an unnamed lady that immediately follows it. Her song is alluded to by means of a fragmentary citation;[19] his song is given in its musical and verbal entirety, so that lyric performance coincides temporally with narrative event.

The way in which the lyric pieces of the *Remede de Fortune* simultaneously exist as such and as constitutive elements of the narrative (advancing the story line, even generating "new" narrative developments) is most elaborately illustrated in the course of the private meeting between Amant and his lady that follows the breakup of the dance. The episode (ll. 3517–3872) begins as the lady takes Amant aside and asks for an explanation of his earlier behavior with regard to the *lay*. Amant's long reply (ll. 3551–3714) contains his first open avowal of love. He begins by retelling the story of the birth of his love, how from the moment when he first saw his beloved she became "examplaire et voie / De tout ce que faire devoie" (ll. 3585–86) ("model and guide in all I should do"). He goes on to tell how his love experience generated love poetry: "lay, complainte, ou chançon estrange" (l. 3596). Significantly, the order in which the three exemplary lyric forms are listed here by Amant reflects that in which they have previously appeared in the *Remede*. The potential arbitrariness of the ordinal relationship among the various fixed forms suggested in ll. 401–6 is here, I think, revised, in accord with the *Remede*'s self-presentation as an ars poetica. At the same time, it is important to note that the *chançon estrange* (l. 3596) ("original song") here presented as the product of the first-person protagonist, clearly evokes the *chant roial* sung by Esperance, which was repeatedly described as *nouvel* (ll. 1975–76, 1984). Again, the identities of the various speaking lyric subjects in the *Remede* are subsumed under that of Machaut-*poète:*

Si m'avisay que je feroie
Selonc ce que je sentiroie
Pour vous et a vostre loenge
Lay, complainte ou chançon estrange . . .
Et me sembloit chose plus belle

De dire en ma chançon nouvelle
Ce qui mon cuer destraint et serre,
Que par autre guise requerre.
Si fis un lay dou sentement
Que j'avoye au commencement.
(ll. 3593–96, 3599–3604)

So I decided that I would compose, according to my feelings toward you and in praise of you, a *lay, complainte,* or original song . . . and it seemed to me better to tell in my new song what was oppressing and wringing my heart than to try by some other method. So I composed a *lay* about the feelings I had at the beginning.

We have here the thematization of a specifically lyric poetic inspiration and composition that are thus incorporated into the identity of the lover-protagonist at the same time as they serve to differentiate him from the *poète,* the global author both of the intercalated lyrics and of the dit as a whole. Further, the fact that this (first-person) discussion of a lyric poem takes place in the context of (indeed, by means of) narrative poetry stresses an opposition between the two that, as we have seen, has functioned throughout the *Remede de Fortune* to emphasize the dit's status as verbal artifact, as patterned language, as well as to intensify the implicit presence of the *poète* in his text.

This implicit presence is further emphasized by the process of what might be called "narrative doubling." Amant (qua protagonist) is now recounting to his lady what he has already recounted (qua narrator) to the reader at the beginning of the dit. It is the act of narration as such that is thereby emphasized—and the existence of the *Remede de Fortune* as structured narrative. In addition, a kind of implicit textual self-referentiality (and self-authorization) is set up as the "truth" of what the lover-protagonist recounts to his lady is guaranteed by the fact that it has already been recounted from a different perspective (i.e., that of the narrator/reader) and vice versa.

Amant continues his narration (or renarration), telling why he fled in tears when his lady asked him who had written the *lay* and how he arrived in the garden where he made his *complainte* against Fortune. Amant then tells how Esperance "comforted" him and gave him the courage to approach the lady. This brings the "narrative doubling" to a close, as we are now back at the "present" moment, the situation that had prompted Amant's retelling in miniature of the plot of the dit. He thus proceeds (ll. 3683 ff.) to make a flawlessly courtly *declaration* of love (presented as prompted by the insistence of Esperance). Amant ends his speech by commingling his identity as lover and as love poet when he invokes his lyric poem (i.e., his *virelay* of ll. 3451–96) as a guarantee of the truth of his sentiment:

Et s'il vous plaist, ma dame chiere,
A regarder la dairreniere
Chançonnette que je chantay,
Que fait en dit et en chant ay,
Vous pourrez de legier savoir
Se je ment ou se je di voir.
(ll. 3705–10)

And if it please you, my dear lady, to consider the last little song I sang, of which I composed both words and music, you can easily tell whether I'm lying or speaking the truth.

This reference implicitly presents Amant's lady as a reader of the *Remede* qua narrative sequence, and thus foregrounds the reader's status as such: For this is the only context in which the temporal designation *dairreniere* makes sense. At the same time, the opposition between the verbs *chanter* and *faire* (ll. 3707–8) highlights that between protagonist and *poète,* Amant and Machaut.

Significantly, the lady's first response is to question Amant about his identity as a lyric poet, asking if he really composed the *lay* himself (ll. 3725–28), before going on to question him about his love for her and the truth of the episode with Esperance that he has just narrated. Amant, after reaffirming the truth of all his statements, reformulates his declaration of love, stressing that he speaks only in the name of Esperance. The lady replies that she will obey Esperance (whom she praises at length) and accepts Amant as her lover, granting to him "loyaument de m'amour l'otroy" (l. 3846) ("faithfully the gift of my love").

As the lovers' meeting ends and Amant is about to depart, his lady's final amorous glance is "si vray et d'un si doulz langage, / qu'elle retint mon cuer en gage" (ll. 4101–2) ("so true and of such sweet meaning that she kept my heart as hostage"). The lyric inspiration of the eighth intercalated song (the seventh with musical accompaniment) of the *Remede de Fortune* is thus made part of the narrative progression, i.e., it is generated directly from a moment in the sequential unfolding of the narrator's love experience:

Dont si liés fu et si joyans
Que de tous les biens fu joians . . .
Et pour la joye que j'avoie
Ce rondelet fis en ma voie.
(ll. 4103–4; 4107–8)

I was so happy and overjoyed by [the lady's parting glance] that everything made me happy . . . and for the joy I felt I composed this *rondelet* as I went along.

Once again, the explicit generic designation functions to mark the lyric insert as such within the context of the discourse system of narrative verse. This procedure is completed by the other half of the frame: "Quant j'eus finé ce rondelet / Je me mis en un sentelet" (ll. 4117–18) ("When I'd finished this *rondelet,* I took a little path"). In addition, a lapse of narrative time is created to accommodate the performance of the lyric, at the same time as narrative temporality is reflected in the very verbal structure and thematic content of the *rondelet:*

> Dame, mon cuer en vous remaint,
> Comment que de vous me departe.
> Par fine amour qui en moy maint,
> Dame, mon cuer en vous remaint.
> Or pri Dieu que li vostres m'aint,
> Sans ce qu'en nulle autre amour parte.
> Dame, mon cuer en vous remaint,
> Comment que de vous me departe.
> (ll. 4109–16)

> My lady, my heart stays with you, although I myself must leave you. With true love I bear within, my lady, my heart stays with you. Now I pray God that your heart will love me, without being shared with any other. My lady, my heart stays with you, although I myself must leave you.

This is the last intercalated lyric poem in the *Remede de Fortune*, and it coincides with the apex of the narrator's amatory success within the context of the story line.

The final episode in the narrative of Amant's love affair is far from an unqualified success. On returning to his *dame* (l. 4141), Amant is greeted with indifference. She appears *changie* (l. 4154) ("changed") and seems to be attempting to ignore him. All his former joy vanishes at this reaction, and Amant falls into painful doubt and *grant merencolie* (l. 4163) ("great melancholy"). He is unable to arrive at a satisfactory or unambiguous interpretation of her behavior: "je ne pos onques le voir / De la mensonge concevoir" (ll. 4171–72) ("I could never distinguish the true from the false"). When he seeks an explanation, demanding that she tell him outright if she has ceased to love him, the lady assures him he has no reason to worry and excuses her previous coldness on the grounds that it was a ruse to deceive the *médisants* ("slanderers"):

> Car je le fais pour le milleur
> Et pour mieus celer vostre amour,
> Car qui en amour ne scet faindre,

Il ne puet a grant joye ataindre.
(ll. 4199–4202)

I do it for the best and in order to conceal our love better, because a lover who does not know how to feign cannot attain great joy.

Amant intensely wants to believe his lady, but the episode closes somewhat ambiguously.[20] Amant maintains the same verbal attitude towards her as before, but all he has is the "hope" that he is loved. The authenticity of the poet-protagonist's love experience within the context of the story line seems to be put into doubt, or at the very least, rendered problematic.[21] The final verbal attitude of courtly devotion that the narrator explicitly adopts thus takes on an artificial, conventional *literary* aspect.

At the very end of the *Remede de Fortune*, in his concluding declaration to Amours in the Epilogue, the poet-narrator goes on to cast the dit as a whole as a lyric offering to his lady, who, he hopes, will receive it favorably and whose love he hopes to obtain:

Et certes, je le doy bien faire,
Quant tu me donnes tel espoir
Qu'adés mieus recevoir espoir,
Et que ma douce dame chiere
De bon cuer et a lie chiere
Verra ce dit qu'ay mis a rime,
Comment qu'assez nicement rime.
Et cil espoir qui en moy maint,
Qu'encor ma chiere dame m'aint
Mon cuer si doucement resjoie
Qu'en grant santé et en grant joie
Li change mal, u tu me dis
Que pris en gré sera mes dis.
Or doint Dieus qu'en bon gré le prengne,
Et qu'en li servant ne mesprengne.
(ll. 4286–4300)

And it is certainly proper that I do so, since you give me such hope that I constantly hope for better, and that my dear sweet lady will see with good heart and happy countenance this dit that I have rhymed, even though I rhyme rather poorly. And this Hope within me, that my dear lady loves me, so sweetly cheers my heart that its sorrow is changed to great joy and comfort, when you tell me that my dit will be welcomed by her. Now may God grant that she accept it gladly, and that I never err in serving her.

Thus at the very end of the dit, all that the first-person narrator possesses qua lover is hope, i.e., he is in the same situation as at the beginning and middle of the dit. But if his status as lover has not changed, this is not the case with his status as poet: The dit has been written and this fact is repeatedly emphasized in the Epilogue while the poet-narrator's love seems to be reduced to an increasingly literary hope of being loved, with which he proclaims himself satisfied. It is significant that, while references to the dit and to Amours are in the present indicative, or the *passé composé,* references to the lady and the personal love experience associated with her are in the subjunctive or the future. In sharp contrast to the vagueness (reflected in the very tense structure of the Epilogue) of the narrator's final situation as a lover is the "fact" that the *poète*'s service to Amours has produced the *Remede de Fortune*. As was the case with the clerkly element of the narrator's identity, the courtly love–poet element, as it appears in the Epilogue, overlaps to a large degree with the figure of the *poète*. This final expansion of the narrator figure also distances him from the first-person account of his love experience that has formed the basis for the dit's story line. This love experience thus takes on a final literary (rather than experiential) cast. At the same time it is implicitly presented as, above all, poetic subject matter.

The implicit primacy of the relationship *poète* / text that emerges from the Epilogue serves to authorize a reading of the *Remede de Fortune* as a poetic *liber exemplorum* ("book of examples"): for the series of lyric poems (of songs) embedded in (and integrated into) the narrative functions as an exemplary collection of fixed forms. There is one superlative example of each of the major lyric forms of the fourteenth century—which were to become fixed after Machaut for at least three generations, and which are presented here as models to be imitated. It is in this sense that the *Remede de Fortune* is to be read as an implicit ars poetica. And it is only in the context of such a reading that the full significance of the didactic orientation of the Prologue becomes evident. Further, an important correspondence emerges between the level of plot and the didactic level of the dit: just as the narrator-protagonist fails as lover but succeeds as poet, so the *Remede de Fortune* fails as an *ars amandi* but succeeds as an ars poetica.

The *Remede de Fortune*'s character as an ars poetica involves the most elaborate and authoritative self-presentation of the *poète* in his text, as well as the most radical differentiation of the *poète* from the first-person narrator-protagonist, whose identity he subsumes. It is thus highly significant that this crucially important aspect of the dit results from a visibly literary activity (even "experience") on the part of the *poète:* the self-conscious transformation of an Old French literary tradition, extending back to the early thirteenth century—that of the narrative work with intercalated lyrics.[22]

The *poète*'s service to Amours (even within the context of the narration of a first-person love experience) thus appears, above all, as poetic service, a multifaceted literary activity that can incorporate a wide variety of experiential perspectives into a greatly expanded lyric identity. The structure and character of the *Remede de Fortune* function to present this *poète* figure himself as exemplary, to present Machaut as an *exemplum poetae*, a model to be imitated. The authority that implicitly guarantees this presentation is, in the broadest sense, lyric-based. It resides nowhere else than in the identity of the *poète* himself.[23]

In conclusion, I would like to suggest that there is an important series of structural relationships among the eight intercalated lyrics (seven set to music and one—the *prière*—without musical accompaniment) of Machaut's *Remede*. It seems to me that the overall organization of the dit suggests four pairs of lyric pieces, in terms of the following variables. First, the *lay*[24] is answered and "corrected" by the *virelay* (*chanson balladée*) in the sense that the inscribed performer (Amant) and the subject matter (Amant's direct love experience) are the same in both cases, while the inscribed audience involves in the first case, the *absent* lady; and, in the second case, the *present* lady. What we seem to have here, diegetically speaking, is a repetition of the same subject matter, "marked," as it were, the first time for failure; the second time for success. The second pair of lyric set pieces that I envisage in this context involves the *complainte* and the *prière*. In the first case, the diegetic Lover reacts negatively to Fortune and Love; in the second case, the same Lover reacts positively. The basic structural relationship is thus palinodic. The third pair I would like to propose involves the *chant roial* and the *balladelle*. The character Esperance performs both of these songs (the only two she is credited with at the level of the plot). In both cases the inscribed audience is Amant alone. In a very real sense, these two lyric pieces represent the beginning and the end of Amant's "cure" at the diegetic level. The fourth and final pair involves the *balade* and the *rondelet*. Both are composed and performed by Amant in isolation; the *balade,* after the departure of Esperance; the *rondelet,* after the departure of Amant's lady. In both cases, the lyric gives expression to Amant's intense happiness as a result of his interaction with the lady in question.

The relationships among the four pairs of lyric set pieces are indicated below in the Appendix, which also attempts (in schematic fashion) to take into account the diegetic or intratextual discursive context of each. The fact that the *Remede*'s lyrics may be seen as interrelated in this kind of complex patterning is one more indication of the degree to which this work involves a lyric anthology functioning simultaneously as such and within the context of a narrative progression.

Appendix

Lyric Set Pieces in Guillaume de Machaut's *Remede de Fortune* (c. 1349): Structural and Discursive Patterns, in Pairs

1. ***lay*** (ll. 431–680) performer: Lover inscribed audience: Lady (indirect)	***Qui n'aroit autre deport***
2. ***complainte*** (ll. 905–1480) performer: Lover inscribed addressees: Amours and Fortune (absent)	***Tieus rit au main qui soir pleure***
3. ***chant roial*** (ll. 1985–2032) performer: Esperance inscribed audience: Lover (direct)	***Joye, plaisance, et douce nourreture***
4. ***balladelle*** (duplex ballade) (ll. 2857–92) performer: Esperance inscribed audience: Lover (direct)	***En amer a douce vie***
5. ***balade*** (ll. 3013–36) performer: Lover (alone)	***Dame, de qui toute ma joie vient***
6. ***prière*** (ll. 3205–3348) performer: Lover inscribed addressees: Amours and Esperance (absent)	***Amours, je te lo et graci***
7. ***virelay*** (*chanson balladée*) (ll. 3451–96) performer: Lover inscribed audience: Lady (direct)	***Dame, a vous sans retollir***
8. ***rondelet*** (ll. 4109–16) performer: Lover (alone)	***Dame, mon cuer en vous remaint***

Notes

1. For the didactic function of the intercalated lyrics of the *Remede de Fortune* see Ernest Hoepffner, ed., *Œuvres de Guillaume de Machaut*, 3 vols. (Paris: Société des Anciens Textes Français, 1908–21), 2:xxxiv–liv; Armand Machabey, *Guillaume de Machaut: La Vie et l'œuvre musical*, 2 vols. (Paris: Richard-Masse, 1955), 1:50–51; Daniel Poirion, *Le Moyen âge II: 1300–1480* (Paris: Arthaud, 1971), pp. 192–94; William Calin, *A Poet at the Fountain: Essays on the Narrative Verse of Guillaume de Machaut* (Lexington: University of Kentucky Press, 1974), p. 70; and Kevin Brownlee, *Poetic Identity in Guillaume de Machaut* (Madison: University of Wisconsin Press, 1984), pp. 37–39, 60–63. For descriptions of the various fixed forms in the *Remede*, see Daniel Poirion, *Le poète et le prince: L'évolution du lyrisme courtois de Guillaume de Machaut à Charles d'Orléans* (Paris: Presses Universitaires de France, 1965), and Lawrence Earp, "Scribal Practice, Manuscript Production, and the Transmission of Music in Late Medieval France." Ph.D. diss., Princeton, 1983.

2. For an important general treatment of the "poetics of insertion" in medieval French literature, with special reference to Guillaume de Machaut, see Jacqueline Cerquiglini, "Pour une typologie de l'insertion," and "Le montage des Formes: L'exemple de Guillaume de Machaut," *Perspectives Médiévales* 3 (1977): 9–14, 23–26. See also Cerquiglini's groundbreaking study, *"Un Engin si soutil": Guillaume de Machaut et l'écriture au XIVè siècle* (Paris: Champion, 1985), esp. pp. 23–103. Calin, discussing the intercalated lyrics of the *Remede de Fortune* as a group (pp. 71–72), considers that "they form part of a larger narrative pattern, in which they are completely integrated" (p. 71). See also Lawrence Earp, "Scribal Practice," Ph.D. diss., Princeton, 1983, pp. 276–83.

3. I will thus not be dealing with the specific musical form of the seven songs except in the most tangential manner. See Friedrich Ludwig, "La Musique des intermèdes lyriques dans le *Remede de Fortune*" (in Hoepffner, ed., *Œuvres*, 2:405–13), and Earp, "Scribal Practice," pp. 276–83. See also Umberto Malizia, "Guillaume de Machaut: Le Sette *Chansons* del *Remede de Fortune*," *Quaderni di filologia e lingue romanze* 6 (1984): 11–48. The present essay is concerned, however, with the status and function of the one intercalated lyric that is not set to music (i.e., the *prière* (ll. 3205–3348) in terms of the key *structural* role played by the set of lyric intercalations considered as such.

4. For the significance of the term *poète* as applied to Machaut see Brownlee, "The Poetic *Œuvre* of Guillaume de Machaut: The Identity of Discourse and the Discourse of Identity," in *Machaut's World: Science and Art in the Fourteenth Century: Annals of the New York Academy of Sciences* 314 (Oct. 1978): 219–33; and *Poetic Identity*, pp. 3–23.

5. The analysis that follows elaborates and expands certain ideas originally set forth in my book *Poetic Identity in Guillaume de Machaut*. I am grateful to the University of Wisconsin Press for permission to reprint parts of that book in this new context.

6. For a discussion of the narrative structure of the *Remede de Fortune* see Calin, *Poet at the Fountain*, pp. 55–74; and Brownlee, *Poetic Identity*, pp. 39–60. For the import of the lady in the *Remede de Fortune* as well as for Machaut's concept of courtly love, see Douglas Kelly's important study *Medieval Imagination: Rhetoric and the Poetry*

of Courtly Love (Madison: University of Wisconsin Press, 1978), esp. pp. 100–103, 121–23, 130–37. For a trenchant analysis of the relationship between narrative, lyric, and iconography in the *Remede*, see Sylvia Huot, *From Song to Book: The Poetics of Writing in Old French Lyric and Lyrical Narrative Poetry* (Ithaca, N.Y.: Cornell University Press, 1987), pp. 249–59, 275–79. Huot's study also investigates the literary implications of the codicological and iconographic differences between the *Remede* in Bibliothèque Nationale, fonds français 1586 and 1584.

7. All citations and English translations are from James I. Wimsatt and William W. Kibler, eds. and trans., *Guillaume de Machaut: "Le Jugement du roy de Behaigne" and "Remede de Fortune,"* music edited by Rebecca A. Baltzer. Copyright 1988 by the University of Georgia Press, Athens. Reprinted by permission. Line numbers follow in the text.

8. I take the term *diegetic* from Gérard Genette, *Figures III* (Paris: Seuil, 1972), where *diégèse* is defined as "l'univers spatio-temporel désigné par le récit" ("the spatio-temporal universe designated by the narrative"), and *diégétique* as "qui se rapporte ou appartient à l'histoire" ("that which refers or belongs to the story") (pp. 238–41, 280).

9. For the *lay* as a technical achievement see Hoepffner, ed., *Œuvres*, 2:xxxvii–xxxviii. For a rhetorical and thematic analysis of the *lay* see Kelly, *Medieval Imagination*, pp. 102–3.

10. I am grateful to Jacqueline Cerquiglini for suggesting this to me. See also the protagonist's later use of *lire* when he recounts this incident to the lady who had provoked it: "Car, ma dame, vous m'appellastes / Et [le] *lire* me commandastes. / Si le vous *leu* de point en point" (ll. 3609–11, emphasis added) ("For, my lady, you summoned me and commanded me to *read* it; and I *read* it to you from beginning to end").

11. See Anne Hagopian van Buren, "Reality and Literary Romance in the Park of Hesdin," in *Medieval Gardens*, ed. Elizabeth McDougall (New York: Dumbarton Oaks Research Library and Collection, 1986), pp. 117–34. See also, Marguerite Charageat, "Le Parc d'Hesdin: Création monumentale du XIIIe siècle," *Bulletin de la Société de l'histoire de l'art français* (1950): 94–106.

12. See Hoepffner, ed., *Œuvres*, 2:xxxii–xxxiii.

13. Boethius, *The Consolation of Philosophy*, Book 1, *Meters* 1–3 and *Proses* 1–3. See Hoepffner, ed., *Œuvres*, 2:xxi–xxii.

14. The crucial importance of song in the *prosimetrum* Boethian model is, of course, highly relevant for the *Remede de Fortune*.

15. For the function and import of this kind of code in Machaut, see Cerquiglini, "Syntaxe et Syncope: Langage du corps et écriture chez Guillaume de Machaut," *Langue Française* 40 (1978): 60–74.

16. In this connection, it is significant that the narrator-protagonist is first identified (in the rubrics) as L'Amant (the Lover) in the two passages that frame the *chant roial* of the *bele dame*. From this point on, he is consistently referred to by this title (in manuscripts A and F, as reproduced by Hoepffner). Earp ("Scribal Practice," pp. 395–99) gives a useful table containing transcriptions of the rubrics and descriptions of the miniatures in the major manuscripts of the *Remede*.

17. This *prière,* in my opinion, functions as an integral part of the series of intercalated lyric set pieces around which the *Remede* is structured (see Appendix). A

suggestive consideration of why it alone is not given a musical setting is made by Margaret Switten (in "Guillaume de Machaut: Le *Remede de Fortune* au carrefour d'un art nouveau," *Cahiers de L'Association Internationale des Études Françaises* 41 [1989]: 101–18): "la tristesse, selon le nouvel art, ne se chante pas. La musique étant une science de la joie, il convient que la *prière,* qui efface la *complainte,* ne soit pas notée, car seul le silence accueillera dorénavant la souffrance de l'amant. . . . La douleur sera réduite au silence, figurée par la *prière;* la joie alimentera un nouvel art social, polyphonique—l'*ars nova*" (pp. 113, 115–16) ("sadness, according to the new art, is not sung. Since music is a joyful art, it makes sense that the *prière* (which displaces the *complainte*) should not be set to music, for henceforth only silence will greet the lover's suffering. . . . Pain will be reduced to silence, figured by the *prière;* joy will nourish a new—polyphonic—social art: the *ars nova*.").

18. This was a "professional" matter of some importance to Machaut, who consistently preferred the term *chanson balladée*. See Poirion, *Le Poète et le Prince*; pp. 327–29. Poiron gives particular attention to the *virelay* from the *Remede de Fortune*. See in addition, Hoepffner, ed., *Œuvres*, pp. xlix–lii.

19. Hoepffner tellingly describes Machaut's usage of this *refrain* as both the "commencement et fin d'une chanson qu'une dame chante en dansant" (*Œuvres*, 2:liii) ("beginning and end of a song that a lady sings while dancing").

20. Kelly (*Medieval Imagination*, pp. 100–105, 130–37) views the *Remede de Fortune* as the first of Machaut's poems in which his new conception of *fin 'amor* is set forth in detail. The dit's "fundamental idea" is, in Kelly's terms, "the primacy and sufficiency of hope in love," which is presented "schematically" in the *lay* and developed "systematically" in the speeches of Esperance (p. 102). This cogent interpretation of the content of the *Remede de Fortune* is, to my mind, highly relevant to Machaut's self-presentation as *poète* in the dit and to the related presentation of love as poetic subject matter. However, the opposition between Amant (the narrator-protagonist) and Machaut (the *poète*-author) that is built into the structure of the dit must be taken into account in a consideration of the work qua amorous doctrine. This opposition allows the final representation of Amant's situation as a lover to be insolubly ambiguous while, at the same time, Machaut's "sublimation of courtly love" remains intact as poetic "ideology."

21. This is reinforced by the fact that Amant's belief in the truth of his lady's words is clearly shown to depend, not on the truthfulness of their content, but on the identity of their enunciator (see esp. ll. 4219–51). Cerquiglini suggestively discusses the significance of this key discursive distinction for Machaut's poetics in "Syntaxe et Syncope," and, in more general terms, in "*Un Engin si soutil*," pp. 181–200.

22. For a discussion of the progressive development of this tradition, especially with reference to first-person narration, see G. B. Gybbon-Monypenny, "Guillaume de Machaut's Erotic 'Autobiography': Precedents for the Form of the *Voir-Dit*," in *Studies in Medieval Literature and Languages in Memory of Frederick Whitehead*, ed. W. Rothwell (Manchester: Manchester University Press, 1973), pp. 133–52. In the *Remede de Fortune* we have an expansion of the range of this tradition accomplished by transposing it into what might be called the fourteenth-century didactic register: the seven intercalated lyrics are presented as exempla forming together an ars poetica. At the same time Machaut is transforming a specifically literary model from within this

tradition: the *Dit de la panthère*, where the idea of using intercalated lyrics as poetic exempla appears, as it were, in embryo. See Ernest Hoepffner, "Les Poésies lyriques du *Dit de la panthère* de Nicole de Margival," *Romania* 53 (1920): 204–30 (esp. 226–30).

23. In this respect it is revealing to compare the *Remede de Fortune* (written before 1349), in which an ars poetica is fully integrated into (indeed presented by means of) a narrative poem, with the *Art de dictier* (Art of versifying—written in 1392) of Machaut's disciple Eustache Deschamps. In the later work we have a rhetorico-poetic treatise written in expository, didactic prose in which lyric poems (sometimes incomplete) are presented as illustrations of compositional rules. Machaut's single, all-inclusive poetic discourse (deriving from his identity as *poète*) is no longer felt to be sufficient for the purpose of writing "about" poetry. In addition, the ars poetica that was (perhaps necessarily) implicit in Machaut becomes explicit in Deschamps. Finally, Deschamps's model lyric pieces are presented without musical settings—they are not sung.

24. In this context, I consider of necessity only the initial performance of the *lay* within *Remede*'s plot line, which coincides with its complete textual citation. The second performance of the *lay* at the level of plot (ll. 690–95) is entirely presented by indirect description rather than direct citation.

Sylvia Huot

2. From Life to Art: The Lyric Anthology of Villon's *Testament*

François Villon's *Testament*[1] is made up of 186 huitains and 19 fixed-form compositions, interspersed throughout the huitains at irregular intervals: 16 ballades (including 1 double ballade) and 3 rondeaux. It is in the huitains that Villon establishes the testament format, provides a sketchy autobiographical (or pseudoautobiographical) framework, enumerates his many bequests, and comments upon the world in which he lives and the characters who populate it. The fixed-form poems are closely allied to the huitains: they may continue the protagonist's meditations on a given subject, be placed in the mouth of some other character who has been introduced in the preceding huitain(s), or be offered as bequests under conditions specified in the huitains. They bring into focus the thematic concerns of the *Testament*—love and sexuality, language, old age, death—while the surrounding huitains supply details concerning the identity of the lyric protagonists, the situation that led to the composition of the poem, or the circumstances under which it is to be performed. In this way the fixed-form compositions participate variously in the thematic context of the *Testament*, in the implied social context of a projected performance, or in the implied autobiographical context of the poet-protagonist's life. The versification clearly sets the ballades and rondeaux apart from the huitains, inviting analysis of these pieces as a special poetic program within the *Testament*: a small lyric anthology of fixed-form compositions embedded within the larger quasi-narrative framework of the huitains. It is with the series of fixed-form compositions that the present study is concerned.

As will be seen, the lyric anthology of the *Testament* comprises a remarkable variety of voices. The lyric *je* undergoes a series of transformations, as does the relationship between the voice of the huitains and that of each successive lyric insertion. As a result, the collection can be mapped in terms of these shifting voices and discourse configurations. The principles of unity and coherence in the *Testament* have been a subject of much scholarly debate; it is a poem that resists easy analysis.[2] The fixed-form compositions can easily be extracted to stand on their own merits as anthology pieces, and it is generally assumed that many if not all of them had already been composed and circulated before Villon decided to incorporate them into the *Testament*. If these poems retain a certain autonomy, however, they nonetheless work together and play off one another within the context of the *Testament*. The *Testament* resonates with a cast of voices ultimately generated from and grouped around that of the authorial *je*, locus of unity for the work as a whole. Villon's deft manipulation of poetic voice is such that he succeeds in creating an authorial voice that is liberated finally from identification even with the persona of the *Testament*. The death of the protagonist that is recorded in the *Testament* is at the same time the creation of this transcendent poet figure, since the persona "Villon" is shown to pass from life into the realm of art and poetry.

As a frame text containing a series of poems set apart by their versification, the *Testament* belongs to a well-established poetic tradition, extending back to the early thirteenth-century *Roman de la Rose, ou de Guillaume de Dole* of Jean Renart. Following Renart, the inclusion of lyric selections in both prose and verse narratives was a popular practice.[3] These lyric pieces could be presented as performance pieces within a social context, as privately sung expressions of feeling, or as written texts composed by the narrative protagonist in order to document a particular experience, his own or that of a patron. In texts of the latter sort, such as Guillaume de Machaut's *Fonteinne amoureuse* or Jean Froissart's *Prison amoureuse*, the frame narrative explores the relationship between the authorial figure who creates a poem and the character who appropriates it as a written or oral expression of his or her own experience. By narrating the processes of composition, performance, and written dissemination of lyric pieces, the romance or the dit with lyric insertions provides a commentary on the genesis of a particular lyric corpus, and on the processes of performance and textual transmission.

Though Villon is clearly situated within this tradition, his use of the testament format is unique, and an analysis of the *Testament* must account for the particular statement that this format allows him to make.[4] My reading will begin with a brief look at the overall thematic development of the interspersed ballades and rondeaux. I will then examine the relation between the frame text and the fixed-form compositions through a detailed examination of the figures of poet, protagonist, performer, and audience, focusing on the poems offered as bequests. In this way it will be possible to assess the structural and thematic function of the fixed-form compositions within the *Testament* as a whole, as well as the relevance of the testament format to Villon's enterprise as lyric poet.

A decontextualized reading of the *Testament*'s poems seems at first to present a somewhat disjointed program, shifting kaleidoscopically from one thematic configuration to another and back again.[5] A given poem is thematically linked to several others that may or may not appear in sequence, and each of which in turn has its own set of links. The result is a network of overlapping structures that does not lend itself to linear analysis. We can nonetheless establish relationships among poems and trace the transformations effected within thematically linked groups. (To facilitate this process, a list of the fixed-form compositions of the *Testament* appears as an appendix.) Order will fully emerge only when we can look upon the *Testament* as a whole in which certain elements answer to certain other elements, creating an overall effect larger than the sum of its parts.

A number of Villon's themes converge in the ballade "Ne que monnoye qu'on descrye" (No less than cried-down money), in which La Belle Héaulmière, an aging madam who has lost her physical charms, exhorts her prostitutes to take advantage of their youth. As a feminine reflection on the mercantile quality of male-female relations, "Ne que monnoye" finds its immediate response in the antifeminist sentiments expressed by the *Testament*'s masculine narrator in the ballade "Bien eureux est qui riens n'y a" (Happy is he who has nothing to do with it). "Ne que monnoye" receives a different sort of response in the ballade written in the voice of Villon's mother, "En ceste foy je vueil vivre et mourir" (In this faith I wish to live and die): as in "Ne que monnoye," we find the meditations of an old woman approaching death, but the optimistic piety of the mother contrasts with the cynicism of La Belle Héaulmière. The sentiments of "Ne que monnoye" return in the ballade "Sans empirer, ung povre secourir" (Without injury, to help a poor man), where Villon offers his lady friend "Marthe" advice very similar to that voiced by La Belle Héaulmière. The rondeau "Mort j'appelle de ta rigueur" (Death, I appeal your rigor) and several of the subsequent ballades continue to explore male-female relationships. The world of La Belle Héaulmière reappears, finally, in the two ballades, only seventy lines apart, "En ce bordeau ou tenons nostre estat" (In this brothel where we make our living) and "Tout aux tavernes et aux filles" (All to taverns and girls). The latter in particular, in which the aging, streetwise narrator offers the hard-won lessons of his life to the *enfants perdus* [lost boys], clearly echoes "Ne que monnoye" and provides the most explicit masculine counterpart to the figure of La Belle Héaulmière. "Ne que monnoye" and "Tout aux tavernes" provide a frame within which are contained all of the other poems devoted to amorous pursuits of one sort or another. The two frame poems work together to present an older couple, able to reflect on the great game of love but no longer full participants; while many of the poems contained between them show us other couples, still in their youth, engaged in this "game."

The poems of old age are themselves framed by poems devoted explicitly to death: the three "ubi sunt" ballades near the beginning of the *Testament* and the final fixed-form compositions, that is, Villon's epitaph (a rondeau) and the two ballades announcing his death. The theme of male-female counter-parting is prefigured in the opposition of male and female subjects in the first two poems: "Mais ou sont les neiges d'anten?" (But where are the snows of yesteryear?), a meditation on mythical and historical ladies of bygone days, and "Mais ou est le preux Charlemaigne?" (But where is the bold Charlemagne?), a parallel meditation on men of the past. The transition from poems of death to poems of love and sexuality is effected by "Ne que monnoye," in which the topics of old age and death generate reflection on past amorous relations. Love and death are then reunited in "Mort j'appelle de ta rigueur," the lament for a lost loved one; this poem of mourning for a woman finds its masculine counterpart in the following ballade, "L'ame du bon feu maistre Jehan Cotart" (The soul of the late good Master Jean Cotart). "Mort" lies at almost the precise textual midpoint of the *Testament*, so that death is the focus of the fixed-form compositions both at the outer edges and at the center of the collection.

Following "Tout aux tavernes," the transition back to poems of death is made by the rondeau "Au retour de dure prison" (Upon return from harsh prison), which continues the theme of male-female relationships in somewhat different form: the protagonist laments his treatment at the hands of Lady Fortune. The reference to prison in this context recalls and inverts the poetic topos of *prison amoureuse* ("amorous prison"), exemplified in Villon's own work in the opening passages of the *Lais*. There, the protagonist needed to escape the allegorical prison of unrequited love to which he had been condemned by a real lady; here, it is an allegorical lady who has condemned him to languish in a real prison. Likewise, the death that threatened the protagonist in *Lais*, stanza 5, was purely metaphorical; here, it is real. In this way "Au retour" transforms the theme of amorous relations into that of imprisonment and death. We are now brought full circle, with a return to the themes with which the *Testament* started and with which it is soon to close.

The closing of the circle, however, also brings about a change of focus. The movement from "Ne que monnoye" to "Tout aux tavernes" takes us from Villon's female counterpart to his male persona; the movement from the initial ballades to the final ones takes us from the general condition of humanity to Villon's condition in particular. This direction is already suggested in the discussion of Villon's own impending death in the huitain immediately following the "ubi sunt" poems. In the final ballades, his death is no longer hypothetical but real. The penultimate ballade, "Je crye a toutes gens mercys" (I cry mercy to all people), inverts the "ubi sunt" motif of the opening group, where the lyric protagonist directed his attention to the many dead and enumerated a seemingly endless list of names of those who have passed away. In "Je crye a toutes gens mercy," the *je* is dying, and he lists the many categories of people still alive, to whom he bids farewell. This lyric *je*, defining itself against the living on the one hand and the dead on the other, is the focal point of the *Testament* and the source of its coherence.

Because of the centrality of this first-person voice, the final ballade,

"Quant de ce monde voult partir" (When he wanted to leave this world), has perplexed some readers. In "Quant de ce monde," the death of Villon has already taken place, and a new poetic voice emerges, one dissociated from the protagonist of the *Testament*. The appearance of this seemingly new lyric *je* has led to speculations that the ballade may be the work, not of Villon, but of a later writer.[6] However, close reading shows that this poem is essential to the function of the fixed-form compositions as a group within the *Testament*. It brings the themes of love and death together one final time in the figure of Villon the protagonist, and it completes the narrative of his joys and sorrows. It also completes the formation of Villon the author, whose identity is defined by the collection as a whole. While questions of authorship can be nearly impossible to determine with certainty, the poem's integral role within the *Testament* provides a stronger argument, to my mind, than the assertion that Villon, a highly sophisticated poet, could not have written a poem in which he refers to himself in the third person and narrates his own death.[7]

To demonstrate the importance of the final ballade, we must first address the question of just what death means in the context of the *Testament*. The first clue comes in the "ubi sunt" ballades. Here, the female characters range from mythical figures, such as Echo, to historical figures, such as Heloise and even Villon's near contemporary, Joan of Arc. The male characters are all historical figures, but a similar blend of myth and history is present in the figure of Charlemagne, a real person elevated to mythic status through the many fictional adventures ascribed to him in literary tradition. All these characters are placed on equal footing, subject to the question "ubi sunt?" Whether these figures existed at one time or not, none survives except in the stories told about them. More specifically, these characters exist in the text of Villon's *Testament*. To die is to enter the realm of art, for it is in texts and images that the past lives on.[8]

The analogy between death and art is renewed in the central rondeau, "Mort," in which the lyric protagonist states that, having been deprived of his heart through his lady's death, he must either die himself or go on living without life "comme les ymaiges" (l. 988) ("like images")—a point to which I will return below. The process of passing from life into literature is also portrayed in the ballade that follows, "L'ame du bon feu maistre Jehan Cotart." In this ballade Villon identifies a biblical tradition of drinkers and ensures Cotart's entry into this tradition by supplying him with a text commemorating his capacity for drink. Villon's petition that Cotart be admitted into the heavenly company of imbibers is self-fulfilling: in his ballade, the four great drinkers of history are conjoined for all time in a single poetic construct.

It is in light of these remarks that we may understand Villon's own death. In huitains 176–78, Villon describes his projected tomb, which is to include both a visual image (a portrait) and a text, the rondeau "Repoz eternel donne a cil" (Grant to him eternal rest). This epitaph transforms the persona of the *Testament* into a third-person character and presents his essential qualities in distilled form. The oxymoronic quality of the *Testament* is nowhere more apparent than it is here.[9] The mixture of dictions in the epitaph achieves an expressive power beyond what any single diction could attain. At once comic and moving, it formulates the heights and depths of Villon's experience; it is truly a monument to the persona of the *Testament*, who retains full dignity among prostitutes and thieves. The final ballade, in turn, is the logical culmination of the poetic construct created by the *Testament* as a whole: "le povre Villon" ("poor Villon") undergoes his final transformation into a poetic subject and so leaves the world of the living to enter that of art.

As I suggested above, the voice of the fixed-form compositions and its relationship to the persona "François Villon" changes constantly throughout the *Testament*, and is deserving of closer analysis than it has received thus far. The ballades and rondeaux offered as bequests provide a field for the study of the relationship between the voice of the fixed-form and its relationship to that of the huitains. One can trace a cyclical pattern, hitherto unnoticed, in this group of poems, in which a progressive dissociation of voices is followed by a reidentification. In this way Villon explores the varieties of authorial presence in the lyric text.

The two poems at the beginning and end of this cycle, the ballades "En ceste foy je vueil vivre et mourir" and "En ce bordeau ou tenons nostre estat," have been described in an article by Karl Uitti.[10] Uitti's analysis of "En ceste foy" focuses on the fusion of Villon's learned poetic diction with the colloquial diction of his mother, resulting in the conjoined voice of mother and son. As he points out, the mother-son persona is represented in the envoi acrostic, "VILLONE": a feminine form of the author's name. That this represents a purely poetic construction of mother and son is underscored by the fact that "Villon" is an assumed name and not a family name, hence not the name that Villon actually shared with his mother. The author's participation in the poem and his relationship with its female recipient are assured by the performance that he envisions for it: its realization is the conjunction of mother's voice and son's poetry. Moreover, the mother-son relationship so vital to the creation of the poem is mirrored within it by the Virgin and Christ.

In the ballade that follows, "Sans empirer, ung povre secourir," Villon's participation in the poem, as well as his relationship with its female addressee, are more problematic. The fusion of male and female in a single *je* that we saw in the preceding poem, has given way to a *je-vous* opposition, and the relationship between *je* and *vous* is far from simple. The poem itself provides a space for textual coupling. The acrostics of the first two stanzas, FRANCOYS and MARTHE, specify the identity of *je* and *vous* respectively, and allow for the presence of the two personae in the textual fabric. There is, moreover, a symmetrical disposition of these personae within the poem. The first two stanzas delineate the effects of the lady's behavior on the male protagonist. But stanza 1, bearing the name FRANCOYS, concentrates on the qualities of the as-yet unidentified woman; stanza 2, carrying the name MARTHE, concentrates on the experience of the male persona. The relationship between the two finally emerges with the second-person pronouns and verbs of stanza 3. The female partner, until now present only in the third person as a disconnected series of attributes in stanza 1 and as a name in stanza 2, is finally addressed directly. As the poet reproaches her, he conjures up the vision not only of her old age but also of his own: the two are inseparable. This shared experience, if no other, binds the two characters together. This sense of parallel, if not entirely fused, experience is reflected in the scrambled acrostic VJJLVONS: a suggestion of the plural form "Villons."[11] The lack of harmony in the relationship is reflected in the impossibility of fully resolving the two parties into a single acrostic like the VILLONE of the preceding poem. Nonetheless, male and female personae are close counterparts.

The disharmony within the relationship emerges most clearly from the actual message of the poem, as well as from the attached huitains. Villon complains that this lady has consistently refused his advances and remained, for him, untouchable. The gap between *je* and *vous* is one that can only be bridged poetically, in the manipulation of words and images and in the language of direct address. Indeed, according to the huitains, Villon will not himself deliver this message to Marthe; it is to be delivered by Pernet de la Barre. While Villon does not explicitly state that this is to be an oral presentation, the placement of the ballade directly after Pernet's address to Marthe certainly implies that it will form part of his speech to her:

> Il luy dira sans plus enquerre:
> "Orde paillarde, dont viens tu?"
> BALLADE
> Faulse beaulté qui tant me couste chier.
>
> [He will say to her without further inquiry,
> "Filthy good-for-nothing, where are you coming from?"
> BALLADE
> False beauty that has cost me so dear.]
>
> (ll. 940–42)

In this projected scenario, the voice reciting the words will not come from within the poem but will be provided by a third party, and it is inescapable that, as the words become his, the identity of the lyric *je* is obscured.

The extremely tight configuration of "En ceste foy" has been loosened. The reciprocal relationship of poet-son and performer-mother has become a triangle: the completion of the relationship between lover and beloved is contingent on that between poet and performer, and therefore on that between performer and audience. In the rondeau "Mort," this process of dissolution is carried even further. Here, *je* and *elle* have been irretrievably separated by death: there can be no further communication between them, not even through intervening performers. Now the relationship can be realized only within the text, as a poetic construct.

"Mort" is not presented as the record of Villon's experience; it is bequeathed to Ythier Marchant, who is required to prepare it for performance by setting it to music, and who thus presumably becomes the referent for the lyric *je*. It is his life rather than Villon's that is to provide the interpretive context for this poem. But the information concerning Ythier given in the preceding huitain elicits a very strange reading of the rondeau. The suggestion that the *elle* of the rondeau actually refers to more than one person—"ses anciennes amours" (l. 975) ("his former loves")—robs the rondeau of any force as a serious lament, since its tragic quality depends on the uniqueness of the lost relationship. In this light, the protestations of grief are a sham. The classic diction, deprived of sincerity, exemplifies the abuse of language at the hands of those who ape courtly modes of expression without fulfilling the prescribed role. The designation of Ythier as recipient for this poem is in effect an exposure of Ythier's unjustified pretensions to courtliness.

Such treatment of Ythier parallels that accorded him in *Lais*, stanza 11, where, as Villon reminds us (*Test.*, l. 9971), he left Ythier his *branc d'acier* ("steel sword"), to be redeemed for *ung escoz huit solz* ("the sum of eight sous") and then shared, or perhaps disputed, with Jehan le Cornu. The absurdity of the "gift" reflects, again, on the aristocratic pretensions of Ythier, who must stoop to such means as this in order to arm himself. The word *branc* can also be interpreted as a reference to sexual potency, through an interpretation of the sword as a phallic symbol.[12] The supposed gift is actually an exposure of Ythier's impotence; that he must buy his sexual power further points to the type of woman that suits him. The *Testament* legacy recalls and continues the *Lais* passage: to bestow the lament on Ythier suggests that his amorous relations are permanently over, while the plural reference to his "loves" reminds us of the transient nature of these relationships.[13] Allied with the melodramatic nature of the suggested musical accompaniment, these suggestions shatter the courtly image of Ythier as grieving lover and turn lament into parody.

All of the bequest poems are of course designed for presentation or performance after Villon's death, hence in his absence. But the poet lives on in his poems, which enable him to be present in word if not in body. In the first, the recital of the poem by his mother affirms the voice created in the poem as well as his bond with her. In the second, Pernet de la Barre's recital or delivery of the poem still succeeds in transmitting Villon's words to their intended recipient, even if at one remove. With the performance of "Mort" by Ythier Marchant, Villon's stately lament is significantly altered. Just as in the *Lais* the sword took on a ludicrous aspect with obscene overtones once it passed into Ythier's hands, so here the courtliness of the rondeau is undercut. The poet is present in his poems only insofar as his voice is brought to life by readers and performers, his representatives. Too great a disjunction between the voice of the poet and that of his representatives means that the former may be completely obscured by the latter.

In the next bequest poem, the ballade "Et c'est la fin pourquoy sommes ensemble" (And that is the purpose for which we are together), the unity of the couple is reestablished. Unlike "Sans empirer," "Et c'est la fin" is not the means of making contact within an otherwise frustrated relationship. It celebrates a relationship of ongoing harmony, the marriage of Robert d'Estouteville and Ambroise de Loré. The acrostic of the first two stanzas, AMBROISE DELORE, once again ensures that the identity of the *vous* is defined within the textual fabric itself; the identity of the *je* is to be supplied by Robert's presence in his delivery of the poem to Ambroise. As in "En ceste foy," the *je-vous* relationship within the poem corresponds exactly to that governing the projected performance.

In this case, however, Villon is excluded. "Et c'est la fin" does not represent a poetic fusion of Villon with either Robert or Ambroise. It is, nonetheless, his tribute to both of them, and the ballade thus implicitly relates the poet to the *je-vous* unit.[14] The situation reverses that found in "Sans empirer." There, the lover-poet must rely on a performer to deliver the message he has formulated; here, the lover-performer must rely on a poet to formulate the message he is to deliver. In that respect, "Et c'est la fin" is similar to "Mort"; it differs from "Mort" in that the language and the *je-vous* relationship correspond to, rather than conflict with, the narrative context provided by the immediately preceding huitain. "Mort" presents a situation where poet and performer are at odds; in "Et c'est la fin" they cooperate.

In the ballade "Il n'est tresor que de vivre a son aise" (There is no treasure like living at one's ease), bequeathed to Andry Courault, the lyric *je* is once more identified with that of the huitains. But the voice that speaks to us from inside the poem is no longer elaborating upon his own affairs. Rather, as in "Jehan Cotart" and "Soient frictes ces langues ennuyeuses" ("May these bothersome tongues be fried"), the *je* is an observer and a codifier of the world around him. "Il n'est tresor" opens with the description of a portly canon and his lady friend, whose luxurious life is compared to the simple existence of the pastoral couple Franc Gontier and Helen; the first person appears only in the eighth line, with "les vy tous deux" (l. 1480) ("I saw them both"). The effect of this delay is that the *je* does not appear to construct the scenario; instead he assumes the role of voyeur, attached to the completed scene from the outside.[15] Villon's *je* participates in the internal dynamics of the ballade, but not in the fictional world of the canon or of Franc Gontier.

Nor is the audience included in these fictional worlds. The performance situation suggested by the direct address of the second stanza—"Lequel vaut mieulx? Lict costoyé de cheze? / Qu'en dictes vous?" (ll. 1490–91) ("Which is better? A bed with a chair beside it? What do you say?")—is not, as it is in the other poems of male-female union, an extension of the poetic world. Instead, Villon invites his readers, and Andry Courault in particular, to join him in contemplation of, and judgment on, the two scenes he has evoked. Again, the poetic text is the means of establishing a relationship between a *je* and a *vous,* but this relationship is not itself the subject of the poem. The couples who constitute the poetic focus are simply representatives of poetic types. The subject of debate is two opposing styles of life and love, associated with two opposing styles of poetry, which *je* and *vous* alike examine, identifying themselves with one or the other. In "Sans empirer" the poet-lover relies on a performer to address his audience-beloved; in "Et c'est la fin" the performer-lover addresses his audience-beloved with words provided by the poet; and in "Il n'est tresor," lover and beloved recede into the poetic world, while poet and audience join forces as readers of that world.

In the ballade "En ce bordeau ou tenons nostre estat," the conjoined *je* of ballade and huitains is reestablished as protagonist of the love world. As Uitti rightly stressed, the envoi acrostic VILLONE again signals the fusion of the poetic persona "Villon" with a female persona. The poem itself thematizes sexual coupling, and stresses the extent to which Margot and her lover are exact counterparts: "Je suis paillart, la paillarde me suyt" (l. 1622) ("I'm a good-for-nothing, the good-for-nothing woman follows me"); "L'ung vault l'autre, c'est a mau rat mau chat" (l. 1624) ("One is worth as much as the other, it's a bad cat after a bad rat"). But although Villon stipulates that the ballade is to be read to Margot, she is not directly addressed within it. "En ce bordeau" thus differs from "Sans empirer" and "Et c'est la fin" in that the relationship of lover and beloved does not provide the *je-vous* relationship that governs performance. Instead, the *je-vous* relationship is purely that of poet and audience. Indeed, the rhetorical question of the envoi, "Lequel vault mieulx?" (l. 1623) ("Which is worth more?"), repeats the question posed some 130 lines earlier in "Il n'est tresor." "En ce bordeau" picks up and continues the theme of critical reading, as the poet reenters the poetic world to present to his audience the spectacle of himself in union with his beloved. Thus "En ce bordeau" offers a new perspective on love poetry, that of the bawdy song, and yet another facet of the ever-shifting configuration of lover and beloved, poet and audience.

One more bequest poem remains to be considered, the rondeau "Au retour" presented to Jacques Cardon. As in the earlier rondeau "Mort," the pathos of Villon's lament is subverted by the bequest. We realize again that the poem's power of reference to its original author is lost in its appropriation by others after his death. In the immediately preceding huitain, Villon proposes that the text be sung to a bawdy tune, suggesting "Marïonnecte" or "Ouvrez vostre huys, Guillemete" (Open your doorway, Guillemete). Neither tune has the proper metrical structure for the piece, and both are wholly inappropriate to the classic courtly diction of "Au retour." Even if we assume that the prison in question might really be an amorous one, "Ouvrez vostre huis, Guillemete" is hardly the plaint of a courtly lover. As Eugénie Droz remarked, "C'est comme si on nous proposait de chanter les vers de Mallarmé sur un air de jazz" ("It is as though it were proposed to us to sing one of Mallarmé's poems to a jazz tune").[16] One can only assume that the personality of Jacques Cardon is such that to identify him with the *je* of the rondeau is to alter completely the sense of the text. *His* lament, no matter how high-flown the language, will be no more than a vulgar street song.

This treatment of Jacques Cardon is similar to that accorded him in *Lais*, stanza 16. There, Villon wishes his "friend" fine clothing and rich food. The gift is tempered, though, by the inclusion of acorns (food for pigs) and by the additional "gift" of daily litigation. Jacques Cardon is presented as a pretentious and ill-tempered man, given to personal excess. The rondeau, with its reference to prison, continues the theme of legal battles; like the presence of acorns in Cardon's daily meal, the bawdy melodies deflate the aristocratic pretensions of a man who would fancy himself worthy of serious lament. The erroneous generic appellation *bergeronette* further suggests Cardon's lack of sophistication with regard to courtly poetry, while the possible sexual implications of *prison* point to his lack of success in amorous pursuits. The function of "Au retour" in the *Testament* and in relation to the *Lais* is parallel to that of the other bequest rondeau, "Mort."

This analysis clarifies the contribution of the fixed-form compositions to the varied and complex world of the *Testament*. We find an aging, cynical madam; Villon's aging and pious mother; his recalcitrant lady friend; a virtuous wife; a feisty prostitute. Ambroise de Loré and Robert d'Estouteville are *l'esprevier* (l. 1378) ("the sparrowhawk") and *son per* (l. 1381) ("its mate"), while Margot and her pimp are *mau rat* and *mau chat* (l. 1624) ("bad rat and bad cat"); yet each couple represents a perfect conjoining of male and female that finds expression through a particular poetic language. It is this perfect correspondence of male to female, and of experience to language, that affords to each its particular dignity within the poetic world of the *Testament*. On the other hand, the lack of correspondence between the experience of Ythier Marchant or Jacques Cardon and the poetic language each would appropriate robs the language and the persona of dignity. Through this distinction, Villon establishes for his world a social hierarchy that is determined poetically, rather than one based on the hierarchies of extratextual society.[17]

In addition to offering windows on Villon's poetic universe, the fixed-form compositions of the *Testament* offer a series of variations on a basic lyric construct. The poems may function as communication within a strictly delimited context: the solitary world of prayer, the love world of a couple, or the larger but still select community whose special interests are addressed by the poem. Villon may identify himself with the *je* of the poem, or he may lend his voice to another, either male or female. Other poems hold up the world of a particular character, couple, or group before a more general audience; in such cases, Villon may locate himself either within the poetic world or outside of it. The one constant is the identity of the author, creator of all poetic voices and personae. From the multiplicity of poetic stances emerges the voice of the poet, who, though frequently associated with members of the poetic world (most closely and most frequently with the protagonist of the huitains), is not ultimately contained by that world. This authorial voice, generated by the dynamics of the composite text, speaks in the final ballade. It is in this manner that Villon the protagonist is subsumed by an anonymous poetic voice and goes on living as a textual figure after death has removed him from the world of experience, the world of performance and communication.[18]

In this respect, Villon continues a tendency already apparent in the work of such poets as Guillaume de Machaut, Jean Froissart, and Christine de Pizan.[19] In the works of these writers too the role of love poet is separated from that of lover or singer. In Machaut's *Fonteinne amoureuse*, Froissart's *Prison amoureuse*, or Christine's *Duc des vrais amans*, the poet recedes from the empirical world of love experience and oral performance to assume the more specialized role of writer. Villon has taken this process one step farther: the separation between poet-narrator and first-person protagonist is so complete that the former can narrate the death of the latter.

It is the nature of a testament that it charts an interim moment between life and death, wholeness and dissolution. The possessions of the dying protagonist appear here as such for the last time. The testament is the instrument of their dispersal; it is, by definition, the protagonist's last statement to the world at large. Villon's *Testament* distributes not only the objects of his private world but also his poetic corpus. As each individual poem is appropriated by readers and performers, the corpus breaks apart, and its reference to Villon is weakened. The identity of a specific poetic ego provides the unifying force that holds a poetic corpus together; the corpus in turn records and represents this ego. Neither the persona nor the poetic corpus, as such, can exist independently of each other.

The *Testament*, as a written compilation, is proof against this dissolution.[20] The creation of epitaph and monument for the dying persona of the *Testament* parallels the creation of the textual artifact. The collection demonstrates the extent of Villon's poetic versatility; the themes of language and art, love and sexuality, old age and death knit the collection together. By presenting his world in the form of a testament, Villon transforms what for other poets might have been a lyric anthology, or a love story with lyric insertions, into a dynamic model of textual transmission. The *Testament* bridges the gap between composition and dissemination, showing us the relations not only between the poet and his texts but also between the poet and those who read, hear, or perform them.

Appendix: The Fixed-form Compositions of the *Testament*

"Mais ou sont les neiges d'anten?" ballade, ll. 329–56
"Mais ou est le preux Charlemaigne?" ballade, ll. 357–84
"Autant en emporte ly vens," ballade, ll. 385–412
"Ne que monnoye qu'on descrye," ballade, ll. 533–60
"Bien eureux est qui riens n'y a," double ballade, ll. 625–72
"En ceste foy je vueil vivre et mourir," ballade, ll. 873–909
"Sans empirer, ung povre secourir," ballade, ll. 942–69
"Mort j'appelle de ta rigueur," rondeau, ll. 978–89
"L'ame du bon feu maistre Jehan Cotart," ballade, ll. 1238–65
"Et c'est la fin pourquoy sommes ensemble," ballade, ll. 1378–1405
"Soient frictes ces langues ennuyeuses," ballade, ll. 1422–56
"Il n'est tresor que de vivre a son aise," ballade, ll. 1473–1506
"Il n'est bon bec que de Paris," ballade, ll. 1515–42
"En ce bordeau ou tenons nostre estat," ballade, ll. 1591–1627
"Tout aux tavernes et aux filles," ballade, ll. 1692–1719
"Au retour de dure prison," rondeau, ll. 1784–95
"Repoz eternel donne a cil," rondeau, ll. 1892–1903
"Je crye a toutes gens mercys," ballade, ll. 1968–95
"Quant de ce monde voult partir," ballade, ll. 1996–2023

Notes

1. All references to Villon's *Testament* and *Lais* are to Jean Rychner and Albert Henry, eds., *Le Testament Villon*, Textes Littéraires Français (Geneva: Droz, 1977), 2 vols. All translations are mine.

2. Italo Siciliano, for example, has argued that the *Testament* represents a somewhat disordered conflation of independent elements, in *François Villon et les thèmes poétiques du moyen-âge* (Paris: A.-G. Nizet, 1967), pp. 445–57. His position is refuted by Claudine Gothot-Mersch, who sees the *Testament* as a deliberately disparate and digressive, but unified, work, in "Sur l'unité du *Testament* de Villon," in *Mélanges Rita Lejeune* (Gembloux: Duculot, 1969), 2:1411–26. For further discussion of the structure of the *Testament*, including a summary of the various solutions proposed in the history of Villon criticism, see A. J. A. van Zoest, *Structures de deux testaments fictionnels: Le "Lais" et le "Testament" de François Villon*, Publications de l'Institut d'Etudes Françaises et Occitanes de l'Université d'Utrecht, 3 (The Hague/Paris: Mouton, 1974).

3. See Jacqueline Cerquiglini, "Pour une typologie de l'insertion," *Perspectives Médiévales* 3 (1977): 9–14; G. B. Gybbon-Monypenny, "Guillaume de Machaut's Erotic 'Autobiography': Precedents for the Form of the *Voir-Dit*," in *Studies in Medieval Literature and Languages in Memory of Frederick Whitehead*, ed. W. Rothwell (Manchester: Manchester University Press, 1973), pp. 133–52; Douglas Kelly, *Medieval Imagination: Rhetoric and the Poetry of Courtly Love* (Madison: University of Wisconsin Press, 1978), pp. 239–56; and my *From Song to Book: The Poetics of Writing in Old French Lyric and Lyrical Narrative Poetry* (Ithaca, N.Y.: Cornell University Press, 1987), pp. 106–34 and passim. For comments on lyric anthologies of the thirteenth, fourteenth, and fifteenth

centuries, see Jacqueline Cerquiglini, "Quand la voix s'est tue: La Mise en recueil de la poésie lyrique aux XIVe et XVe siècles," in *La Présentation du livre: Actes du colloque de Paris X—Nanterre (4, 5, 6 décembre 1985)*, ed. Emmanuèle Baumgartner and Nicole Boulestreau, Littérales: Cahiers du Département de Français, 2 (Nanterre: Centre de Recherches du Département de Français, 1987), pp. 313–27; and my *From Song to Book*, pp. 46–80.

4. Ilse Nolting-Hauff comments on the novelty of lyric insertions in a testament format and terms Villon's *Testament* "eine Anthologie seiner selbst" ("an anthology of himself"), in "Selbstbekenntnis und Selbstironie in Villons *Testament*," *Poetica* 2 (1968): 181.

5. David Kuhn outlines a thematically based division of the last twelve ballades into three symmetrically ordered sequences of four, in *La Poétique de François Villon* (Paris: A. Colin, 1967), pp. 375–78. Kuhn's analysis brings out many important features of the ballades and their interrelationships, but it cannot be regarded as a definitive solution to the arrangement of the *Testament*. Any one of the ballades in question can just as easily be linked with ballades outside its particular group.

6. Helmer Lång, "Villon's *Testament* and the *Ballade pour servir de conclusion*," *Symposium* 9 (1955): 308–23. Dieter Ingenschag refutes Lång's reading of the penultimate ballade as a statement of penitence, which had formed the basis for his argument that it is specially suited to close a testament, in "Pragmatische Form und lyrische Besetzung: Zur Konstitution von Ballade und Testament bei Deschamps und besonders Villon," in *Literatur in der Gesellschaft des Spätmittelalters*, ed. Hans Ulrich Gumbrecht with Ursula Link-Heer and Peter M. Spangenberg, Grundriß der romanischen Literatur des Mittelalters, Begleitreihe, vol. 1 (Heidelberg: Carl Winter/Universitätsverlag, 1980), pp. 182–85.

7. Karl D. Uitti argues that the final line of the closing ballade completes the unfinished opening sentence of the *Testament*, in "A Note on Villon's Poetics," *Romance Philology* 30 (1976): 191–92. Kuhn argues that the closing ballade is closely tied to the rest of the *Testament* and distinguishes between the close of the testament and the close of the poem: "La 'leçon' et l'Epitaphe sont les derniers legs d'un vrai testament, tandis que les ballades finales terminent et résument à la fois un poème, un testament satirique, et une entreprise littéraire" ("The 'lesson' and the Epitaph are the last bequests of a real will, while the final ballades at once sum up and end a poem, a satiric will and a literary undertaking") (*Poétique de Villon*, p. 377).

8. Charles Mela finds the "ubi sunt" ballades "le lieu qui défie la mort: la mémoire, et le moyen de la préserver; la parole poétique" ("the place that challenges death: memory and the means of preserving it; poetic language"), in "'Je, Françoys Villon . . .'" in *Mélanges Jean Frappier*, Textes Littéraires Français 112 (Geneva: Droz, 1970), 2:784.

9. On the mixture of opposing registers in the *Testament*, see the excellent study by Evelyn Birge Vitz, *The Crossroads of Intentions: A Study of Symbolic Expression in the Poetry of François Villon* (The Hague/Paris: Mouton, 1974). Claudine Gothot-Mersch discusses Villon's manipulation of a disparate and digressive style in "Sur l'unité du *Testament* de Villon," in *Mélanges Rita Lejeune*, 2:1411–26.

10. Uitti, "A Note on Villon's Poetics," pp. 187–92.

11. Previous critics have identified the acrostic of the third stanza as an imperfect

form of VILLON, ignoring the final *s*: see Rychner and Henry's note on vv. 958–64. The full acrostic VJJLVONS is suggested by Uitti ("A Note on Villon's Poetics," p. 188). It may seem strange that a single acrostic name should refer simultaneously to two different people, but there is precedent for such a device. In particular, thirteenth- and fourteenth-century poets sometimes created anagrams that were supposed to produce the names of both the poet and his lady or, alternatively, the poet and his patron. See my *From Song to Book*, pp. 162–63, 191, 288–90.

12. See Vitz, *Crossroads*, pp. 30–31.

13. Kuhn discusses the *Testament* legacy to Ythier Marchant as a continuation of that in the *Lais* (*Poétique de Villon*, pp. 425–26). Kuhn points out that Villon explicitly refuses to state the name of Ythier's "former loves" and suggests that this name is "folly," "filth," or "shame" (p. 425).

14. Gabriel Bianciotto discusses the historical events alluded to in "Et c'est la fin" and argues that the ballade and immediately preceding huitain express Villon's friendly relations with Robert d'Estouteville, in "A propos du *Testament* de Villon: Troïle et Robert d'Estouteville (vv. 1369–1377)," *Mélanges Jean Frappier*, 1:115–32.

15. This effect is discussed by Kuhn in *Poétique de Villon*, pp. 361–62.

16. Eugénie Droz, "Les Chansons de François Villon," *Mélanges de musicologie . . . Lionel de La Laurencie*, Publications de la Société française de la musicologie, ser. 2, vol. 3–4 (Paris: Droz, 1933), p. 31; my translation.

17. On Villon's reconstitution of society, and his views on its moral order or lack thereof, see Vitz, *Crossroads*, pp. 111–31.

18. In the words of Charles Mela: "Villon enterre 'le povre Villon' (vv. 1997–98), en même temps qu'il se dédouble dans la formule significative où se découvre la vérité de son mensonge. . . . Emportant dans la tombe ce dont il a su se libérer, il éclate de rire et termine sur un bon mot" (in "'Je, Françoys Villon . . . ,'" p. 796). ("Villon buries 'poor Villon' [ll. 1997–98] at the same time that he doubles himself in the meaningful formula where the truth of his lie is revealed. . . . Bearing into the tomb that from which he had managed to free himself, he bursts out laughing and closes on a witticism"). Precedents for the association of the close of a poetic text or corpus with the poet's death can be found in manuscript compilations of the works of Rutebeuf and Adam de la Halle, in the works of Machaut, and in the *Roman de la Rose*; see my *From Song to Book*, pp. 71, 218, 262, 265–66.

19. For a brief but illuminating discussion of Froissart and Villon as heirs to a poetic tradition partially shaped by Machaut, see Kevin Brownlee, *Poetic Identity in Guillaume de Machaut* (Madison: University of Wisconsin Press, 1984), pp. 211–14. On the poet figure of Machaut's *Fonteinne amoureuse* and Froissart's *Prison amoureuse*, see also my *From Song to Book* pp. 293–301, 311–16.

20. See Mela, "'Je, Françoys Villon . . . ,'" p. 790.

George Joseph

3. Lyric Sequence as a Condition of Meaning: Various Arrangements of Marot's Poems from "Certaines oeuvres qu'il feit en la prison"

A lyric sequence is a continuous or connected series of poems that follow one another in some kind of order. In Clément Marot's poetry maverick poems often disrupt sequences based on principles such as hierarchy, chronology, and genre, but the effect is often to create meaning and a new kind of order through a playful and suggestive dialectic with the very sequences that are undermined.

Marot's poems pertaining to his first imprisonment appear in this kind of give-and-take arrangement, whether it be the 1534 "Certaines oeuvres qu'il feit en la prison" (Certain works that he wrote in prison), where they are published together, or in the 1538 *Oeuvres*, where they appear scattered in smaller groups.[1] In both instances, there is a witty manipulation of what has been called the reader's "wandering viewpoint."[2] Since a reader can take in Marot's text only bit by bit, each new segment causes the reader both to revise (not necessarily discard) perceptions of what has just been read and to project an expectation of what will come next. The purpose of this essay is to track the stops and starts of such a progressive reading of the sequences into which the prison poems are arranged.

"Certaines oeuvres qu'il feit en la prison"—1534

That a play on sequence is a factor of meaning becomes especially apparent as we reconstruct the story of Marot's imprisonment on the basis of the prison poems themselves. Sequences are important not only insofar as they provide objective facts about persons, places, times, and things, but also to the extent that they color value judgments—whether people were friendly or unfriendly and events were justified or unjustified. In these cases, then, sequences suggest a moral analysis as well as an objective "history" of experience.[3] In the 1514 edition the poems appear in the following order:

1. "Le Rondeau qui fut la cause de sa prise"[4]
   (The Rondeau that was the cause of his arrest)
   Marot denounces his mistress's infidelity.
2. "La Ballade qu'il feit en prison"
   (The ballade that he wrote in prison)
   Marot protests that his mistress had him arrested in revenge for his denunciation of her.
3. "Epistre qu'il envoya à Bouchard, docteur en Theologie"
   (Epistle that he sent to Bouchard, Doctor of Theology)
   Marot protests that he has been unjustly imprisoned on charges of Lutheranism and asks for Dr. Bouchard's assistance.
4. "Rondeau parfaict composé apres sa delivrance & envoyé a ses amys"
   (Rondeau parfait composed after his deliverance and sent to his friends)
   Marot celebrates his release from prison and thanks his friends for their help.
5. "Epistre à son amy Lyon"
   (Epistle to his friend Lyon)
   Marot turns to his friend Lyon Jamet for help in getting out of prison.

A cursory glance at the titles of these poems reveals the inadequacy of chronology as the guiding principle of the sequence. Although the title of the group, "Certaines oeuvres qu'il feit en la prison," creates the expectation that the works that are to follow were written while the poet was biding his time in captivity, "Le Rondeau qui fut cause de sa prise," the reason for Marot's imprisonment, was of necessity written beforehand. The "Rondeau parfaict composé apres sa delivrance & envoyé a ses amys" was clearly written afterwards. One is tempted to jump to the conclusion that the titles are a sloppy afterthought on the part of Marot or his publisher, Roffet.[5] Yet we shall see in the ensuing discussion that the 1534 arrangement, including the play in sequence between the titles, is rich in meaning for the reader who takes the text seriously.

From freedom to captivity

Although the "Rondeau qui fut la cause de sa prise"[6] is clearly a poem written before the arrest, its presence in the collection does not necessarily contradict the claim that the poems of Marot's series represent "oeuvres qu'il feit en la prison"; rather, it can indicate that the rondeau is a kind of introduction or prelude that orients the reader in regard to the rest of the sequence.

The rondeau is simply a denunciation of Marot's mistress for her blatant fickleness:

Car je ne puis son maulvais bruyt cacher
Si seurement qu'elle ne se descache
    Comme inconstante

(ll. 13–15)

For I cannot hide her bad reputation
As surely as she reveals herself
    Fickle

There is no mention of prisons, police, or crimes—except of course those of the insatiable mistress: "Il luy fauldroit (au train qu'à mener tasche) / Des Serviteurs à journée et à tasche" (ll. 6–7) ("She would need (at the rate that she tries to live) / Several Servants all day and at work"). The title, therefore, is an invitation to speculate on the ways in which the rondeau led to Marot's imprisonment.

The next poem in the series, "La Ballade qu'il feit en prison" (*OD*, LXXX), reveals the connections. There we learn that because of the rondeau, Marot's *amye* ("friend") denounced him to the authorities. Marot goes on to say how he was arrested and imprisoned, and then laments his fate.

In this fashion the rondeau and ballade suggest the history of Marot's imprisonment from the time of his freedom to the moment when he was languishing in prison thinking about the past. The order of the two poems is motivated by a twofold chronology, and both are important in the rest of the sequence: (1) The titles, which present the ballade as having been written after the rondeau, imply that the poems are arranged in the order in which they were written. (2) The poems also follow the chronology of events. We shall see below how the text both follows these two chronologies and plays against them.

Taken together, the rondeau and the ballade trivialize the prison episode, which seems to be the result of a lovers' spat rather than a serious matter of politics, religion, or criminal justice. Since we have never been able satisfactorily to determine the identity of Marot's mistress, it is easy to suspect a poetic cover-up or to consider the whole love affair as a metaphor for the kind of injustice that Marot suffered.[7]

Be that as it may, the structure of the betrayal sets up a series of relationships that create a point of reference for the rest of the sequence. Marot's denunciation of his mistress's infidelity is a violation of the code of so-called courtly love, according to which one never casts aspersions on one's beloved. Regardless of the truth of his accusation, Marot writes a type of poem associated with *faux amants* or *losangiers*—slanderers who destroy a woman's reputation.[8]

Yet while Marot may not be an entirely innocent victim because of his uncourtly conduct, he considers his mistress's response an overreaction. By means of the rhyme, he underscores the fact that although he was writing only (*seulement*) about her fickleness, she lost no time in paying him back heatedly (*chauldement*):

> Ung jour rescripviz à m'Amye
> Son inconstance seulement;
> Mais elle ne fut endormie
> A me le rendre chauldement.
> Car des l'heure tint parlement
> A je ne sçay quel Papelard
> Et luy dict tout bellement:
> Prenez le, il a mangé le Lart!
> (ll. 1–8)

> One day I wrote to my Friend
> Just about her fickleness,
> But she was not asleep
> When it came to heatedly getting back at me.
> Because immediately she contacted
> Some hypocrite
> And said to him outright:
> Take him, he has eaten the lard!

We shall see below how the theme of the guilty but unjustly treated victim, as well as that of the treacherous female, function in regard to the unity of the sequence.

The refrain, "Prenez le, il a mangé le Lard," has been taken to mean that Marot transgressed the traditional Lenten abstinence from meat and meat products such as lard.[9] Michael Screech, however, maintains that we are to ignore the associations with meat in the expression *manger le lard*. Not only does he make a distinction between *meat* and *lard,* he also maintains that we are to take the expression only in the specific figurative sense of "criminal offense." Such a figurative interpretation receives intertextual confirmation, since *manger le lard* recalls a ballade by Eustache Deschamps ("Sachiez qui a mangié le lart": "Know who ate the lard") concerning the duc de Berry's treasurer, Bétissac, who was imprisoned for embezzlement. This reading, then, implies that Marot received a criminal punishment for his noncriminal offense against his mistress. However, such an interpretation, while possible, becomes, in the context of the sequence, no more than an initial expectation that must be revised.[10]

In the poem that follows the ballade in the sequence, the "Epistre qu'il envoya a Bouchard, docteur en Theologie" (*Epîtres* IX), the "crime" for which the mistress denounced Marot takes on a religious dimension:[11]

> Donne response à mon present affaire,
> Docte Docteur. Qui t'a induict à faire

Emprisoner, depuis six jours en ça,
Ung tien amy, qui onc ne t'offensa?
Et vouloir mettre en luy crainte & terreur
D'aigre justice, en disant que l'erreur
Tiens de Luther? Point ne suis Lutheriste
Ne Zuinglien, & moins Anabatiste:
Je suis de Dieu par son filz Jesuchrist.
(ll. 1–9)

Give an answer to my present case,
Learned Doctor. Who got you to have
Thrown into prison, six days ago,
A friend of yours who never offended you?
And to want to put fear and terror in him
Of bitter justice, by saying that I subscribe to
Luther's error? I am not Lutheran
Nor Zwinglian, and even less an Anabaptist:
I am of God by his son Jesuchrist.

The name *Bouchard* in itself creates a link between Marot's religious defense and the refrain of the preceding ballade. Appearing only in the title of the epistle—immediately after the last repetition of the refrain of the ballade—"Bouchard" rhymes with *lard*. "Bouchard" also rhymes with *art* from the verb *ardre* ("to burn"), which Marot uses in the envoi to the ballade:

Prince, qui n'eust dit plainement
La trop grand chaleur dont elle art,
Jamais n'eust dit aucunement:
Prenez le, il a mangé le Lart.
(ll. 25–28) [12]

Prince, if someone had not said plainly
The too great heat of which she burns,
Never would she have said in any way:
Take him, he has eaten the Lard.

Thus, Bouchard, a theologian whose mouth (*bouche*) burns (*art*) with slander, recalls the vengeful female who overreacts *chauldement* out of emotional motives rather than serious considerations. The poem continues in this vein later when Marot asks the doctor to rein in his anger ("refrains de ton couraige l'ire," l. 20), and to be his friend:

A tant me tais, cher Seigneur nostre Maistre,
Te suppliant à ce coup amy m'estre.
Et si pour moy à raison tu n'es mis,
Fais quelcque chose au moins pour mes amys,

En me rendant par une horsboutée
La liberté, laquelle m'as ostée.

(ll. 33–38)

Thus I stop, dear Lord our Master,
Begging you on this occasion to be my friend.
And if for me you are not disposed to reason,
Do something, at least, for my friends,
In giving me back by a release
The liberty that you have taken from me.

Because of the place of the epistle after the ballade, the request for Bouchard to be an *amy* establishes the theologian in a situation between the treacherous female *amye* of the ballade and the *amys* whom Marot now mentions and whom he will address in the next poem. One hesitates at this point to say that Marot's *amys* are all masculine, given the special relationship we know that he had with Marguerite de Navarre and other prominent women at the royal courts of France and Ferrara. The sequence as we shall see, however, evolves from a treacherous female friend to a trustworthy male one.

Liberation

As in the first two poems of the sequence, Marot casts himself in the role of a partially guilty victim while protesting his imprisonment in the "Rondeau parfaict composé apres sa delivrance & envoyé a ses amys" (*OD*, LXIV). Marot admits that he has "fasché la Court Rommaine" ("angered the Roman Court")—which I take to be the papal curia—but he is more upset by the fact that he was treated like a criminal than he is interested in defending his orthodoxy. In the following passage, we see that for Marot the absurdity of his imprisonment comes from the fact that he, who has always associated with "good" people (*Des bien famez*), has been thrown into prison with common crooks (*meschans*):

Pourtant, si j'ay fasché la Court Rommaine,
Entre meschans ne fuz oncq alloué.
Des bien famez j'ay hanté le dommaine;
Mais en prison pourtant je fuz cloué.

(*OD*, LXIV, ll. 9–12)

However, if I have angered the Roman Court,
Among common crooks never was I numbered.
Of good people have I frequented the domain;
But in prison, however, I was nailed.

The tension between criminal punishment and religious offense is also alluded to in the following lines, which are among the very few that are backed up by documents outside the poem: "J'eus à Paris prison fort inhumaine; / A Chartres fuz doulcement encloué" (ll. 17–18) ("I had in Paris a terribly inhuman prison; / In Chartres, I was gently secured").

Marot was first arrested by the civil authorities and then transferred to the jurisdiction of Bishop Guillard of Chartres on charges of "nonullis excessibus, delictis et criminibus, etiam haeresis" ("for several aberrations, transgressions, crimes, and also heresy") [13]

The double connotations of the polyvalent *manger le lard* as both a criminal and a religious offense may refer to both dimensions of this curious historical conflict between criminal and ecclesiastical jurisdictions, rather than to one or the other. In that case it would be an irony of literary history that the expression has divided interpretors rather than bringing them together (see note 10).

The *rondeau parfait* continues to underscore the central role of Marot's friends and enemies in the prison episode. Addressed to Marot's friends, it concludes with this joyous expression of gratitude:

> Au fort, Amys, c'est à vous bien joué
> Quand vostre main hors du parc me ramaine.
> Escript & faict d'ung cueur bien enjoué
> Le premier jour de la verte Sepmaine.
> (ll. 21–24)

> The main point, Friends, is that it's a good play on your part
> When your hand brings me back out of the park.
> Written and done with a greatly joyful heart
> The first day of the green Week [the first day of May]

This passage clearly states the central point that Marot has been developing throughout the prison sequence: Whereas he freely admits his guilt, he shows that his imprisonment and liberation were more of a personal affair between his enemies, his friends, and himself than a matter of true justice.

The end of the 1534 sequence.

We have already seen that the title of the *rondeau parfait* contradicts the title of the sequence "Certaines oeuvres qu'il feit en la prison," since it tells us that Marot wrote the poem after his liberation. One could have considered the poem a postlude—hence not an invalidation of the title—just as the rondeau that began the series was a prelude.[14] Marot, however, plays a new game with the reader because this poem is a displaced postlude.

The "Epistre à son amy Lyon" (*Epîtres*, X) is the last poem of the sequence, although it gives the impression of having been written before the *rondeau parfait*. It is Marot's attempt to enlist Lyon Jamet's help in getting out of prison. The epistle departs, therefore, from the twofold arrangement of the prison sequence according to both the order in which the poems were written and the chronology of historical events.[15]

Although the epistle to Lyon is out of chronological order, its place after the *rondeau parfait* strengthens the theme of friendship running through the sequence. To pass from the request for Bouchard to be a friend to a peal of thanks addressed to friends for liberation suggests that Bouchard threw his support behind—or at least did not hinder—the efforts of Marot's friends to obtain Marot's liberation. Furthermore, by putting the epistle to Lyon Jamet last, Marot—whatever his relations with his patroness Marguerite may have been elsewhere—balances the treacherous and imprisoning world of female friendship of the opening poem in the sequence with a liberating, safe, and trustworthy world of male camaraderie in the concluding poem.[16] The place of the poem also contrasts the worst of friends with the best of friends. We shall further consider the implications of this arrangement in the discussion of the 1538 edition of the epistles below.

The epistle to Lyon Jamet not only identifies a special male friend, it adds another dimension to the expression *manger le lard*. We have seen that the expression refers figuratively to the crime of theft or embezzlement. We have also seen how the epistle to Bouchard and the *rondeau parfait* cause the reader to add a vague religious dimension to the offense to which the expression refers. In the epistle to Lyon, Marot now implies that the word *lard* is in fact a synecdoche for *meat*:

> Cestuy Lyon, plus fort qu'ung vieulx Verrat,
> Veit une fois que le Rat ne sçavoit
> Sortir d'ung lieu, pour autant qu'il avoit
> Mangé le lard & la chair toute crue.
>
> (ll. 16–19)

> This Lion, stronger than an old Boar,
> Once saw that the Rat did not know
> How to get out of a place, inasmuch as he had
> Eaten the lard and the flesh completely raw.

The glory of this playful passage is the many-faceted meaning of the expression *toute crue*. On one level, it simply means "raw." On another, it could mean "literally." (Consider the modern expression *parler cru*—"to speak plainly") In this sense, for Marot to say "Mangé le lard & la chair toute crue" is to say that by *lard* he really means *chair* ("meat"), so that the offense that tainted Marot with the heresy of Lutheranism and angered the Roman court would be that of eating meat. Since eating meat was only an offense during appointed times of abstinence (usually times of fasting), it would seem that Marot was accused of eating meat during a forbidden season or day, but this is a leap of interpretation that cannot be justified in terms of the text alone.

Let us recall that Marot, in an adaptation of Aesop's fable "The Lion and the Mouse," casts himself in the role of an imprisoned rat who begs for the assistance of his friend Lyon (the lion, of course). As Marcel Françon has observed, the mention of eating meat could be a natural extension of the rat metaphor.[17] Thus at the very moment when Marot seems to be revealing the truth, we find ourselves embroiled in the complications of figurative discourse.

At this point, a reader, at 450 years remove from the events to which the prison poems refer, must admit that the texts in themselves do not tell all. We cannot affirm with certainty the exact nature of Marot's religious crime. Only in referring to other texts do we see that a leap to the conclusion that Marot was arrested for eating meat during Lent can be justified.

By the time that Marot published his poems in 1534, there had been two imprisonments, one in 1526 and one in 1532. We know little more about the 1526 imprisonment than the fact that there was the strange conflict between criminal and ecclesiastical jurisdictions mentioned above. However, in 1532 Marot and several others were arrested, "estans chargez d'avoir mangé de la chair durant le temps de Karesme & autres jours prohibez" ("being charged with having eaten flesh during the time of Lent and other prohibited days").[18] Thus by the time Marot published the poems in 1534, formal accusations against him were such that the reader would have extended the expression *manger le lard* from a reference to criminal guilt to that of breaking the laws of abstinence during Lent or some other prescribed time.[19]

As we look back over the sequence as a whole, we see that although the poems do not serve us well in terms of the precise details concerning Marot's imprisonment, they are much more eloquent about Marot's own feelings and opinions about his experience. The identity of Marot's mistress is shrouded in mystery—hence, the whole love-affair-gone-sour may well be little more than a metaphor for Marot's relations with the religious authorities. The exact nature of Marot's misdeed is also unclear beyond the fact that he most certainly offended what he called *la Court Rommaine* ("the Roman Court"). However, the sequence of poems makes it very clear that despite the guilt that Marot acknowledges either directly or indirectly, his imprisonment is more the result of personal enmities than of crimes or serious religious offenses. It is also clear that Marot takes great offense at being treated like common riffraff.[20] In a word, both the individual poems of the sequence and their arrangement communicate Marot's protest that his punishment did not fit his crime.

The 1538 arrangements

In the 1538 edition, the prison poems are scattered into three different sections. In one case the new arrangement is not as meaningful as the earlier one; in another it justifies some of the earlier readings; and in a third it leads to a new reading.

First of all, the two rondeaux appear in the 1538 version of the previously published *Adolescence Clémentine* at the end of the section of poems of the same genre. Here the order seems completely arbitrary except for the fact that the *rondeau parfait* by its difference from the preceding *rondeaux simples* creates a feeling of closure.[21] Otherwise, Marot has placed these poems at the end of the section simply because they were the last rondeaux he had written in his "adolescence."

For the same reason, the verse epistles to Bouchard and Jamet are the last two poems in the section of the *Adolescence* epistles. The order in which they appear does comply with a traditional interpretation of the poems, that Marot wrote to Jamet when help from Bouchard was not forthcoming.[22] Chronology, however, is not necessarily the reason that Marot placed the epistle to Jamet last. The *Adolescence* epistles are arranged in hierarchical order, as I have shown elsewhere, so that here the doctor of theology takes precedence over a court secretary.[23] Furthermore, now that we see the possible effects based on a reading of the poems as if they were written one after the other, we can better appreciate the delicacy of the 1534 arrangement, in which the placement of the *rondeau parfait* between the two epistles leaves the question of Marot's success with Bouchard completely open.

Only the new arrangement of the ballades seems richly meaningful. Not only does it justify the leap of interpretation that would have *manger le lard* refer to the breaking of religious abstinence, it also suggests other religious dimensions. In the 1538 edition, Marot provocatively places the ballade with the refrain "Prenez le, il a mangé le Lart" in a sequence of religious poems that refer to feasting and fasting in relation to the Christian calendar:

1. "Du Jour de Noel" (On Christmas Day—*OD*, LXXVII)
2. "De Caresme" (On Lent—*OD*, LXXVIII)
3. "De la Passion nostre Seigneur Jesuchrist" (On the Passion of Our Lord Jesus Christ—*OD*, LXIX)
4. "Contre celle qui fut s'Amye" (Against she who was his friend—*OD*, LXXX)
5. "Chant Royal de la Conception" (Chant Royal of the Immaculate Conception—*OD*, LXXXVI)

Themes of feasting and fasting run throughout the series. The ballade on Christmas draws on a popular ballade, the refrain of which is "Le pain au fol est le premier mangé" ("The bread of the fool is the first that is eaten").[24] It portrays shepherds singing a call to see the newborn baby Jesus. The ballade on Lent that follows is a call to silence and fasting in honor of the season. The ballade on the crucifixion does not deal with feasting and fasting but is immediately followed with the famous "Prenez le, il a mangé le Lart." Thus we see Marot accused of having *mangé le lard* just after we have read of the crucified Christ and meditated on the appropriateness of celebrating at Christmas and fasting during Lent. Once again the interpretation of eating a meat product during a period of fasting and abstinence suggests itself.

There are other implications of placing the ballade with the refrain "Prenez le, il a mangé le Lart," between a song of the crucifixion and the *chant royal* on the immaculate conception. The Immaculate Conception, it should be recalled, is the doctrine that the Virgin Mary in order to be the mother of Christ must have somehow been free of the original sin characteristic of humanity from the time of her conception—hence the refrain of the chant royal, "Le digne couche où le Roy reposa" ("The worthy bed where the King lay in state").[25] The poems surrounding the ballade invite the reader to compare the rejected lover and his fickle mistress with Christ crucified and the sinless Virgin Mary. Such considerations lead to several perceptions of Marot's identity, but rather than discard one in favor of another, the reader should appreciate the humorous contrast between them. Marot, who claims innocence, may be casting himself in a role parallel to the crucified Christ, but the reader, who knows of the poet's guilt, might be more inclined to see Marot as one of the thieves (perhaps the forgiven one) crucified with Christ.

At first reading, the fickle mistress does not come out so well. Her actions seem particularly dark in relation to the immaculately conceiving mother portrayed in the following poem. Here the expression *manger le lard* takes on new significance. In contrast to the sinless mother of Christ, Marot's friend perverts the maternal role of nurturer as she turns in the poet for an act of eating. However, it is possible to find a peaceful resolution to Marot's anger if we consider both Marot and his mistress as examples of the unfortunate humanity that Marot portrays in the crucifixion ballade as having been led astray. In such ways, the inclusion of the contentious and worldly "Prenez le, il a mangé le Lart" in the midst of serious religious poems strikes a note of the smiling and sophisticated wit to which Marot often resorts in the midst of suffering and humiliation.

We shall probably never be able to reweave the story of Marot's imprisonment into a seamless web. Yet it is important that we play the game of the text and try, for it is only in living the frustrations and manipulations of our desire for a story as we work our way through Marot's witty, contradictory arrangements that we can feel the comfort and release that a prisoner, possibly himself bewildered, could draw from *le plaisir du texte*.[26]

Notes

1. All translations are mine. See *Le Premier Livre de la* Métamorphose *d'Ovide, Item Certaines oeuvres qu'il feit en la prison, non encores imprimey* (Paris: E. Roffet, 1534), the first edition in which these poems appear; and *Les Oeuvres de Clément Marot* (Lyon: E. Dolet, 1538), the last author-approved edition of Marot's collected works.

2. For a discussion of the "wandering viewpoint," see Wolfgang Iser, *The Act of Reading: A Theory of Aesthetic Response* (Baltimore and London: Johns Hopkins University Press, 1978), pp. 108–9.

3. There are many aspects of these poems that have been discussed elsewhere, such as their sophisticated wit, natural style, and religious implications. I shall deal with these points below only insofar as the arrangement of the poems in a sequence reveals new possibilities.

4. References to the poems from modern editions will be given when they are discussed in more detail.

5. It does not matter who really affixed the titles, since critics assume that this edition was published with Marot's approval.

6. Clément Marot, *Oeuvres diverses,* ed. Claude Albert Mayer (London: Athlone, 1966), LXIII. The roman numerals stand for the number of the poem in the volume; citations to this edition will hereafter be provided in text as *OD*.

7. Claude Albert Mayer has observed that Marot's blame of his mistress is an intertextual allusion to François Villon, who attributed his flight from Paris to the disappointments of love. See Claude Albert Mayer, *Clément Marot* (Paris: Nizet, 1972), p. 91.

8. For a discussion of *losangiers,* see Roger Dragonetti, *La Technique poétique des trouvères dans la chanson courtoise* (Brugge: De Tempel, 1960), pp. 272–78). In this respect Marot's condemnation differs from those that Claude Albert Mayer cites from Villon (see preceding note). Villon's disparaging remarks about his beloved at the beginning of the *Lais* (ll. 9–64) fall into the category of acceptable complaints by a disappointed lover. Later in the *Testament* (l. 661), Villon's denunciation of Catherine de Vaucelles for having beaten him does not fall into the category of slander characteristic of the *losangiers.* See François Villon, *Oeuvres,* ed. Auguste Longnon; 4th ed. revised by Lucien Foulet; Notes by A. Lanly (Paris: Champion, 1976). Marot is a guiltier male victim than Villon.

9. *Abstinence,* "the abstention from eating meat or certain meat products" is to be distinguished from *fasting,* "complete or partial abstention from food." The latter consists of such practices as taking only one meal during the day. See P. M. J. Clancy, "Fast and Abstinence," *New Catholic Encyclopedia,* 10 vols., William J. McDonald, editor-in-chief (New York: McGraw Hill, 1967), 5:847.

10. See Orentin Douen, *Clément Marot et le Psautier Huguenot: Etude historique, littéraire, musicale, et bibliographique* (Paris: Imprimerie Nationale, 1878): 1:72–73, and Michael Screech, *Marot évangélique* (Geneva: Droz, 1967), pp. 39–45.

11. The abbreviated title *Epîtres* in the text stands for *Les Epîtres de Clément Marot,* ed. Claude Albert Mayer (London: Athlone, 1958). This poem has caused much ink to flow concerning Marot's true religious loyalties. Discussion of the problem here would take us beyond the scope of this study. I have given my opinion on the subject

as well as references to further reading in George Joseph, *Clément Marot* (Boston: G. K. Hall, 1985), preface, and pp. 4–6, 127–37.

12. It is interesting to note that both the spellings *lart* and *lard* are present in the ballade. In the 1538 edition the spelling of the name is changed to "Bouchart."

13. For more details see Claude Albert Mayer, *La Religion de Marot* (Paris: Nizet, 1973), pp. 11–13.

14. The fact that the two poems that contradict the title are rondeaux is of aesthetic significance. The playful rondeau, traditionally of lower status in the hierarchy of poetic genres than the epistle or the ballade, stands as a poem associated with the easier times of freedom.

15. Pierre Villey imagines that the epistle to Lyon was written after the rondeau as a sort of "retour amusé" ("amused repetition") concerning the imprisonment. Thus, although Villey as a reader revises his expectation that the poems recount events in the order in which they happened, he maintains the conviction that the poems appear in the order in which they were written.

16. Male camaraderie is especially apparent in the long prologue. There, the *renuntio amoris* ("je ne t'escry de l'amour vaine & folle, / Tu voys assez s'elle sert ou affolle" [ll. 1–2]: "I do not write you of vain and foolish love / You see well enough by yourself if it serves or maddens") and the allusion to Jamet's sexual prowess ("Je ne t'escry des Dames de Paris; / Tu en sçais plus que leurs propres Maris" [ll. 11–12]: "I do not write you of the Ladies of Paris / You know more about them than their own husbands") are prime examples of male bonding over and against women conquered behind the backs of cuckold husbands.

17. Marcel Françon, "Marot au Châtelet," *Modern Language Notes* 55 (1940): 1.

18. See Mayer, *Religion de Marot*, p. 15. Lines 17–18 of the *rondeau parfait* refer to this transfer of the prisoner.

19. For arguments against this interpretation see Michael Screech, *Marot évangélique*, pp. 39–41.

20. Marot grounds his outrage in his identity as a poet and member of polite (i.e., court) society even more clearly in "L'Enfer," ll. 310–38. See Marot's *Oeuvres satiriques*, ed. Claude Albert Mayer (London: Athlone, 1962), pp. 53–73. As far as Marot was concerned, membership in the court of France should have shielded him from punishment for offenses committed against the courts of love and of Rome.

21. For an understanding of how a difference of this sort can be taken as a device of closure, see Barbara Herrenstein Smith, *Poetic Closure: A Study of How Poems End* (Chicago, London: University of Chicago Press, 1968), pp. 34, 53.

22. See Mayer, *Marot*, pp. 84–85.

23. For more on the hierarchical order of the *Adolescence Clémentine* epistles, see Joseph, *Marot*, p. 34.

24. See Mayer, *OD*, p. 157 n. 1.

25. See Edward Dennis O'Connor "Immaculate Conception," *New Catholic Encyclopedia*, 7:378–82.

26. See Roland Barthes, *Le Plaisir du texte* (Paris: Seuil, 1973).

Doranne Fenoaltea

4. A Poetic Monument: Arrangement in Book 1 of Ronsard's 1550 *Odes*

By choosing to make his poetic debut in 1550 with a collection of odes, Ronsard clearly called attention to his affiliation with Pindar and Horace, the ancient and prestigious models for lyric poetry to whom he principally compared himself in that collection and to whom he wished to be compared. To emphasize his ties to these precursors, Ronsard explicitly invoked them and drew liberally on their themes, expressions, and overall developments.[1] Further underscoring his debt, Ronsard placed at the beginning of his work thirteen Pindaric odes, using the triadic structure of his Greek model; in addition, the group of four books recalls the total number of books of Horatian odes. This essay hypothesizes that Ronsard also recognized and used principles of arrangement and formal symmetry discernible in the works of the Latin lyric poets. In doing so, Ronsard sought to create for his work a formal and architectural unity similar to that to be found in the work of the poets of Augustan Rome.[2]

The 1550 *Odes* lend themselves to description in terms of the two basic types of pattern found in the works of Augustan poetry, ring and interlocking-ring composition (schematically presented in fig. 1). Defined by recurrence of similar textual expression or allusion, and occasionally by similar structural development, these patterns appear systematically throughout the four books and can be found at all levels of composition: the organization of a single ode; the creation of correspondences among two (or three) odes; and finally, the formation of structuring patterns in the overall arrangement of the book.

For Ronsard's collection as for those of Roman poets, ring patterns generally are confirmed by numerical symmetry. In Roman poetry books, equality of lines or distichs (sometimes with an inequality of one line or distich) appear to confirm ring patterning; in Ronsard's *Odes*, the number of strophes serves a similar function. (This divergence makes sense, since the strophe is the basic structural unit in French poetry, much as distichs are in

Latin verse; we may note in addition that Latin distichs were often translated into strophes in French.)

This essay examines one ring pattern, an interlocking ring in the first book of the 1550 *Odes*, in order to define it and to consider its implications for interpretation.[3] I will not here be concerned so much with the poet's intentions as with patterning that can be perceived in a systematic way by a reader attentive to the formal devices involved. Of particular interest, in addition, is how the effects of the perception of such patterning affects the meaning attributed to the book as a whole and our view of the poet who composed it.

Book 1 of the 1550 *Odes* contains twenty poems. The first thirteen are Pindaric[4] and of varying length: the shortest (the usure or "interest payment," 1.7) has 16 verses and the longest, the ode to Du Bellay (1.9), has 220. Among these poems, strophic length varies considerably, as do rhyme patterns. However, in the Pindaric odes, the meter is consistently heptasyllabic, except in the shortest, the octosyllabic "interest payment" poem; the longest, the ode to Du Bellay, where the strophe and antistrophe are octosyllabic and the epode heptasyllabic; and the final Pindaric ode (1.13), which has a six-syllable line throughout. The six poems that follow are either heptasyllabic (1.14, 1.16, 1.17, 1.19) or octosyllabic (1.15, 1.18), while the final poem (1.20), to the poet's lyre, is decasyllabic.

In terms simply of formal patterning, the "interest payment" poem, by its different meter and structure, prepares for the shift of meter in 1.9 and the later change to the Latin or Horatian ode. The shift of meter in the final Pindaric ode signals a change in a more immediate way and thus has a closural function. Finally, the new meter and longer verse line in 1.20 also appear to help effect closure. Thus, at the level of the book, meter serves both to control the variety of other formal aspects of the lyrics and to signal change; it will become clear that these variations of meter also serve as markers for the overall arrangement of the interlocking-ring pattern.

Thematically, the first eight odes are encomiastic poems addressed to royalty and to glorious ranking members of the nobility, those on whose shoulders fall the protection and defense of the kingdom of France. The following eight are also poems of praise, addressed to poets and humanists,

Fig 1. Ring and interlocking-ring composition.

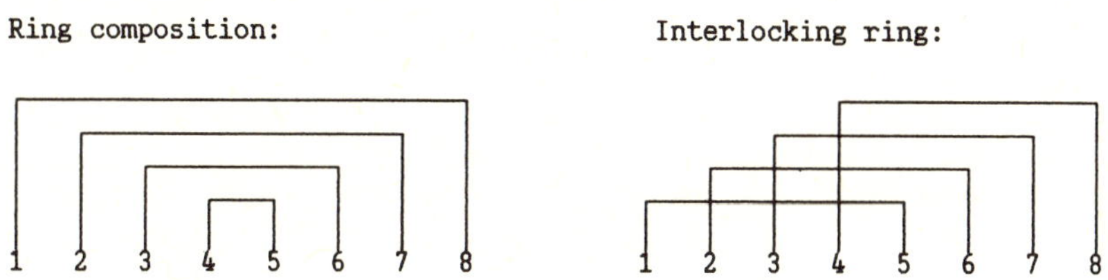

Fig 2. Ring composition, 1.5–1.8.

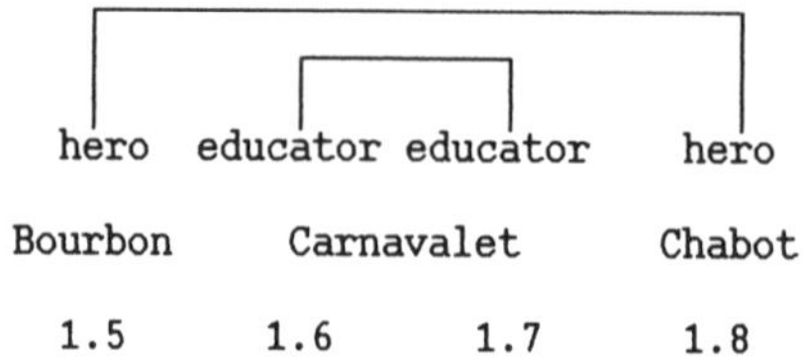

Fig 3. Ring composition, 1.9–1.16.

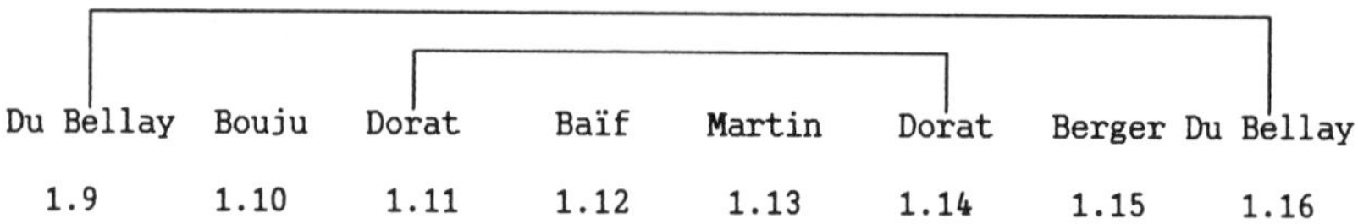

whose role is to make known the grandeur of these royal and noble figures, to promote knowledge, and to extend the arts for the greater glory of France. The final four odes treat a variety of topics.

The initial poems follow rules of (royal) precedence: the first is addressed to the king, the second to the queen, and the third to Madame Marguerite, the king's sister. Next, an ode addressed to the Cardinal de Guise celebrates the priestly function and the status of the church as represented by a noble and high-ranking member of the clergy. Odes 1.5–8 are all addressed to nobles and suggest a ring pattern (fig. 2). The outer odes address glorious defenders of France, François de Bourbon and Guy de Chabot, while the inner ones praise Carnavalet, educator of the nobility in one of their principal and most noble skills, horsemanship. The eight poems that follow, addressed to poets and humanists, also suggest a ring pattern (fig. 3), which underscores the importance accorded in this book to Du Bellay (1.9, 1.16) and Dorat (1.11, 1.14), each of whom receives two poems. (While two poems are also addressed to Carnavalet—like Dorat, an educator—they differ in being consecutive and explicitly and closely linked.) The Pindaric odes of this section suggest the establishment of a hierarchy of poetic genres (similar to the royal and noble hierarchy of the preceding section). Du Bellay is a lyric poet (1.9), 1.10 alludes to epic, and 1.11 describes Dorat, elucidating the ancient poetry that must be mastered in order to perfect French poetry.[5] Baïf (1.12) is the initiator of tragedy in French, Martin (1.13) is a translator of Italian and Latin works in diverse genres, and Bertrand Berger (1.15) is a pastoral and dithyrambic poet.

The first fifteen poems are related thematically through the reiteration of the fundamental idea that praise in elevated verse is the source of lasting renown.[6] Most recall insistently the epicinian and encomiastic odes of which Pindar was the greatest practitioner. The final group of five poems furnishes examples of other functions of poetry in the ancient world: expressing secrets

Fig 4a. Book 1, Interlocking-ring composition.

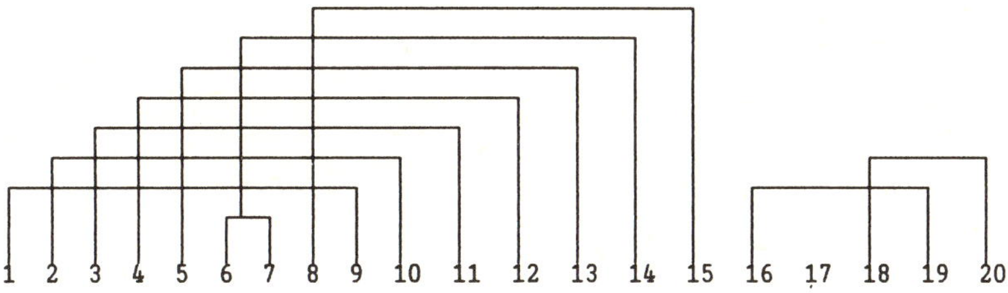

Fig 4b. Book 1, Interlocking-ring composition.

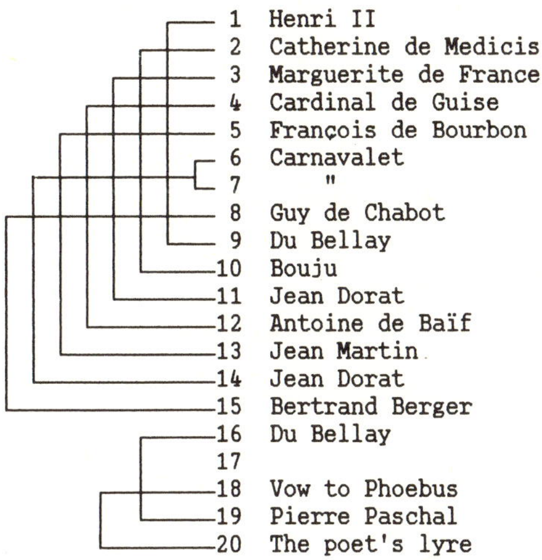

of the cosmos, creating or recreating myth and history, invoking the forces of nature. They also reflect ancient honored genres: epyllion, hymn, prayer or vow (*voeu*).

This description of the first book of Ronsard's *Odes* gives a clear indication of thematic and generic order and grouping, but it does not suggest an overall formal arrangement.[7] Textual and thematic correspondences among poems, most typically in an interlocking ring pattern, are the source of one such arrangement (fig. 4a and b), which will be described in detail in the following pages. In some cases, the correspondences merely serve the overall structure, but in most, they suggest themes, relationships, and values often different from those apparent as one reads individual odes. At the very least, the body of correspondences that emerges is suggestive of overall coherence; indeed, it suggests the presence of a formally significant design, with implications for the work as a whole. This perfectly regular pattern has two distinct parts and generally corresponds to the thematic patterns outlined

Fig 5. Metrical changes, book 1.

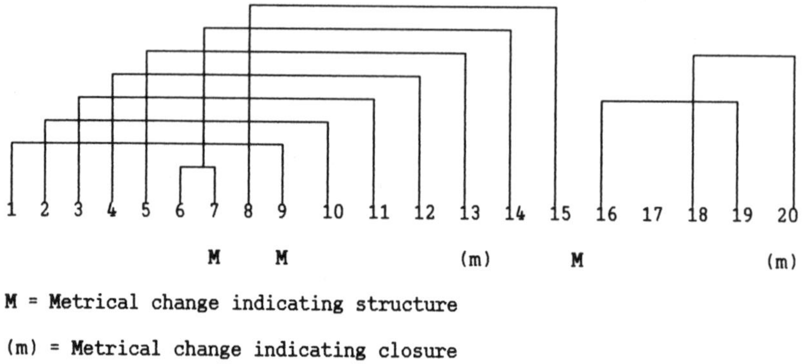

above. There is one noncorresponding poem (1.17) and one case of a 2:1 correspondence, (1.6–1.7 to 1.14); both variations have been described as regular features of Roman poetry books as well.[8]

Metrical changes serve as important indicators for establishing this pattern, for they help to mark the divisions 1.1–1.8 and 1.9–1.15 (fig. 5). The first change of meter occurs in 1.7, which does not have a separate corresponding poem but is the second poem of the 2:1 correspondence. A second change of meter occurs in 1.9, the first backward-looking correspondence. The change of meter in the final Pindaric ode (1.13) appears only to signal closure. As the final ode of the full set of correspondences, 1.15 also has a change of meter, from the dominant heptasyllabic to the octosyllabic.

The numerical correspondences that emerge from this pattern depend on numbers of strophes. There are fifty-nine in 1.1–1.8,[9] again the same number in 1.9–1.15, and the same again in 1.16–1.20, excluding the noncorresponding 1.17. The interlocking-ring pattern thus is "confirmed" by a tripartite division based on strophic equivalences.[10]

The first correspondence, between the odes dedicated to Henry II and to Du Bellay (1.1 and 1.9), is striking. A perfectly regular interlocking ring, created by means of structural and verbal parallels, joins the two strophes of the first ode to the first two (of five) of the second (fig. 6). The same strophes are thematically linked as well, by their systematically corresponding treatment of nourishing sweet song, invocation of the muse, the tie between virtue and poetry, and allusion to the king's appreciation of poetry. The extended praise of royal power embodied in the king and of poetic power embodied in Du Bellay and Ronsard occurs at the same point in the two poems. While the first ode proclaims the grandeur and power of the king and the second the grandeur and power of Ronsard and Du Bellay, the parallels also underscore the contrasting claims made for political-military and poetic power. Where royal might represses and forces submission ("La terre sous eus se plie, / La mer

Fig 6. Textual and thematic links, I.I and I.9.

I.I: AU ROI	I.9: A JOUACHIM DU BELLAI ANGEVIN
En mon dous Nectar j'abreuve (l. 8)	Et pour licher la gloire douce Qui emmielle (ll. 15–16)
[Invocation of the Muse] (l. 21)	[Invocation of the Muse] (l. 17)
[Virtue and song related] (ll. 21–28)	[Virtue and song related] (ll. 17–32)
. . . nostre ROI Duquel la divine oreille Humera cette merveille (ll. 25–27)	. . . les douceurs nompareilles Sçavent flater les oreilles Des Rois (ll. 39–41)
Prenant plaisir d'ouir dire Ses louanges [Jupiter's] à la lire (ll. 33–34)	. . . béans à t'ouir : Seule en France est nostre Lire Que les fredons sache elire Pour les Princes rejouir (ll. 41–44)
[Royal power and superiority of Henry] (ll. 39–54)	[Power of learned poetry and superiority of Ronsard and Du Bellay] (ll. 45–76)
L'horrible foudre des Rois (l. 48)	(Portans la foudre du grand Roi) (l. 57)
pour ma guide apparoistre [Henry] (l. 55)	L'aiant prise pour ma guide [Muse] (l. 77)

I.I: To the King:
With my sweet nectar I quench (the thirst) (l. 8)
. . . our KING, whose divine ear will breathe in this marvel (ll. 25–27)
Taking pleasure in hearing Jupiter's praises on the lyre (ll. 33–34)
The fearful lightning bolt of Kings (l. 48)
to appear as my guide [Henry] (l. 55)

I.9: To Joachim Du Bellay:
the sweet glory that drenches with honey (ll. 15–16)
. . . the incomparable sweet words flatter the ears of Kings (ll. 39–41)
. . . wide open to hear you: In France, only our Lyre knows how to choose the sounds that give joy to Princes (ll. 41–44)
(Carrying the lightning bolt of the great King) (l. 57)
Having taken her for my guide [the Muse] (l. 77)

fiere s'humilie"—ode 1, ll. 43–44; "The earth bows beneath them, the proud sea humbles itself"), poetic power promotes pleasing fertility and expansion ("Où le flanc de Loire ride / Baignant les champs plantureus;"—ode 9, ll. 80–81; "Where the Loire's surface ripples, bathing the abundant fields"). Finally, the correspondence suggests a generic reciprocity: the strong lyricism of the initial ode (underscored by the close parallel at the outset to the beginning of Pindar's *Olympia* 7), is an effect of the art of the lyric poet, the capacity in which Du Bellay, and Ronsard as well, appear in ode 9.

In addition, partly because of the interlocking-ring structure of the ode to Du Bellay, a second set of correspondences appears between 1.1 and the second part of 1.9. This double correspondence is unique to these two poems in the first book and thus suggests the importance to be accorded to the figures and the correspondence. The second series is more complex, formed by a combination of interlocking-ring (fig. 7) and ring composition (fig. 8). The interlocking ring parallels to some extent the first series, while the ring is formed by brief verbal reminiscences. In the recurrent verbal and thematic parallels of the interlocking ring, the praise of the king and the poet occupy the same place in the pattern.

In the comparison thus created between the king and the poet, the poet's capacity to create his own lasting glory gives him an advantage over the king, who must rely on the poet who praises him. And while quantity may not be a criterion of absolute value, the fact that the ode to Du Bellay is more than twice as long as the paired ode to the king is formally suggestive. In the topography of the work at least, the poem to the lyric poet has, clearly, greater relief.

For the second and tenth odes, dedicated respectively to the queen and to Bouju, correspondences are again striking (fig. 9). The chiasmus of the first two and the last two correspondences is tied to allusions to Phoebus. The correspondences emphasize inspiration, ignorance and science, and bad and good poets, rather than praise of the two figures which Ronsard develops according to the rules of classical encomiastic rhetoric. In addition, the poem to Queen Catherine, with its description of the mythic origin of Florence, the praise of her ancestors, and the prophecy of the future dominion of her son, represents a kind of foretaste of epic; Bouju's talent for the epic muse is alluded to 1.10, once again suggesting a generic aspect to the correspondence.

In the odes dedicated to Marguerite de Valois, sister of the king (1.3), and to Jean Dorat (1.11), the textual and thematic correspondences occur at approximately the same point in the second half of each text (fig. 10). The correspondences draw attention to the similarities between the figures, who help prepare the way for new poetry,—the first by battling ignorance, the second by increasing knowledge. As in the first pairing (the king and Du Bellay), different but interdependent (or complementary) roles are attributed to royalty and to poets. The correspondences underscore in particular

Fig 7. Textual and thematic links, 1.1 and 1.9.

1.1: AU ROI	1.9: A JOUACHIM DU BELLAI ANGEVIN
En mon dous Nectar j'abreuve (l. 8)	Romme s'ivrant de leur parler (Dont le Nectar sembloit couler) (ll. 105–6)
Heureus l'honneur (l. 11)	Le saint honneur (l. 109)
Le saint Harpeur de ta gloire, Et l'archer de ta memoire (ll. 18–19)	Ensemble l'effort de sa lance Jointe avecque une belle vois (ll. 119–20)
Muse, bande ton arc dous, . . . Quel Prince fraperons nous, L'enfonçant . . . ? (ll. 21–24)	Mais repren l'arc, Muse, il est tens Guigner au blanc où tu pretens: (ll. 135–36)
De Jupiter les antiques Leurs ecris embellissoient, Par lui leurs chants poëtiques Commençoient, & finissoient, Prenant plaisir d'ouir dire Ses louanges à la lire: Mais HENRI sera le Dieu (ll. 29–35)	Puis que sa louange foisonne En cent vertus propres à lui, A quoi par les honneurs d'autrui Rempli-je ce que je lui donne? Sa gloire sufit pour borner Les vers qui le veulent orner. O bons Dieus . . . (ll. 137–43)

1.1: To the King:
With my Nectar I quench the thirst (l. 8)
Happy the honor (l. 11)
The pious harp player of thy glory, and the archer of thy renown (ll. 18–19)
Muse, stretch thy sweet bow . . . What Prince shall we strike, driving it [the arrow] in . . . ? (ll. 21–24)
The ancients embellished their writings with Jupiter, They began and ended their poetic songs with his name, taking pleasure in hearing his praises on the lyre: But HENRY will be the God (ll. 29–35)

1.9: To Joachim Du Bellay:
Rome, becoming intoxicated with their speech (from which Nectar seemed to flow) (ll. 105–6)
The pious honor . . . (l. 109)
The effort of his lance joined together with a lovely voice (ll. 119–20)
But take up the bow, Muse, it is time to look toward the target you aim to reach (ll. 135–36)
Since his praise abounds in a hundred virtues of his own, to what end do I fill up what I give him with the honors of others? His glory suffices to enclose the verses that seek to embellish him. O good Gods . . . (ll. 137–43)

Fig 7. (*continued*)

N.B. The apparent arbitrariness of the return to the muse (in 1.9, l. 135), which has appeared to critics as an awkwardness (it is also reminiscent of Pindar's technique), is, in terms of the correspondence, very strongly motivated, given the importance of the muse in the definition of the poet's situation.

Fig 8. Textual and thematic links, 1.1 and 1.9.

1.1: AU ROI	1.9: A JOUACHIM DU BELLAI ANGEVIN
Le ciel qui ses lampes darde (l. 39)	Et le souleil . . . Les moindres feus du ciel éface (ll. 155–56)
La mer (l. 44)	la mer (l. 153)
croistre* (l. 54)	croistroit* (l. 151)
Et pour ma guide apparoistre Dessus le front de mes vers (ll. 55–56)	Et sur le front la lampe porte Qui seule la peut eclarcir (ll. 147–48)

1.1: To the King
Heaven that shoots down its lights (l. 39)
the sea (l. 44)
to increase (l. 54)
And appear as my guide on the front of my verses (ll. 55–56)

1.9: To Joachim Du Bellay
And the sun . . . effaces the least lights of the heavens (ll. 155–56)
the sea (l. 153)
would increase (l. 151)
And carries on her forehead [*front*] the light that alone can light the way (ll. 147–48)

the contrast between knowledge and ignorance as it relates to the high lyric poetry that Ronsard advocates.

For the odes dedicated to the cardinal de Guise (1.4) and to Baïf (1.12), textual correspondences are not very strong (fig. 11). Adumbrated at the end of the first, more clearly expressed at the beginning of the second, is the theme of faults of character in the two figures.[11] The correspondence thus suggests that Ronsard may allude discreetly to the presence in the cardinal of the excess that can lead to tragedy, the literary genre in which Baïf ex-

Fig 9. Textual and thematic links, I.2 and I.10.

I.2: A LA ROINE	I.10: A BOUJU ANGEVIN
[Effects of inspiration] (ll. 1–13)	[Repetition]: ravit, Ravissent, ravie* (ll. 13, 15, 17)
D'une ardeur mon ame est pleine (l. 3)	Phebus ravit les neuf seurs (l. 13)
Cherchoit des loups le repaire (l. 24)	Mais mon ame n'est ravie Que d'une brulante envie (ll. 17–18)
[Apollo] Entre ses braz la ravit (l. 29)	Qui par les montaignes chasse Les bestes de çà & là (ll. 27–28)
Le comble de ton sçavoir, Et de tes vertus ensemble (ll. 63–64)	Laissant au peuple ignorant Un brazier le devorant Béant après la vertu (ll. 35–37)
bruiant en mes vers* / tout l'univers* (ll. 73–74)	Phebus [sunrise] (ll. 47–48)
gloire* / memoire* (ll. 78–79)	
Phebus [sunrise, sunset] (ll. 106–8)	tout l'univers* / la trompe de mes vers* / ta gloire* / la memoire* (ll. 60, 62–64)

I.2: To the Queen
My soul is full of ardor (l. 3)
Sought the hiding place of wolves (l. 24)
[Apollo] snatched her up in his arms (l. 29)
The highpoint of your knowledge and virtues together (ll. 63–64)
resounding in my verse; the whole universe (ll. 73–74)
glory; memory (ll. 78–79)
Phoebus (l. 106)

I.10: To Bouju
Phoebus ravishes (enchants) the nine sisters (l. 13)
But my soul is only ravished by a burning desire (ll. 17–18)
Who chases the beasts throughout the mountains (ll. 27–28)
Leaving the ignorant to be devoured by flames and gaping after virtue (ll. 35–37)
Phoebus (l. 47)
the whole universe; the trumpet of my verse; your glory; memory (ll. 60, 62–64)

Fig 10. Textual and thematic links, 1.3 and 1.11.

1.3: A MADAME MARGUERITE	1.11: A JAN D'ORAT
[Sciences of the Muses] (ll. 39–40)	. . . ton sçavoir [ancient poetry] (l. 21)
. . . tu alas trouver Le vilain monstre Ignorance, Qui souloit toute la France Desous son ventre couver. [Description of battle] Le Monstre gist étandu (ll. 53–65)	. . . tu brises l'ignorance, Renommé parmi la France (ll. 23–24)
Callimaq', Pindare, Horace (l. 95)	. . . livres laborieus . . . Alcée (ll. 28, 30)

1.3: To Madame Marguerite
. . . you sought out Ignorance, the ugly monster who once covered all of France with his belly. (. . .) The Monster lies vanquished (ll. 53–65)
Callimachus, Pindar, Horace (l. 95)

1.11: To Jean Dorat
your science / knowledge (l. 21)
. . . you crush ignorance and are renowned throughout France (ll. 23–24)
. . . difficult books . . . Alcaeus (ll. 28, 30)

cels. Despite their faults, both are fortunate in their "nature," which Ronsard chooses to emphasize: the cardinal by his birth into a great family, Baïf by his talent. Once again implicit in the correspondence is the suggestion that a Baïf, although (like Du Bellay or Ronsard) of less eminent birth, stands by his talent in a position of equality with the highest nobility.

The correspondences between the odes to François de Bourbon (1.5) and to Jean Martin (1.13) form an interlocking ring; most occur at almost the same lines in each poem (fig. 12). Despite the great differences between the men and the odes dedicated to them, the correspondences reiterate by-now familiar themes and permit the reader to discover the fundamental relation. Each has brought glory to France, the first by his sword, the second by his pen, but both through the knowledge and excellence of his art, placed in the service of France. Implicitly, the value of nobility in war and of poets in peace is underscored. With the enemy destroyed and peace achieved, the work of rendering France illustrious by excellent praise and by disseminating knowledge can begin.[12] Each poem alludes to *ouvriers* ("workers"): for Bourbon's fame, Ronsard is an *ouvrier* superior to Marot (ll. 9–12), while Martin is praised for his translations, a source of technical knowledge that will make French masons superior to Roman ones (ll. 55–64). This point tends to reinforce the

Fig 11. Textual and thematic links, 1.4 and 1.12.

1.4: AU REVERENDISSIME CARDINAL DE GUISE	1.12: A ANTHOINE DE BAIF
Quand tu n'aurois autre grace Ni autre present des cieus, Que d'estre né de la race De tant de Rois tes aieus, Je trouveroi trop de lieus Pour te bastir une gloire (ll. 1–6)	. . . vertus hautes: Car moi qui suis le sonneur Et le courier des louanges (ll. 4–6)
. . . honneur . . . vertus (ll. 37, 39) Et à qui mon hinne donne Une louange si bonne Criant ta gloire en tout lieu (ll. 44–46)	Je ne porte aus gens étranges Sinon la gloire et l'honneur Que le ciel large donneur Aiant quelque soin de toi T'a departi comme à moi (ll. 7–11)

1.4: To the Most Reverend Cardinal of Guise

If you had no other grace, nor any other gift from heaven, than to have been born of the race of so many Kings, your ancestors, I would find too many places in which to build a glory for you (ll. 1–6)

honor, virtues (ll. 37, 39)

And to whom my hymn gives such worthy praise, proclaiming your glory in every place (ll. 44–46)

1.12: To Antoine de Baïf

. . . high virtues, For I who am the sounder and courier of praise (ll. 4–6)

I carry to foreign lands only the glory and the honor that the generous heavens, showing some concern for you, accorded to you as to me (ll. 7–11)

idea of the interdependence of words and deeds: without Ronsard, Bourbon's victory would be imperfectly sung; without Martin, the buildings of France would be inferior to those of Rome.

The ode to Carnavalet and its "interest payment" (1.6 and 1.7) are strongly bound together, the second acting as a codicil to the first.[13] Both argue that material monuments (marble and bronze, cf. marble and iron) are inferior to the poet's pen, while the end of both poems focuses on the fame to be attained thanks to the strings of the poet's lyre: "ta renommée / Voira les cieus, animée / Par le labeur de mes dois" (ll. 35–37) ("Your renown will reach the heavens, given life by the work of my fingers") and "Le bruit de sa corde animé . . . Fera parler ta renommée / De l'un jusque à l'autre Occident" (ll. 13–16) ("The sound of its living string . . . will make your renown heard from one Western shore to the other"). The corresponding poem (1.14) is the sec-

Fig 12. Textual and thematic links, 1.5 and 1.13.

1.5: LA VICTOIRE DE FRANÇOIS DE BOURBON	1.13: A JAN MARTIN
L'hinne (l. 1) gloire* (l. 4) plume (l. 6)	La fable (l. 1) plume (l. 3) gloire* (l. 5)
[I glorify your virtue by my song] (ll. 13–18)	[Your virtue glorifies you in my song] (ll. 15–28)
[Breadth of renown] (ll. 15–16)	[Breadth of renown] (ll. 23–28)
Reveilla l'honneur de France (l. 42)	. . . tu fis naistre A la France un honneur (ll. 43–44)
[The arts of war] (ll. 43–60)	[The arts of peace] (ll. 45–64)

1.5: The Victory of François de Bourbon
The hymn, glory, pen (ll. 1, 4, 6)
Awakened the honor of France (l. 42)

1.13: To Jean Martin
The fable, pen, glory (ll. 1, 3, 5)
. . . you caused France to give birth to an honor (ll. 43–44)

ond to Jean Dorat. The two principal odes share thematic concerns but have no pattern of textual correspondence. Carnavalet educates young noblemen in equitation (and thus helps prepare them for a role as heroes), while Dorat educates young humanists in letters (and helps prepare them for a role as poets). Both poems assign great importance to education and nurture (the example of Pallas and Bellerophon in the first, the metaphor of the mother in the second), although these individuals follow others who practice these arts to serve the nation. The former presents a more public and exterior form of praise; the latter, the first of the non-Pindaric odes, a more intimate one.

The odes to Guy de Chabot (1.8) and Bertrand Berger (1.15) rely for their correspondence on a sequence of thematic contrasts without textual elements.[14] The ode to Chabot praises the hero's victory, which gains him lasting glory, while the well-known ode to Ronsard's fellow poet Berger draws on the example of antiquity to argue that only the poet's art assures lasting renown to the great of the world. Next, each alludes to Fortune and the changeability of reputation (using the seasons as an example), to affirm in the first the inevitability of changes of Fortune and to honor in the second

Berger's virtue in the face of misfortune. In conclusion, Ronsard returns to the praise of Chabot's "acte si beau," in the first, but in the second, the final poem of the entire series, he rejects, in a classical *recusatio,* an elevated style of song, "un si haut chant," for a more appropriate low style, "Retournez louer ma Cassandre" ("Return to the praise of my Cassandra").[15]

The interlocking-ring pattern of the first three quarters of book 1 of the *Odes* has two dimensions. First, a hierarchical order emerges, and each successive figure adds an element to the overall definition of the class. Thus, the nobles are largely presented in terms of victories and power (the king, his sister, Bourbon, Chabot) or in terms of their contribution to the social order that generates them and that they preserve (the queen, the cardinal, Carnavalet). The poets and humanists are presented in terms of their creative power and the (generic) area in which they exercise their talents. Second, we discover a systematic formulation of relationships among the nobles and the poets, with a notable degree of correspondence between the members of the pairs as representative figures and in terms of the poetic genre appropriate to them. Both groups are systematically presented in the light of their "virtue," and the cumulative effect is to make clear the interdependence between them.

At the same time, the patterning underscores a relatively systematic set of values that has more to do with poetry and knowledge than with the figures who receive the poet's praise. These values, brought out by the textual correspondences themselves, draw attention to Ronsard's high view of poetry and the poet's role. They set forth a definition of true poetry, nourished by virtue and knowledge, to be distinguished from the verse of ignorant poets. They affirm its capacity to ensure lasting renown and emphasize its creative and constructive role and its fertility, because it is rooted in the deeds of the powerful undertaken for the good of France. The survival of great deeds and heroic figures is thus a function of the grandeur of the poets who praise them; throughout, Ronsard's use of the Pindaric mode suggests that he has adapted the epicinian and encomiastic hymns to national victories instead of games; he insistently underscores the importance of the new poets for the expression of greatness and valor.

The final poems of book 1 show a separate short interlocking-ring pattern, with very strong textual correspondences. The second ode to Du Bellay (1.16) and the penultimate ode, to Pierre Paschal (1.19), are joined by the only marked example of a ring pattern (fig. 13), here suggestive of impending closure.[16] While the verbal reminiscences are not very close, the odes formulate very similar ideas, pointing up the importance of poetic activity and renown. The ode to Du Bellay describes the new type of poet, whom he and Ronsard represent, while Paschal's knowledge and gift for oratory are emphasized. The central textual block relating the two poems reflects the concern with inspiration (Du Bellay) and art (Paschal) in successful expression, but it is clear

Fig 13. Textual and thematic links, 1.16 and 1.19.

1.16: A JOACHIM DU BELLAI ANGEVIN	1.19: A PIERRE PASCHAL
Nous mariant au troupeau Que le saint Parnase adore (ll. 7–8)	De moi, t'elevant parmi L'honneur des troupes celestes (ll. 35–36)
Ils chantent par l'univers D'une vois où dieu abonde (ll. 19–20)	Soufflés oultre l'univers Par le vent de ma parolle (ll. 27–28)
Un Daimon les acompaigne Sur tretous le mieus instruit, Lequel en songes la nuit Sans nul travail les enseigne, Et demidieu ne dedaigne De les aller informant, Affin que l'homme en dormant Toutes sçiences appreigne (ll. 25–32)	Ce m'est une sainte peine Chanter l'homme en qui les cieus Ont renversé tout le mieus De leur influence pleine, Quand sa clarté merveilleuse Maugré l'obscur se fait voir Par les raions du sçavoir De sa langue mielleuse (ll. 13–20)
Qui commença l'alience De corps, & d'ame entre nous (ll. 61–62)	La cheine qui entrelasse Ton esprit avec le mien, Et mon nom semblable au tien Commande que je le face (ll. 9–12)

1.16: To Joachim Du Bellay
Joining us to the flock that holy Parnassus adores (ll. 7–8)
They sing throughout the universe with a voice in which god's presence is plentiful (ll. 19–20)
A Demon, the most knowledgeable among them, accompanies them [poets], and in dreams at night without any effort teaches them, and although a demigod, he does not disdain to inform them so that man may learn all sciences as he sleeps (ll. 25–32)
Who initiated the alliance of body and soul between us (ll. 61–62)

1.19: To Pierre Paschal
I, raising you up among the honor of the heavenly flock (ll. 35–36)
Blown throughout the universe by the wind of my word (ll. 27–28)
It is for me a pious burden to sing the man into whom the heavens poured all the best of their influence, (now) when his marvelous clarity, in spite of the darkness, is to be seen thanks to the rays of knowledge sent forth by his honeyed tongue (ll. 13–20)
The chain that links your spirit with mine, and my name, which resembles yours, orders me to do so (ll. 9–12)

Fig 14. Textual and thematic links, I.18 and I.20.

I.18: VEU A PHEBUS APOLLON	I.20: A SA LIRE
Phebus (l. 1)	Phebus (l. 1)
seurs* [= Muses] (l. 7)	neuf seurs (l. 2)
[Calm fever] (ll. 13–18)	[Calm Jupiter's armed fire] (ll. 9–16)
[Illness of a lady]	[Illness of the lyre] (ll. 25–26)
[Heal the sick] (ll. 18–21)	[Heal the sick] (ll. 27–32)
[Collect plants] (ll. 43–60)	[Collect (*piller*) verses] (ll. 31–32)
[Gratitude] (ll. 79–80)	[Gratitude] (ll. 57–60; ll. 65–68)
[Phoebus's lyre] (ll. 83–84)	[Ronsard's lyre and lute] (ll. 57–72)

I.18: Vow to Phoebus Apollo
Phoebus (l. 1)
sisters [= Muses] (l. 7)

I.20: To His Lyre
Phoebus (l. 1)
nine sisters [= Muses] (l. 2)

that despite Paschal's exceptional nature (vv. 14–17), there remains a qualitative difference between the lyric poet and the great orator, who remains dependent on the poet's art to ensure his lasting renown.

Finally, the vow to Phoebus Apollo (I.18) and the ode to the poet's lyre (I.20) form an interlocking ring pattern (fig. 14). Framed by brief verbal ties at the beginning and end of both odes, a structural parallelism traces themes of sickness, health, and cure in the central sections. The first poem is a prayer for health, and the second a thanksgiving tribute for health restored. Where *valeur* is attributed to Phoebus in medicine, it is attributed to Ronsard in poetry. Both the god (of medicine *and* poetry) and the inspired poet reestablish health and harmony after a period of illness, due in the first instance to a physical fever, resulting from a lack of harmony among the humors, and in the second to the neglected instrument, the untuned and mildewed lyre. The parallel is clear: as good health (bodily harmony) is restored through the divine physician's art, so good poetry (the harmonious lyre) depends on the inspired poet's. And a healthy lyre is a source of the harmony that calms warlike passions and turns men away from the arts of war (ll. 9–16, 41–48) for the well-being of the nation and the greater glory of poetry. Ronsard states clearly that having praised the victories of kings, he turns to loftier, even worthier, concerns. The correspondences thus reinforce the high value attributed to poetry and to the learned and inspired poet.

As a whole, the interlocking-ring pattern draws attention to the interdependence of heroes and poets. Were it not for the latter, the deeds and virtue of the former would remain unknown. Nonetheless, those deeds and that virtue remain the stuff of high poetry, and without glorious deeds and the circumstances they create, great poetry would be impossible. The emphases suggested by the correspondences also draw attention to Ronsard's ideas about poetry, its sources and functions, at the outset of his career. The hypothesis explored here,—that an examination of the *Odes* with an eye to strictly formal pattern can reveal aspects of meaning less readily discernible through other approaches,—does suggest, even at this relatively simple level of analysis, that attention to structural elements can be productive. One can put off, for later discussion, the question of the poet's conscious incorporation of such patterns, and the issue of the possibility of elucidating other patterns, and other sorts of patterns, in the work: the question, in other words, of the signification of the reader's creation of patterns that may or may not be part of the poet's program. The patterns presented here reveal to what extent, and how systematically, book 1 of the *Odes* is concerned with defining certain relationships, whether or not Ronsard consciously sought to do so. They may also be, in their pervasiveness, a subtle part of the poet's program to "sell" the wares he presents more overtly in a number of odes, in particular in the ode to Bertrand de Berger (1.15). Even if not consciously elaborated, they reveal with great clarity Ronsard's concerns with the mutual dependence of heroes and poets and with the relation between the fertility of genius (the creative and inspirational aspect of poetry that manifests itself in delightful variety) and the discipline of art (represented in the control of techniques that give coherence to the virtue and the values inherent in poetry at its highest). Together, they are the means by which the poet builds a verbal monument to ensure the survival of his work. It is by the achievement of a harmonious balance that Ronsard justifies his implicit boast in the final ode of the entire collection to have equaled Horace's "Exegi monumentum aere perennius" ("I have erected a monument more lasting than bronze") in a later age: "Plus dur que fer, j'ay fini mon ouvrage" ("Harder than iron, my work I have finished").[17]

Notes

1. For the documentation of these ties, consult the notes in Paul Laumonier, ed., Pierre de Ronsard, *Oeuvres complètes* (Paris: M. Didier, 1973), 1:61–166; Laumonier, *Ronsard, poète lyrique*, 2nd ed. (Paris: Hachette, 1923), pp. 26–69; 291–429 passim. The

text used throughout the present study is Laumonier's and will hereafter be cited as *Oeuvres*. All translations are mine.

2. For a clear and rigorous résumé of such patterning devices, consult Helena Dettmer, *Horace: A Study in Structure* (New York: Olms, 1983), ch. 1.

3. For related studies, see my "La Pensée architecturale de Ronsard dans les *Odes*," in *Littérature et architecture, Interférences* 16 (1988): 47–57; "Les modes d'organisation des *Odes* de 1550," in *Ronsard en son IVe centenaire: II, L'Art de poésie* (Geneva: Droz, 1989), 91–100; and *Du Palais au jardin: L'Architecture des Odes de Ronsard* (Geneva: Droz, 1990).

4. With the possible exception of 1.7 (the poem appended to 1.6 as *usure* or "interest payment"—because, says Ronsard, he has offered it later than he should have). It is not triadic, but Laumonier argues that it is nonetheless Pindaric (*Oeuvres*, p. 100; *Ronsard*, p. 298). Throughout, poems are numbered according to book and poem; 1.7 designates Book 1, poem 7.

5. Dorat's poetry, written in Latin and Greek, goes unmentioned. Since Ronsard's goal, like Du Bellay's in the *Deffence et Illustration*, is to enhance the French language, there may be a political motivation to Ronsard's silence here.

6. The overwhelming attention to the power of poetry to confer immortality is reflected in a recurrent cluster of words, generally placed at the rhyme (here and throughout marked by an asterisk), which reinforces the idea: front, vers*, univers*, gloire*, victoire*, memoire*. Most of these terms appear in 1.1, 1.2, 1.4, 1.5, 1.6, 1.8, 1.10, 1.20, and they are present to a lesser degree in 1.9, 1.12, 1.14, 1.15, 1.17 (glorieuse*, victorieuse*), and 1.19).

7. We are accustomed to thematic and generic arrangements and perceive them readily; because strictly formal arrangement is generally less significant for the modern reader, it is not sought out and therefore less easily perceived.

8. Dettmer, *Horace*, ch. 1.

9. Fifty-eight may be a more correct total. Laumonier points out in his notes to the ode that in the 1550 edition, 1.7 is presented without a separation between the two huitains, and argues, on the grounds that several of the Pindaric odes have long strophes, that the poem seems best considered a single long strophe. Whether the poem is seen as composed of one or two strophes, the general principle of numerical correspondences is observed. Dettmer (*Horace*, ch. 1) argues that an inequality (or *inconcinnitas*) of one element in the numerical symmetry is characteristic of first works.

10. This particular kind of equivalence does not seem to have a precedent in Roman collections. Non-corresponding poems generally do not figure in the numerical symmetry of Roman poetry books, as is also the case here.

11. Laumonier, in *Annales Flechier* 1909, pp. 277ff. and *Oeuvres*, p. 75. The Cardinal's character, according to Laumonier, was marked by his being "insolent dans la grandeur."

12. In 1550, the hope of peace was strong and the moment to undertake these tasks propitious. Horace's similar situation in Rome when the doors of war were closed may underlie the general implications.

13. See *Oeuvres*, p. 298. The word *usure* appears only in these two places in book 1. See A. E. Creore, *A Word-Index to the Poetic Works of Ronsard* (Leeds: W. S. Maney and Son, 1972), s.v. usure. The title refers back to l. 24 of the preceding poem, and the antistrophe of the ode to Carnavalet (where *usure* occurs) shares four rhymes with it.

Corresponding to l'enclume* / plume*, renommée* / animée* (in ode 6, ll. 32, 34–36), we find l'enclume* / plume*, animée* / renommée* (in ode 7, ll. 5, 7, 13, 15).

14. The relaxation in the final correspondences of the strong textual linking apparent earlier in the sequence constitutes a formal indication that the pattern is drawing to a close.

15. The ode to Berger is closely modeled on Horace, whereas the principal model for preceding poems is Pindar. This shift appears to constitute another signal of change at the end of the first section of the pattern.

16. What Barbara Herrnstein Smith calls "terminal modification" in *Poetic Closure: A Study of How Poems End* (Chicago: University of Chicago Press, 1968).

17. Horace, *Odes* 3.3, l. 1, and Ronsard, *Odes* 1.20, l. 1.

Catherine Ingold

5. Order and Affinity in the Seasonal Sonnets of Saint-Amant

Each apparently composed at a different time and under different circumstances, Saint-Amant's four seasonal sonnets are reunited in the third volume of his *Oeuvres*.[1] Noting the otherwise chronological order of the collection, Jean Lagny remarks, "Quant aux quatre sonnets des saisons, il est normal de les voir réunis juste après l'épitre [à Villarnoul]" ("As for the four seasonal sonnets, it is normal to see them grouped right after the Epistle [to Villarnoul]").[2] A legitimate question may be raised, however, as to whether this order indicates a real affinity, or is merely a convenient grouping, not unprecedented at the time, of superficially parallel sonnets.[3]

The question of the degree of affinity of the sonnets in the cycle leads in interesting directions. As we begin to examine each sonnet in terms of the developmental principles and the image systems that underlie its developmental structure, a number of similarities between the sonnets become apparent. As an underlying metaphorical structure is revealed in each sonnet, a profound affinity among the sonnets at the metaphorical level appears increasingly plausible. What follows is a discussion of each sonnet, leading to a general assessment of similarities and, beyond that, of thematic unity in the sonnet series. (See the appendix at the end of this chapter for full sonnet texts and translations.)

"Le Printemps aux environs de Paris"

In the spring sonnet, the subject is introduced by evoking an allegorical love tryst between two mythological personages, Zephyrus and Flora. After the somewhat précieux opening statement (ll. 1–2) that expresses the speaker's feeling that Flora (spring) is at the very least a worthy object of admiration, he elaborates, asserting her beneficial effect: "On voit à son éclat les soins s'esvanouir / Comme les libertes devant l'Oeil que j'adore."

Though banal, the simile is functional: by establishing correspondences between the poet's love life and elements of the vernal scene, it moves the poem from the purely abstract realm of mythology to that of individual affective experience. In equating Flora's *éclat* (which banishes care) to the glance of his own beloved (which banishes liberty), the speaker identifies light (*éclat*) with visual contact and facial expression. The shared characteristic of Flora's *éclat* and the beloved's "eye" is erotic stimulus, and indeed it is the description of spring's erotic impact that occupies the remainder of the sonnet.

Not only does the Zephyrus parallel in the introductory simile establish the speaker's capacity to react to the vernal scene by relating his perception to his inner experience, but above all it foreshadows a key developmental device of the sonnet: an analogy between elements of nature and amorous couples.

Understanding the function of the Zephyrus simile is necessary to define the role of the first quatrain, which introduces five essential components of the sonnet: (1) the general topic—the charms of spring; (2) the focus within the broader theme—erotic impact; (3) the principal motif—an affective link between the poet and the spring scene; (4) the dominant structural device—sustained analogy with an amorous couple; and (5) the fire-light image system, which both unifies the sonnet and augments its intensity.

The second quatrain develops the main theme. Describing Spring's admirable qualities, the speaker confirms his initial thesis: that Flora (Spring) is a worthy object of infatuation. On the surface, this development consists of describing a static situation (the spring scene) in which the speaker is present. It can be broken into two parts: the first, corresponding to the second quatrain, deals with the speaker's own reaction to vernal flora and fauna; the second—the first tercet—portrays the interaction of the elements themselves.

The *je* appearing in the last line of the first quatrain is taken up again in the opening two lines of the development: "Qui ne serait ravi d'entendre sous l'Aurore / Les Miracles volants qu'au Bois je viens d'ouïr?" A smooth transition to the development is effected in part by a parallel in the use of the third and first persons: "On voit . . . j'adore"; "Qui ne serait . . . je viens d'ouïr." The use of *qui ne* implies, somewhat more strongly than before, the presence of an audience (however vaguely invoked) that must be convinced of the rightness of his response. The *qui ne* thus functions as "you, in my place." The *je* emphasizes the personal nature of the description, while the indeterminate third person emphasizes its universality.

Another means of creating continuity between the two quatrains is imagery: the *éclat* of spring and the Aurore of line 5 both suggest the initial appearances of a bright light. (Note the identical position of Flora and Aurore in the quatrains.) That the returning birds burst into song at the first light of dawn is noteworthy both as effective use of synesthesia and because it exemplifies the beneficial effects of Spring's arrival. Thus, the birdsong announces not only day but Spring itself, so that the speaker's (and the flowers') reaction in the following lines responds to the advent of Spring as much as that of dawn.

The analytical approach used to separate and observe the various manifestations of spring is applied here to the speaker's own emotions: his heart (pure sentiment) reacts to the morning birdsongs by opening or blossoming in rhythm with the flowers. Dormant sentiments are called forth, so that his neglected lute (the creative impulse) responds in kind to the music that he hears.

The responsiveness of the speaker's emotions to natural phenomena is a more effective reprise of the précieux simile of lines 3 and 4. He seems to observe his own reactions to vernal phenomena and to consider them interacting with the springtime elements he is describing. (This is not, however, a prelude to losing himself in nature, but a preparation for the pathetic fallacy developed in the tercets.) The word *répondre* in the last line of the quatrain emphasizes the motif of interaction and communication.

In the tercets, the interaction motif continues, but with yet another change. First, two mythical beings interacted; then, the speaker and nature; now, the action shifts to the natural elements themselves, paired off to represent increasingly intense gestures of a courtship. The complex of images introduced in the first quatrain reappears with greater density: erotic interplay expressed as visual contact / facial expression and as fire and light.

The series of exchanges begins in line 9 with an invitation to courtship: "L'herbe sourit à l'Air d'un air voluptueux." The couple formed by "l'Air" and "l'herbe" recalls the first pair, Zephyrus and Flora, and like them unites ether and vegetation. Reaffirming his role as observer (*j'apperçois*), Saint-Amant progresses to a description of a caress between two traditionally and physically incompatible elements: "Le doux feu du Soleil flatte(r) le sein de l'Onde." This paradoxical union of fire and water marks movement from visual exchange (a smile) to physical interplay (a caress) emphasized by fire-light imagery of increasing intensity. The incipient light of dawn is now a "doux feu": the agent, not merely the stimulus, of the caress.

The erotic progression continues in the second tercet with a kiss: "Le soir et le matin la Nuit baise le Jour." Once again, Saint-Amant creates an amorous couple by joining two diametrically opposed elements. Night and Day, traditionally seen as struggling for control of the heavens, here are lovers to whom evening and morning provide opportunities to embrace. This coupling of Night and Day has several important functions. From the structural viewpoint, the most obvious is the culmination of the "couple" series in a paradoxical embrace, global in scope, that justifies the conclusion in the next line that "Tout aime." The coupling also serves to introduce circularity to the developmental pattern: up to this point, the dominant motion of the sonnet has been that of awakening and expansion, of rebirth. The only temporal reference has been to dawn. Here, the action of the sonnet is placed into a larger context. Morning now becomes only one of two pivotal points of time; dawn and dusk are counterpoised. In this way, the interaction of Day and Night prepares for the last two lines, which close the sonnet on multiple levels.

On the level of a purely enumerative descriptive structure, the phrase "tout aime, tout s'embrase" in line 13 sums up the reaction of the elements to the emotive stimulus of springtime. In the coda both the courtship itself and its ancillary fire-light imagery reach a culminating intensity. The juxtaposition of "tout aime" and "tout s'embrase" seems to equate the two verbs, definitely linking the image system to the courtship progression. Thus, "s'embrase" serves as the pivotal image of the coda. Its dual meaning (literally, to catch fire and burn: thus, to be destroyed; and metaphorically, to become inflamed with passion) serves as a logical stepping-stone to the final paradox of erotic death. "Mourir d'amour," signifying the critical moment of the love act, closes the erotic sequence that began with the renaissance of emotions (especially of the sexual instinct) stimulated by the arrival of spring. In its broader and more literal interpretation, however, the final line of the sonnet recognizes the relative and transitory nature of the vital cycle that the sonnet celebrates. As night and day follow each other, so do birth and death. Beneath the playful eroticism of the spring sonnet, the speaker retains a cheerful awareness of the impermanence of the scene that he evokes with such vigor.

"L'Ésté de Rome"

The introductory quatrain of this sonnet, like that of "Le Printemps," signals the dominant trait of the season to be addressed. In the case of the spring sonnet, the characteristic is erotic impact; here it is burning heat. In announcing this heat by a rhetorical question, "Quelle étrange chaleur nous vient ici brûler?"[4] the speaker immediately reveals his perception that the heat is a bizarre phenomenon visited upon the inhabitants of the region (himself included) as a kind of burning plague. He emphasizes the unwonted intensity of the heat by proposing two hyperbolic hypotheses to account for it—also couched as rhetorical questions. Both hypotheses involve dislocation: in the first, the speaker wonders if he and his comrades have somehow been displaced to a tropical clime where such heat would be more normal; in the second, he postulates a recurrence of a mythological cataclysm: Phaeton's ill-fated chariot ride, in which the sun itself was wrenched from orbit, then scorched the earth. In spatial terms, the two questions may be summarized as "which is out of place—are we or is the sun?" The aspect of summer heat presented here is one of excess and inappropriateness: the normally beneficent warmth of the sun has been intensified, perhaps through dislocation, and has become destructive.

The allusion to Phaeton is extremely important, for it suggests several primary aspects of the vision of summer subsequently developed in the sonnet. First, it enlarges the scope. Phaeton's ride is to droughts and heat waves what Noah's Ark is to floods: an archetype of unparalleled catastrophe. But certain details of the Phaeton myth are revealing. The poem emphasizes Phaeton's outstanding character trait—imprudence. His excessive self-confidence and rejection of moderating advice leads to widespread destruction and to his own death by Zeus's thunderbolt. Phaeton thus symbolizes destructive excess and loss of control. In terms of fire-light imagery, he is both source of fiery destruction and victim of divine wrath in the form of fire. One can see all of these aspects of the myth either echoed or augmented at some point in the sonnet, so that Phaeton's ride serves as one of the underlying contexts of the sonnet, just as fire and light are underlying metaphorical images.

In the second quatrain, the poem progresses logically from overtly speculating on the nature and source of the heat wave to describing its effects. The earth is first envisioned as a whole, living being, panting and rending itself in agony under the burning rays; the fire image functions as a celestial weapon. Portrayal of the sun in terms of "rayons" rather than as a "grande torche aithérée" ("great ethereal torch"), as in Ronsard's "De la venue de l'Esté" (Of the coming of Summer),[5] conveys the impression of burning missiles hurled at a hapless victim (*La Terre*), producing gaping wounds (*s'entre-fend*). Thus drained of its vital juices, the earth shrivels (*se ride*).

The description of the metamorphosis that follows this burning attack narrows the visual field by focusing on the *champ romain* (the first time that the referent of *ici* in line 1 becomes clear). The plain is transformed into a "sable aride" from which "nulle fraîche humeur ne peut s'exhaler." This last line combines the image of dehydration ("nulle fraîche humeur") with suffocation ("ne peut s'exhaler"), introduced earlier by *panteler*, to yield a vivid account of the final throes of death by roasting. This descriptive passage forms a curiously simultaneous account of different events: the present heat wave that the inhabitants are enduring; the scorching of the earth during Phaeton's ride; and Phaeton's own death by thunderbolt, suggested by "l'ardeur des rayons." On one level (conveyed both explicitly and mythologically), the earth is a victim; on another, that of the speaker's experience, the earth thus transformed becomes an environment that in turn inflicts discomfort on the speaker and his comrades. The perception of being "transported" arises from the radical change in the setting; the earth, moribund, is no longer capable of nurturing its inhabitants, and has become a desert devoid of life-giving moisture.

In the tercets the speaker elaborates on the drying of the roman plain by describing the evaporation of the Tiber. The reference to death is no longer oblique: "Les furieux regards de l'âpre Canicule / Forcent même le Tibre à périr comme Hercule." The description of the Tiber's death is strikingly parallel to that of the earth's agony: the earth was "contrainte" by "l'ardeur des rayons;" here it is the "furieux regards" of the Dog Star that force the Tiber to perish. In the evident identification of *rayons* with *regards* is manifested once again the intertwining of light images and images related to visual contact and facial expression. Whereas in the Spring sonnet, the *éclat* of Spring recalled to the poet the "Oeil que j'adore," in this sonnet the two images share a common malevolent intensity. The angry stare and the burning ray are equally destructive.

The Dog Star's "furious" stare is both a reflection of the madness of Phaeton's actions and an explicit reference to the divine displeasure suggested by the imagery of the sonnet up to this point as well as by the Phaeton myth itself. The reference to Hercules emphasizes the theme of excess that incurs fatal consequences. (Hercules, it will be recalled, led a life fraught with continual indiscretions, even crimes, followed by retributions—e.g. the Twelve Labors.) But the key element of the Hercules myth for this sonnet is not so much the pattern of his life as the manner of his death: Hercules, like Phaeton, perished by fire. More precisely, he threw himself onto a pyre to escape the burning torment of the poisoned mantle. A herculean death is thus an appropriate end to the agony portrayed in the quatrains.[6]

Further examination of the two mythical deaths offers insight into the sonnet's metaphorical frame of reference. The burning mantle is the instrument of Hercules' death as the chariot of the sun is of Phaeton's. Both instruments are provided by well-intended second parties (Hercules' wife, Phaeton's father) in an attempt to secure or affirm a previously existing relationship. In the case of Phaeton, Helios turns over the chariot against his better judgment in order to assure Phaeton both of his parentage and of his father's love. In the case of Hercules, Deianira sends him the mantle believing it has the power to end his infidelity. Thus, both myths provide examples of misguided affection with fatal consequences. This goes far toward explaining the presence of the dislocation hypothesis in the opening lines: the sonnet is a study of love—not only sexual but also paternal-filial—distorted by some action on the part of the eventual victim. The dual view of the earth as both sufferer and cause of suffering reflects the mythical situation in which death results from a fatal error on another's part, but has its true causal origin in the actions of the victim himself, so that death manifests divine retribution—an inevitable triumph of the measure and order that have been assaulted.

The locative emphasis of line 11 leads us to a discussion of the spatial structuring of the sonnet. The placement of the final death scene "dessous l'ombrage sec des joncs, et des roseaux" narrows the field of vision even further, completing a process that pervades the sonnet. Beginning on a global scale, the speaker evokes the entire earth as a suffering victim. Next, he limits his description to the roman plain, and then to the Tiber itself. Within the narrow bounds of the riverbed, he evokes smaller details—rushes and reeds. Each stage of the progressively narrowed visual field is clearly linked by image or by metaphor to the previous one. The dry shade suggests shelter from burning and from dryness, but the shade of the reeds, like the plain, has lost its capacity to refresh.

The progressive shrinking of the poem's perspective functions first of all as a structuring device: among the structural devices recognized by Barbara Herrnstein Smith,[7] it might be classed as a spatially based serial structure. Saint-Amant's substitution of space for time as the framework for the sonnet's progression is particularly interesting. The temporally progressive narration of the myths on a metaphorical level is accompanied by the spatial progression of the drought: as a drying puddle shrinks toward its center, so the sonnet shrinks toward the final refuge of the last drop of moisture: the shaded marshes of the Tiber's riverbed.

The final tercet, which serves as the coda, invites scrutiny in light of the spatial structuring: in principle, it must terminate the spatial sequence while unifying the various image patterns and metaphors of the sonnet.

The first line of the coda, "Sa qualité de dieu ne l'en saurait déffendre," refers to the Tiber: the divinity traditionally ascribed to this river is not proof against the devastating force of the drought. But the comparison of the Tiber's death to that of Hercules leads the reader to apply the statement to the other deaths that the sonnet describes: Phaeton's as well as Hercules'. The coda reinforces an underlying theme of the sonnet: imprudence and excess struck down by a superior order. Hercules and Phaeton, although sons of gods, eventually confront their own mortality.

The second and third lines of the tercet contain the essential, final paradox of the sonnet: "Et le vase natal, d'où s'écoulent ses eaux, / Sera l'urne funeste, où l'on mettra sa cendre." Again, the metaphor refers to the riverbed of the Tiber, which is both the womb (source) and the funeral urn. But the word *cendre* can mean either dust or ashes; thus it sums up and ends the death-by-fire narration on its multiple levels. Spatially, the urn image is particularly successful. It reduces the shrinking visual field of the sonnet to its smallest point and, by evoking a closed space, precludes further spatial changes. The image is strikingly similar to the crystalline "Tombeau précieux" that closes the winter sonnet.

The symbolism of the vase and urn is more difficult to fix, for it admits (and must admit, in order to be complete) a number of possible meanings. It harks back to the metamorphosis of the roman plain in the second quatrain, serving as yet another link in the earth-plain-river continuum and completing the metamorphosis theme begun in the hypotheses of the introduction. The paradox of a life source transforming itself into a funeral urn encompasses as well the leitmotiv of divine disfavor: the two mythical personages of the sonnet derive their source from divine pleasure, both having been fathered by deities. The myth of Phaeton deals with the son of Helios, source of all light, who thus embodies the life-giving aspect of light. Helios is also, however, the unwilling cause of Phaeton's death and of general destruction because he permits Phaeton's ride. Interestingly, it is only by this allusion that the Summer sonnet touches on the creative-generative power of light so strongly emphasized in the Spring sonnet. Rather, the Summer sonnet picks up on the closing paradox of the Spring sonnet: ". . . le Monde / Ne renaît . . . que pour mourir d'amour," and exploits it fully. Love, both conjugal (Hercules-Deianira) and filial-paternal (Phaeton-Helios), is the source of life but, when excessive and misplaced, leads to suffering and death. The dislocation hypotheses that open the Summer sonnet thus point us toward the hidden narrative that the images reveal: a tale of love's distortion and its fatal consequences.

"L'Automne des Canaries"

As in the Spring and Summer sonnets, Saint-Amant characterizes the subject of this poem by referring to light in conjunction with mythological personages: the *gloire* of Bacchus and Pomona. With stronger locative emphasis than in the other sonnets (*côtaux, vallons, territoire*), he sets the scene in a uniquely privileged region, favored by two deities of the harvest. The joint reference to Bacchus and Pomona serves first of all to characterize the region as an abundant and fruitful one, since this is their shared connotation. It pinpoints the aspect of the Bacchanalian legend that dominates the sonnet: the harvest itself, rather than the dementia and self-destruction that are also associated with Bacchus. Moreover, it signals an underlying leitmotiv, the coexistence of divergent aspects, that recurs elsewhere in the sonnet—particularly in the coda. Pomona is a peculiarly tranquil and restrained nymph who shuns lovers, prefers the orchard to the forest, and accepts a husband only as a partner in cultivation. The qualities that she symbolizes are completely alien to the unbridled sensuality of Bacchus, and yet it is their joint patronage that produces the cornucopian abundance of the region described.

The "riche honneur" of the territory reflects the glory of its patron gods as it characterizes the region itself: the term *honneur* conveys the early meaning of "adornment" as well as the current meaning of "honor." The gods' patronage honors the region by adorning it with fruition, made possible by their protecting it from "l'effort des rudes Aquilons."

The fire-light image system, which functions so prominently in the other sonnets to convey widely divergent impressions, undergoes a peculiar metamorphosis in this sonnet. By association with fruit (and particularly with its "golden" ripeness), the *gloire* of Bacchus and Pomona is transposed from the purely visual to the gustatory domain. (This synesthetic transformation is reminiscent of the morning birdsong of the Spring sonnet.) There seems to be a sense here of the transformation of the fire and light of the Summer and Spring sonnets into a more fecund creative force. Moreover, Saint-Amant's predilection for gustatory imagery in expressing sensual pleasure has become a literary commonplace. Here, he effects the transformation (or rather the association, for the light images do not disappear) as a means of expressing yet another aspect of nature, that of pure enjoyment.

The remainder of the sonnet up to the final two lines is devoted to a description of the fructiferous *honneur* of the region and at the same time narrates the homage that the land offers to its patron deities. Two aspects of the development are particularly noteworthy: the relative paucity of reference to the poet's own reaction to the scene he is describing (the reference to "nous" in line 8 serves primarily to emphasize the exotic sweetness of the dates, to which France's only equivalent is honey); and the "y" that, repeated constantly, underlines the locative rather than the seasonal emphasis of the introduction.

Saint-Amant begins his description by simple enumeration of some of the fruits of the region (figs, muscats, peaches, melons) that "couronnent ce dieu qui se délecte à boire."[8] These first two lines of the second quatrain establish the reciprocal nature of the relationship between the region and its patrons: the gods favor the region, which in turn pays homage to the gods. In describing this homage, Saint-Amant uses a device seen earlier in the Spring sonnet: each act in the series is carried out by a different element of the island flora. After the fruits have crowned the god, the palms, "sacrés à la victoire," bow deferentially ("s'y courbent"). The feudal relationship between the region and its deities is manifested in the link between Bacchus's crown of fruit and the similar fruited crowns of the palm trees, which by their very weight forces them into a reverential posture. The "riche honneur" of fecundity thus entails a burden of tribute.

The comparison of the fruits of the palms to honey emphasizes the gustatory imagery introduced by the phrase "se délecte à boire." And in the first tercet, Saint-Amant employs yet another image to evoke the sweet juiciness of the region's fruits. The "doux suc" of the sugarcanes, which recalls the "miel" of the preceding line, is transformed into ambrosia. This drink of the gods recalls even more specifically Bacchus's delectation.

The cane image ties together a number of themes. The "or plein d'ambroisie," which undoubtedly refers to the reddish-golden heads of the sugarcane, relates on the thematic level to the coronation images interspersed through the sonnet: the honeylike dates, the fruits that "couronnent" Bacchus, the "honneur" of the territory, and the "gloire" of Bacchus and Pomona. The crown image is the catalyst of the several stages of the homage paid by the earth to the gods: first the act of coronation, then the reverential bow, and finally in this tercet the rendering of offerings as the ambrosia (somewhat hyperbolically) spurts skyward from the crown itself.

One interesting feature of the first tercet is the site of the sugarcane thicket: "non dans les marécages, / Mais sur des flancs de roche." The tremendous fecundity of the region is emphasized by the apparent paradox of a sap-producing crop drawing its sustenance from bare boulders. The canes of the autumn sonnet invite comparison with the reeds of the summer sonnet, whose situation is precisely the reverse: the reeds, which normally form marshes in the river basin of the Tiber, yield in the summer drought only a dry shade, while the canes, growing on bare rock, are bursting with vital juices. The contrast between the cane and reed images typifies the diametrical opposition between important aspects of the two sonnets: in the Summer sonnet, the drought derives from a fundamental disharmony between earth and heaven so that the upward thrust personified in the Phaeton and Hercules legends is doomed to destruction, and is answered with destructive thrusts from heaven. The harmony between heaven and earth illustrated in the Autumn sonnet is fructiferous, producing life rather than death, and is thus reminiscent of the mood of the Spring sonnet.

The first line of the second tercet links the descriptive/narrative body of the sonnet to the coda, as it does in the other three sonnets as well. The *orange* (both the tree and the fruit) is the last in what is superficially an enumeration of the fruits of the region. It is tightly linked to the preceeding line by the homophony between *l'or* of line 11 and *l'or* of *l'orange,* as well as by association (golden color, fruit-bearing plant of prodigious fecundity). In addition, the particular characteristic of its growth that is used to illustrate its fecundity makes the transition to the closing paradox of simultaneity. The fact that the orange both buds and matures "en même jour" conveys the idea of bountiful production of fruit, and can be read as a telescoping of the life cycle resulting in increased yield. More importantly for the sonnet's thematics, the phenomenon demonstrates the coexistence of various stages of the life cycle at the same moment and emphasizes the unbroken continuity of the cycle. These concepts are emphasized in the coda: "Et durant tous les mois on peut voir en ces lieux / Le printemps et l'été confondus en l'automne."

The most direct interpretation of the coda is that it summarizes the consequences of the gods' protection from winter's ravages that was noted in the opening lines. Since the region is forever exempt from the rude north winds, the climate is a perpetual cycle of spring-summer-fall, but one in which all stages of development are simultaneously and continuously manifest. If we recall Saint-Amant's particular portrayals of spring and summer, however, the cycle seems somewhat more complete: the fall fruition that the sonnet describes would result from a combination of spring's harmonious coupling and summer's burning intensity. (Recall the ancient belief that the death of the seed must precede germination.[9] In this case the "vase natal" becoming the "urne funeste" would be a necessary prelude to renascence.)

When we take into account the sonnet's vision of spring and summer, the coda joins the paradox of simultaneity with that of the coexistence of opposites. This latter paradox is suggested by the joint reign of Bacchus and

Pomona (not usually associated in mythology), and by the dual nature of Bacchus himself. The fall sonnet evokes a privileged place in which the gentlest and the most destructive aspects of nature have been brought to a fruitful harmony, a completion of the cycle begun in the spring.

"L'Hyver des Alpes"

In "L'Hyver des Alpes" there is a sharp deviation from the general structural pattern of the other sonnets—a deviation that under Barbara Herrnstein Smith's theory on "how poems end" might well be considered a closing device. Rather than beginning with an introductory statement or question, the poem launches directly into an enumerative description of winter's visual delights that continues unbroken through the quatrains, forming a single sentence. It is after this description that the speaker gives us his general impression of the season, which in the other three seasonal sonnets forms the introduction.

In the first quatrain, the now-familiar fire-light imagery is employed with unusual density: "atomes de feu," "brillent," "étincelles," "lustre." Once again this image system creates an impression totally different from that of the preceding sonnets. Here the images are of sparkle rather than of heat; they lack both the erotic intensity of the Spring sonnet and the burning force of the Summer sonnet, and they contrast with the golden fecundity of autumn's glory by their lack of substance and productivity. The images have neither mass nor duration: "atomes de feu" are infinitesimally small; the "étincelles d'or, d'azur et de cristal" evoke the minute, momentary flashes seen when turning a diamond in the light. The modifiers are important: the crystals reflect the sun (*l'or*) and the sky (*l'azur*). Their reflective quality is emphasized in the third line of the sonnet: the poem specifies that "*l'Hiver, au Soleil,* d'un lustre oriental / Pare ses cheveux blancs" (my italics). Winter, then, adorns its hoary head with the sun's reflected fire, and acquires a "lustre *oriental,*" evoking a similarity between the glitter of winter's *parure* ("adornment") and the light of dawn. While the two are similar in the sense that both proceed from the sun, the evocation of dawn contrasts sharply with the references to old age: Winter's hair is not only white, but thinning—scattered by the winds. The view of Winter presented in this first quatrain is that of an aging season that replaces its own disappearing glory with a *parure* borrowed from the sun in order to reacquire the appearance of youth and vigor.

In the last line of the second quatrain, the speaker introduces in the first person his reaction to the scene that he has just described. The pleasant visual expression ("si doux à mes yeux") elicits a response in kind: the twinkle of pleasure in his eyes answers the glittering particles of the first quatrain. This passage recalls a similar one in the Spring sonnet in which the speaker responds in kind to birdsongs by taking up his lute. In a highly visual sonnet, it is a fleeting example of the leitmotiv of visual contact–facial expression that appears in the four sonnets with varying degrees of prominence.

The speaker's response in the last line of the quatrain leads to a further subjective characterization of the season in the first tercet. He reaffirms, in more general terms, that "Cette Saison me plaît," and specifically cites "la froideur" as one of its attributes. In this way he emphasizes the purely visual nature of the sparks that emanate from the snowy scene: they yield no warmth. If only by proximity, he seems to associate the crystalline clarity of the air with its coldness. The sonnet continues in this vein as he elaborates on his impression of Winter: "Sa Robe d'innocence, et de pure candeur / Couvre en quelque façon les crimes de la Terre." Here the reference to a celestial garment in line 5 becomes more explicit: the "beau Coton du Ciel" is now a "Robe d'innocence" whose purity (specifically related to whiteness by the term *candeur*) hides the earth's crimes. The progressive modification of the decorative function throughout the sonnet is evidenced by the verb used: first *parer,* then *habiller,* and finally *couvrir*. The ornamentation has become a disguise.

The final tercet presents substantial critical problems because of the existence of two entirely different versions. The normal course is to accept the later, revised tercet, since presumably it arose from the poet's dissatisfaction with the earlier one; however, it seems useful here to examine the earlier one as well, since it reveals something of the original direction of the sonnet; moreover, the later version is substantially inferior to the earlier one in the degree of thematic integration to the sonnet as a whole.

The later tercet recalls the divine protection of the autumnal sonnet; it draws on the leitmotiv of facial expression–visual contact ("l'Olympien la *voit* d'un front humain"—my italics) that occurs in the other three sonnets and parallels the poet's jovial twinkle in line 8. Its link with the rest of the sonnet is in the logical conclusion of divine favor that results from the masking of the earth's crimes by a "robe d'innocence." The conclusion seems overly facile; it attributes to the Olympian a total lack of perspicacity by ignoring the apparent, rather than substantial, nature of the earth's innocence. But the lack of integration of the coda with the rest of the sonnet is the real source of difficulty here. There is no connection to the light imagery and the decorative elements that establish the major themes of the sonnet. Moreover, the reference to thunder introduces an auditory image into an almost exclusively visual poem. The earlier tercet also lacks the necessary elements of closure: references to finality are notable by their absence, as is any element of paradox. Jove's restraint is unqualified and not temporally limited; the past tense renders it even less apt for closure, making it more of a historical footnote than an arrestation of development.

The earlier tercet, more successful in several ways, contrasts the winter to the unpleasant heat described in the Summer sonnet: "Au prix du dernier chaud ce temps m'est gracieux." The contrast seems to go beyond a question of temperature. One salient characteristic of the winter that Saint-Amant portrays is its lack of any emotion or feeling, its apparent sterility. Winter's appearance of purity is cold, in the sense of being deathlike or at least dormant: that it does not seem so to the poet is due to the reflection of sun on the snow that creates a "lustre oriental," an impression of vitality or of temporary rejuvenation. The use of the word *gracieux*—in addition to expressing the poet's own enjoyment of the season—revives the theme of divine favor: graciousness includes the idea of grace, the free granting of a gift regardless of the merit of the recipient. Saint-Amant thus revives the theme of divine favor of the original coda, but in a much attenuated form.

With the mention of the possibility of the speaker's death, "Et si la Mort m'attrappe en ce chemin de verre," the sonnet moves definitively toward closure. The path of glass recalls the "pavé transparent" of the first quatrain, but with the emphasis shifted from its beauty to its danger: glass suggests fragility as well as slipperiness.

The final line of the sonnet sums up the paradox of the season: "Je ne saurais avoir qu'un Tombeau précieux." The tomb, recalling still more strongly the funeral urn of the Summer sonnet, effectively closes the paratactic development of the sonnet, both as an image of closed space and as an evocation of death. (The displacement of the introduction does not substantially modify the structure of the sonnet, since its theme may be deduced early in the development.) The coda also provides the final step in the serial development on the metaphorical level. The series consists of the progressive envelopment of the earth, which is first adorned, then clothed, then covered, and finally entombed—a process quite similar to the preparation of a body for burial. The image of the "Tombeau précieux" comprehends the dual aspects of the envelopment sequence, that of entombment and that of adornment. In doing so, it summarizes the paradoxical impression of winter: the absence of real life and the glittering *parure* that lends it an appearance of vitality.

The Seasonal Series

At this point, it seems clear that each sonnet is far more than a vivid description of a season: each deals with a particular aspect of human and divine relationships—an aspect suggested by the attributes of the season itself. It is equally clear that there exist multiple links in patterning, theme, and image between the sonnets. The problem that remains to be addressed is that of the unity or coherence of the sonnet series—if indeed such a series can be said to exist.

The ostensibly paratactic structure of the Spring sonnet tends to conceal a structure considerably more rigorous. It may be said that the structure of the Spring sonnet is that of a narrative sequence whose sequentiality is not immediately apparent. Characteristics of the narrative development that are of note include the use of the following devices: (1) verbal sequences that establish the narrative; (2) a series of agents (here, couples) rather than a single agent, which further conceals the narrative; (3) imagery dominated by fire, light, and facial expression; (4) space as a reinforcing element (an expanding visual field); (5) closure by paradox and reference to death.

If we take this as a model, the other sonnets fit remarkably well into the pattern: the Summer sonnet shares all five of the development characteristics present in the Spring sonnet, although the use of multiple agents is less visible and is supplemented by a sixth device—use of mythological referents—that enriches the metaphorical texture of the sonnet.

In the Fall sonnet, the first three devices are clearly visible, with some modification of the imagery. As in the Summer sonnet, use of mythological referents is an ancillary device, while space functions less as a structural device than as a key element in defining the thematic emphasis: the Fall sonnet is less about autumn and more about the Canaries as a privileged place.

The Winter sonnet in the earlier variant clearly exhibits all five of the development characteristics present in the Spring sonnet. The use of space as a reinforcing element is limited to the use of enclosure as a terminal device along with paradox and reference to death. The later variant, like the Autumn sonnet, lacks a reference to death, but includes the use of a mythological referent.

The degree of uniformity among the sonnets in their metaphorical structures and the devices used is quite remarkable, especially considering their believed dates of composition. Clearly, they are related; but can the four sonnets then be called a series with an overarching structure? It would appear so. Each of the four sonnets deals fundamentally with some aspect or stage of the natural (life) cycle: Spring portrays the awakening of life and the beginning of the procreative process; Summer shows the increasing intensity of the Spring sonnet attaining the apogee, at which point it burns itself out (both consumes and consummates), preparing for the fruition of the Autumn, which requires the participation of both aspects (Bacchus and Pomona) to achieve its prodigious fecundity. Winter's envelopment and entombment of the earth both terminates the series and, as presented by Saint-Amant in a contrastingly lively perspective, prepares for the reenactment of the cycle. Thus the Winter sonnet, with its multiple closural images, serves as the final step in the series, as do the terminal lines of the individual poems.

The disguise theme of the Winter sonnet is a clever characterization of the sonnets themselves, whose metaphorical narrative structures are quite thoroughly concealed from the casual reader beneath Saint-Amant's more visible descriptive skills—a sparkling trompe l'oeil.[10]

Appendix:

Full texts of the four seasonal sonnets in modernized spelling, with literal English translations (Translations by C. W. Ingold and Noëlle McAlpine)

Le Printemps aux environs de Paris

Zéphyr a bien raison d'être amoureux de Flore;
C'est le plus bel Objet dont il puisse jouir,
On voit à son éclat les soins s'évanouir
Comme les libertés devant l'Oeil que j'adore.

Qui ne serait ravi d'entendre sous l'Aurore
Les Miracles volants qu'au Bois je viens d'ouïr?
J'en sens avec les fleurs mon coeur s'épanouir,
Et mon Luth négligé leur veut répondre encore.

L'herbe sourit à l'Air d'un air voluptueux;
J'aperçois de ce Bord fertile et tortueux
Le doux feu du Soleil flatter le sein de l'Onde.

Le soir et le matin la Nuit baise le Jour;
Tout aime, tout s'embrase, et je crois que le Monde
Ne renaît au Printemps que pour mourir d'amour.

Spring in the Paris Area

Zephyrus is right to be in love with Flora;
She is the loveliest Object that he can enjoy.
With her brilliance one sees cares vanish,
Like liberty before the beloved's Eye.

Who would not be delighted to hear beneath the Dawn
The flying Miracles that I just heard in the Woods?
I feel my heart blossoming with the flowers,
And my neglected lute tries to answer them again.

The grass smiles at the Air voluptuously;
I see from this fertile and twisting Bank
The gentle fire of the Sun caressing the breast of the Wave.

Evening and morning Night kisses Day;
Everything is in love, everything catches fire, and I believe the World
Is reborn in the Spring only to die of love.

L'Été de Rome

Quelle étrange chaleur nous vient ici brûler?
Sommes-nous transportés sous la zone torride?
Ou quelqu'autre imprudent a-t-il lâché la bride
Aux lumineux chevaux qu'on voit étinceler?

La Terre en ce climat, contrainte à panteler,
Sous l'ardeur des rayons, s'entre-fend et se ride,
Et tout le champ romain n'est plus qu'un sable aride
D'où nulle fraîche humeur ne peut s'exhaler.

Les furieux regards de l'âpre Canicule
Forcent même le Tibre à périr comme Hercule,
Dessous l'ombrage sec des joncs, et des roseaux:

Sa qualité de dieu ne l'en saurait défendre;
Et le vase natal, d'où s'écoulent ses eaux,
Sera l'urne funeste, où l'on mettra sa cendre.

Summer at Rome

What strange heat comes to burn us here?
Are we transported to the torrid zone?
Or has some other imprudent fellow dropped the reins
Of the luminous horses that are seen glittering?

The Earth in this climate, forced to pant,
Under the burning of the rays, splits and wrinkles,
And the whole roman plain is nothing but a dry sandscape
From which no cool moisture can exude.

The furious gaze of the bitter Dog Star
Forces even the Tiber to perish like Hercules,
Beneath the dry shade of the rushes and reeds.

His godly nature cannot protect him from it;
And the natal vessel, from which his waters flow,
Will be the funeral urn where his ashes will be placed.

L'Automne des Canaries

Voici les seuls côteaux, voici les seuls vallons
Où Bacchus et Pomone ont établi leur gloire;
Jamais le riche honneur de ce beau territoire
Ne ressentit l'effort des rudes Aquilons.

Les figues, les muscats, les pêches, les melons
Y couronnent ce dieu qui se délecte à boire;
Et les nobles palmiers, sacrés à la victoire,
S'y courbent sous des fruits qu'au miel nous égalons.

Les cannes au doux suc, non dans les marécages,
Mais sur des flancs de roche y forment des bocages,
Dont l'or plein d'ambroisie éclate et monte aux cieux.

L'orange en même jour y mûrit et boutonne;
Et durant tous les mois on peut voir en ces lieux
Le printemps et l'été confondus en l'automne.

Autumn in the Canaries

Here are the only slopes, here are the sole valleys
Where Bacchus and Pomona have established their glory;
Never has the rich honor of this handsome land
Felt the effort of the rough north winds.

Figs, muscats, peaches, melons
Crown this god who delights in drink;
And the noble palm trees, sacred to victory,
Curve beneath fruits that we compare to honey.

The sweet sugarcane, not in the marshlands,
But on the bare boulders forms copses
Whose gold, full of ambrosia, bursts forth toward the heavens.

The orange tree there ripens and buds in the same day;
And during all the months can be seen in this place
Springtime and summer blended into fall.

L'Hyver des Alpes

Ces atomes de feu, qui sur la Neige brillent,
ces étincelles d'or, d'azur et de cristal,
Dont l'Hiver, au Soleil, d'un lustre oriental
Pare ses cheveux blancs, que les vents éparpillent:

Ce beau Coton du Ciel, de quoi les monts s'habillent,
Ce pavé transparent, fait du second métal,
Et cet Air net, et sain, propre à l'esprit vital,
Sont si doux à mes yeux, que d'aise ils en pétillent.

Cette Saison me plaît, j'en aime la froideur.
Sa Robe d'innocence, et de pure candeur,
Couvre en quelque façon les crimes de la Terre:

Aussi l'Olympien la voit d'un front humain;
Sa colère l'épargne, et jamais le tonnerre
Pour désoler ses jours ne partit de sa main.

earlier second tercet:

Au prix du dernier chaud ce temps m'est gracieux;
Et si la Mort m'attrape en ce chemin de verre,
Je ne saurais avoir qu'un Tombeau précieux.

Winter in the Alps

These atoms of fire, that sparkle on the snow,
These sparks of gold, blue, and crystal,
With which Winter, in the Sun, with an Eastern luster,
Adorns his white hair, scattered by the wind;

This lovely Cotton of the Skies, in which the mountains array
themselves,
This transparent pavé made of the second metal,
And this Air clean and healthy, suitable to the vital spirit,
Are so sweet to my eyes that they sparkle with delight.

This Season pleases me, I love the cold of it,
Its robe of innocence and pure candor
covers in some fashion the crimes of the Earth.

Thus the Olympian sees it with a humane brow,
His anger he spares it, and never the thunderbolt
To desolate its days ever left his hand.

earlier second tercet:

At the price of the last heat this weather is gracious to me;
And if Death catches me on this road of glass,
I could have only a precious Tomb.

Notes

1. Saint-Amant, *Oeuvres complètes*, 4 vols., ed. Jacques Bailbé and Jean Lagny (Paris: Didier, 1967), 3:147–50. (Translations into English are by C. W. Ingold and Noëlle McAlpine. Spelling of French text has been modernized for the benefit of readers.)

2. *Oeuvres*, 3:xix.

3. *Oeuvres*, 3:xvii.

4. Variant punctuation: ". . . bruler!" (*Oeuvres*, 2:122.)

5. Pierre de Ronsard, *Oeuvres complètes*, 8 vols., ed. Paul Laumonier (Paris: Hachette, 1921), 2:23–24.

6. For the most generally accepted version of the Hercules myth, see the *Oxford Companion to Classical Literature*, ed. Sir Paul Harvey (Oxford: Clarendon Press, 1951), pp. 201 ff.

7. See Barbara Herrnstein Smith's seminal work, *Poetic Closure: A Study of How Poems End* (Chicago: University of Chicago Press, 1968).

8. The scene as described vividly calls to mind numerous portraits of Bacchus of the period, typified by Caravaggio's 1589 painting of young Bacchus in which the god, crowned with grapes and seated behind a bowl of fruit, holds up a glass of wine. If Saint-Amant did have this picture in mind, it might explain the reference to "ce dieu."

9. E.g., New Testament, 1 Cor. 15:36: "What you sow does not come to life unless it dies."

10. Other studies applying similar critical approaches to these sonnets include portions of Robert Corum's important work on Saint-Amant's nature imagery in his *Other Worlds and Other Seas*, published by French Forum Monographs, Lexington, Ky., 1979 (pp. 115–42); and Francis L. Lawrence's insightful article "Saint-Amant's 'L'Hyver des Alpes': A Structural Analysis," *Romanic Review* 68 (1977): 247–54.

David Lee Rubin

6. Triple Calculus: Notes Toward a Poetic and Rhetoric of La Fontaine's *Fables*, Book 7

Terms and Distinctions

Suite or Potpourri?

Formalists and thematicists alike have long suspected that individual books of La Fontaine's *Fables* are not miscellanies, but possess the singleness, completeness, and integration of poetic or rhetorical wholes.[1] Plausible and seductive as this suspicion may be, it has until recently proven difficult to confirm or deny—no doubt for reasons of method. Leo Spitzer's study of transitions and Jean-Pierre Collinet's of certain double fables are typical: though revealing and suggestive, they are piecemeal and limited in scope. Certain other treatments are more global, but misleadingly reductive: in the case of René Jasinski, to political allegory; in that of Pierre Bornecque, to moral predication. Promising new developments have appeared, however, in the work of Philip Wadsworth, Nathan Gross, and Richard Danner[2] who, with varying emphases and different ends, have seriously attended to the nuances and interplay of structure, narrative viewpoint, and poetic language, as well as ideas and theses. Though deviating (in some respects, quite radically) from the specific methods pursued by Wadsworth, Gross, and Danner, the following study continues the holistic tendency of their research.

Independent Variables

Fundamental to this analysis is an inductive formal description of the fable genre and its principal categories of form, technique, style, and end. As independent variables, these may occur in a wide variety of permutations and combinations.

Magnitude and Modality

Because it is the autonomous discourse of one personage—the narrator or authorial persona—in a single, uninterrupted situation, the literary fable is a species of lyric.[3] Moreover, it is serial in structure, obeying the principle of rigorous sequence; and it is conventional, for both its parts and their arrangement are of extrapoetic[4]—specifically, rhetorical[5]—origin.

Form

The parts of fable are the apologue and the exposition, which in a particular text may be single or multiple. Apologue is a theme-dominated plot or description: it serves primarily to embody an argument. As such, it stands in sharp contrast with an unthemed description or a plot, whose chief purpose is to provide grounds for the arousal of emotion.[6] (Thought, of course, is seldom absent from the latter, and potential emotion may play a role in an apologue; both, however, are subordinate elements. In an unthemed description or action, for example, thought may contribute to or derive from states or their depiction, or from deeds—whether accomplished, discussed, or merely contemplated—and their representation; in an apologue, potential emotion may reinforce a persuasive tendency.) Apologue may be classified in various ways—by the form of its plot[7] or state as well as its general tonality and, above all, by species of logic.[8] Deductive logic, or reasoning from the general to the particular, occurs in complete or partial allegory (e.g., "La Mort et le malheureux" [Death and the wretched man], 1.15);[9] inductive logic, or reasoning from the particular to the general appears in exemplum (e.g., "L'Homme entre deux âges, et ses deux maîtresses" [The middle-aged man and his two would-be wives], 1.17); and analogy, or the establishment of correspondences between relative dissimilars, is found in all other fables. There are at least two subtypes of analogy: the intergeneric (which compares essentially different personages, e.g., animals and humans) and the *intra*generic (which asserts similarities between different categories of the same kinds, whether animal, vegetable or mineral, e.g., "Le Laboureur et ses enfants" [The farmer and his sons], 5.9, where the personages are analogues for all other types of workers). Though almost invariably the most developed element of a fable, apologue is not the principal part: it subserves the exposition, which less indirectly, less figuratively, and less concretely addresses topics, states problems, and affirms or denies facts, concepts, attitudes, or values. Like apologue, exposition may take a variety of discursive forms[10] (i.e., proverb, precept, motto, epigram, maxim, aphorism, apothegm), or a combination of these, which I shall call essay.

Correlations of Formal Variables

The linkage between apologue and exposition may be deductive or inductive. Deduction occurs where the apologue follows, and is a clear, distinct example of the principles enunciated in, the exposition (i.e., "Le Vieillard et ses enfants" [The old man and his sons], 4.18). By contrast, the simplest kind of induction occurs where the exposition follows, and is a plausible inference from the apologue (i.e., "Les Deux Taureaux et la grenouille" [The two bulls and the frog], 2.4). More complex are the critical reconstructions required where the exposition is lacking and the reader must infer it from the apologue alone (i.e., "Le Chêne et le roseau" [The oak and the reed], 1.22) or where a character in the apologue makes a comment that appears to be expository, but is in fact nothing but his own belief, either unshared by the narrator or the implied author, or limited to the point of unreliability as an explanation of the total apologue (e.g., "Le Cochet, le chat, et le souriceau" [The cockerel, the cat, and the young mouse], 6.5), where the issue is not judgment by appearances, as asserted by the mouse's mother, but inappropriate analogy making and the inability to synthesize).[11] The most challenging species of reconstruction occurs where the exposition is present but incomplete, inaccurate, imprecise, or irrelevant as an explication of—or a commentary on—the apologue. The reader must first recognize the insufficiency of the exposition, then reject it, and finally attempt to construct a more adequate formula,[12] again on the basis of apological evidence, while attempting to relate the rejected exposition to the author's technique (i.e., "Les Compagnons d'Ulysse" [The companions of Ulysses], 12.1).[13]

Technique

This study will consider four facets of poetic manner: relative completeness, closure, clarity, and correspondence. Of these, the first three have distinct formal and thematic aspects.

A fable is formally complete if the exposition is comprehensive and explicit, if each narrative apologue has a beginning, a middle, and an end, and if each descriptive apologue touches on every pertinent aspect of the state or condition with which it is concerned. Thematic completeness is coverage by the exposition of all pertinent topics presented in the apologue.[14]

A fable is formally closural if both the apologue and the exposition are internally logical and end on a stable note of finality, however implicit. It is thematically closural if all thematic problems are resolved.[15]

A fable is clear in form if form and format (or representation) coincide;[16] that is: if what appears to be exposition is segregated from the apologue, and is functionally expository rather than apological; and if multiple plot—or state—forms are circumstantially or causally rather than analogically related.[17] Formal clarity also results from stable and finite narrative irony,[18] and from a preference for direct reference rather than allusion.[19] Clarity of theme results from straightforward, stable values, both narrative and authorial.

Finally, correspondence occurs when—without ironic reconstruction—the exposition proves to be plausible, i.e., accurate, categorially complete, and precise.

Style

While fables are chiefly written in low style (i.e., that of familiar conversation and ordinary narrative, descriptive, or expository discourse), local modulations are possible—both vertical (to middle or high style) and horizontal (from one generic code to another).[20] In style, as in technique, it is possible to speak of relative clarity, for ambiguities (especially puns) may occur. Finally, there may be figures, either complete or incomplete, local or pervasive, modulatory or nonmodulatory, supporting or serving as a counterpoint to themes or theses.[21]

End

Though fable is theme-dominated, and thus appeals primarily to the reader's intellect, specific ends may vary widely, depending upon the selection and use of technical and stylistic devices. Here, the chief variables are the assertional versus the problematic and the resolvent versus the nonresolvent. Didactic fables are directly instructive; problematic fables require a reconstructive or "ironic" reading. Resolvent fables explicitly or implicitly contain the last word on the issue at hand; nonresolvent fables explicitly or implicitly leave that issue unsettled. Because of its completeness, closure, clarity, and correspondence, as well as its stylistic monotony and afigurality, the Aesopic mode (as exemplified by virtually the entire work of Phaedrus and such fables by La Fontaine as "Le Renard et la cigogne" [The fox and the stork], 1.18) may be considered assertional and resolvent, thus altogether suitable for enlightenment or guidance of naive readers. In contrast, many fables of La Fontaine (e.g., "Les Compagnons d'Ulysse," 12.1) are incomplete, anticlosural, opaque, or non-correspondent, as well as stylistically diverse, and are laden with puzzling puns or figures. These are problematic and often nonresolvent. Between these extremes is the *Panchatantra*, as well as numerous fables by La Fontaine ("Le Corbeau et le renard" [The crow and the fox], 1.2), for instance, which are problematic, but ultimately resolvent.

Protocol

To discover the poetic organization of book 7, I studied each fable in terms of the framework outlined above. Then, for each category, I identified the norm or mode: that is, the variant of each formal, technical, stylistic, or final factor that appears most frequently in book 7. Thereafter, I undertook a synthesis of all such norms or modes and constructed a normal or modal fable for the entire book. This established, I ascertained the extent to which any particular fable participates in the composite norm or mode by computing a simple ratio of conformity (in which the number of participating elements was divided by the total of all elements). Finally, I inspected the distribution of these ratios for evidence of a pattern in the sequencing of "normal," "deviant," and intermediate fables.

Poetic and Rhetoric in Book 7: The Norm

The normal or modal fable of book 7 has the following array of features:

Form
- Apologue
  - Number: multiple, coordinated by analogy
  - Type: narrative
  - Plot form: moral choice
  - Tonality: burlesque
  - Reasoning: combination of intergeneric and intrageneric analogies
- Exposition
  - Topic: freedom and constraint
  - Values: necessity of art, artfulness, artifice
  - Discursive mode: essay
  - Correlation of Formal Variables: reconstructive

Technique
- Completeness
  - Formal: no omission
  - Thematic: no omission
- Closure
  - Formal: no irresolution
  - Thematic: no irresolution
- Relative Clarity
  - Formal: at least one form-format discrepancy
  - Thematic: no ambiguity of values
  - Correspondence: exposition routinely discrepant

Style
- Height: low
- Modulations
  - Vertical: at least one instance
  - Horizontal: at least one instance
- Relative Clarity: at least one thematically significant pun
- Figures: at least one thematically significant pattern of imagery, metaphor, or symbol.

End: Problematic and resolvent

Varieties of Modal Fable

The highest degree of participation in the norm for book 7 occurs in three fables whose superficial differences are so great as to mask profound similarities. They are "Les Animaux malades de la peste" (The animals stricken by the plague), "Le Héron et la fille" (The heron and the maiden) and "Un Animal dans la lune" (An animal on the moon).

The Systematic Spirit

But for the absence of a form-format discrepancy, "Le Héron et La Fille" is the fable that most conforms to the poetic mode of book 7. Clearly and distinctly double, the fable mockingly narrates, through coordinated intergeneric and intrageneric analogies, an encounter between the unaccommodating nature of things and the characters' rigid, arrogant, and ego-involved fastidiousness (gastronomical in the heron's case, sexual in the woman's). Refusal of aesthetically unacceptable opportunities leads first to the utter frustration of natural needs, and finally—as appetite triumphs over prejudice—to a desperate surrender, an unseemly willingness to settle for options of a type previously spurned. The essayistic exposition (ll. 27–34), which exhorts the reader to be conciliatory rather than difficult, is too simplistic and vague to explicate the pair of apologues, and is thus—from a technical viewpoint—slightly non-correspondent. The notion of *habileté* ("cleverness") (l. 28), however, suggests that there is an art—or in epicurean terms, a calculus—that adjusts freedom of choice to chance, contingency, or the constraints imposed by one's *compte* ("what's right for you") (l. 31). Carefully worked out and scrupulously implemented, the calculus would probably prevent mental pain like that suffered by the protagonists and—within the limits of the possible—would permit security and untroubledness without so complete a betrayal of personal tastes.

Stylistically, the fable is normal. Fundamentally low, it modulates in a key passage to a precious middle level, contaminated by subdued echoes of misogynist satire.

> L'âge la fit déchoir: adieu, tous les amants.
> Un an se passe, et deux, avec inquiétude.
> Le chagrin vient ensuite: elle sent chaque jour
> Déloger quelques ris, quelques jeux, puis l'Amour;
>   Puis ses traits choquer et déplaire;
> Puis cent sortes de fard. Ses soins ne purent faire
> Qu'elle échappât au Temps, cet insigne larron.
>   Les ruines d'une maison
> Se peuvent réparer; que n'est cet avantage
>   Pour les ruines du visage!
> Sa préciosité changea lors de langage
> Son miroir lui disait: "Prenez vite un mari."

> Age lessened her charm: no suitors at the gate.
> In a year, then two, worry was full-blown,
> And discontent: she watched each day give a shove
> And dislodge a few Pleasures, Diversions, then Love:
>   Saw her looks shock and displease.
> Makeup came next, of every kind, but care could not appease

> Or prevent the ravages of time, that infamous thief.
> A house that comes to grief
> Can be repaired. Why can no one grant this boon
> To a face lined like a prune?
> Her pickiness then swiftly changed its tune.
> "Go get yourself a husband quick," her mirror said.
> (ll. 61–72)

Made possible, or merely legitimated by these shifts, certain key terms—*de régime* ("systematically") (l. 11) and *précieuses* ("finicky maidens") (l. 51) and *préciosité* ("finickiness") (l. 71)—imply a variety of notions that characterize the protagonists, who, until their surrender, are inflexibly rule-ridden in their preferences and their actions, as implacable as they are imperious, and closed, both aesthetically and pragmatically. These resonances are echoed in the fable's imagery, metaphors, symbols, and other key terms—e.g., the heron's stiff *longs pieds* ("long legs") (l. 1), his *goût dédaineux* ("disdainful taste") (l. 16), his refusal to [*Ouvrir*] *pour si peu le bec* ("Open my beak for such a trifle?") (l. 22) when gudgeon is available; and the woman's *fièreté* ("pride") (l. 35), her impossibly exacting requirements for a mate (ll. 37–38, 40–41), her closed-mindedness ironically disclosed by the exclamation, *"Ah! vraiment je suis bonne / De leur ouvrir la porte!" ("Ah, what a foolish exercise to open my door to them!")* (ll. 55–56). In extremis, however, both are *heureux* . . . / *heureuse* ("content") (ll. 25, 76)—yielding, delighted, and open to any opportunity that presents itself. Thus, though problematic—requiring the reader to reconstruct its meaning—this double fable is totally resolvent.

Sublunary Considerations

Deviating from the norm in only two respects, "Un Animal dans la lune" ranks second among the modal fables. First, all its coordinated apologues are inductive, rather than analogical. Second, the final apologue, dealing with the political ends and means of Louis XIV, is formally incomplete: the outcome awaits a decision by the king himself.

The first part of the essay-exposition deals with freedom vs. constraint in the domain of knowledge (ll. 1–54). Supported by brief interspersed exempla (ll. 15–22, 29, 35–41, 42–54) narrating the passage of thought from error to lucidity, it argues that unrestrained commitment to, or rejection of, the senses leads inevitably to error and that the sophisticated technique of criticizing sense reports by means of reason *développe le vrai caché sous l'apparence* ("uncovers truth hidden beneath the appearance") (v. 26). The exemplar in this section is not only the narrator, whose experiences as a mitigated skeptic are detailed in the first three narratives, but above all King Charles II of England, who in the fourth narrative discovers that the beast "seen" on the moon by astronomers, presaging war, is nothing but a mouse caught between the lenses of the Royal Society telescope. The second part of the exposition not only seems tacked on to the first but also disrupts the clear distinction and deductive relationship thus far maintained between expository and apological materials. Indeed, it appears that except for the obvious contrast between the two kings—one committed to arts and sciences and the other to war—the second apologue is irrelevant to the poem's philosophical issue. In fact, however, reconstructive analysis shows that it is not. Again, the narrator contrasts freedom and constraint, but now on the political level: unbridled commitment to prestigious wars of conquest, he implies, is not compatible with happiness, here defined as repose and pursuit of the civilizing arts (ll. 55, 66, 72). A critical rethinking of national priorities, he suggests, would produce another policy geared more closely to both of these needs. A deeper and more substantial connection arises from the multiple meaning of line 53. "Dans la lunette était la source des guerres" ("In the glass lay all the source of war in Europe's house") applies literally to perception and interpretation in the first royal apologue and introduces—in a figurative way—the issues of the second. Reading between these lines of muted lament and cautious criticism (presented as an encomium cast in a faintly parodic elevated style), one apprehends that the trouble with Louis XIV is the inadequacy of his moral-political *lunette* ("glass"), (l. 53) which allows him to be dazzled by immediate *gloire* ("glory and acclaim") (l. 56), causes him to operate in an ethical *ombre* ("shadow"), (l. 40), and thus to misidentify the good. As a result, he seeks the unnecessary, short-term pleasures of victory and its fame. What the king requires is a new lens, the moral equivalent of partial skepticism in practical and scientific reasoning, a critical capability that will

> rectifie
> L'image de l'objet sur son éloignement,
> Sur le milieu qui l'environne,
> Sur l'organe et sur l'instrument.
>
> adjust the image by how far it's been sent
> By the compass of its background,
> By the organ and the instrument.
> (ll. 8–11)

With this, he could replace political bedazzlement and impaired moral vision with lucidity, and could craft rational policies capable, like those of Charles II, of assuring the nation's defense while making possible a high level of well-being and culture. Again, the fable is problematic et resolvent.[22]

Status and Art

"Les Animaux malades de la peste," the third-ranking modal fable, deviates from the norm in four respects: if not in fact a proverb, its exposition *is* proverbial, rather than essayistic; the apologue is single rather than double (thus precluding a discrepancy between form and format); and, finally, the apologue is built on an intergeneric analogy.

To believe the exposition, the fable concerns the relationship between power and status, for lines 63–64 conclude from the apologue that the first depends directly upon the second: "Selon que vous serez puissant ou misérable, / Les jugements de cour vous rendront blanc ou noir" ("Your power or weakness will always decide your lot: whether judgments of court will make you white or black"). The narrative contained in the apologue, however, suggests a different state of affairs, which in turn establishes a non-correspondence between the parts and imposes a reconstructive reading. Dealing with the causes and the effects of pramatically sound choices by the guileful lion and *petits mâtins* (slightest cur) (l. 47) but an *un*sound choice by the ass, the plot is concerned with the impossibility of freedom, as the opening lines show with chilling force. Nor is it certain that scapegoating the ass will ward off further destruction by the plague.

In addition to the inaccurate exposition, the narrator's ostensible sympathies and antipathies contribute to confusion. Outwardly favorable to the ass (l. 59) and sarcastic toward the cur, his citations of the lion and the fox (ll. 15–33, 34–42) seem intended to arouse indignation. All of this invites reconstructive reading, because it inverts the customary congruence in the *Fables* between narrative and authorial approval of well-developed survival skills. In fact, one might conclude that because of his faulty reasoning and his axiological distance from the implied author, the narrator stands convicted of unreliability.

Stylistically, the fable is rich in modulations away from its conventional base: the cosmic formulas occurring at the opening (ll. 1–6) suggest a macrocosm of the court, but one that is less tractable and discriminating in its choice of victims; the pompous political rhetoric of the lion's speech testifies to his artfulness as a manipulator of popular feeling; while the simple, direct, and familiar speech in the ass's discourse (ll. 49–54) reflects the victim's lack of resources and foreshadows his doom. There is but one symbolic image, which contrasts social blackness and whiteness. It is somewhat complex, for the status conferred by artfulness (and denied by its absence) is—as the apologue suggests—neither absolute nor fixed, as is the distinction between these ultimately contrasting colors. Other circumstances, other strategies, might culminate in very different valuations. Again, and despite the numerous hermeneutic problems presented by the fable, it is as resolvent as the others in its category.

Varieties of Deviant Fable

Two fables deviate to an extreme degree from the formal, technical, and stylistic norms of book 7. They are "Le Rat qui s'est retiré du monde" (The rat who withdrew from the world) and "La Tête et la queue du serpent" (The head and tail of the snake).

Tossing the Coin

The more deviant of the two, "La Tête et la queue du serpent," unequivocally resembles the mode in only eight respects. It contains two coordinated apologues, both of which are narrative and analogical (the first, intergenerically; the second, intragenerically). On the technical level, there is a form-format discrepancy, since the second apologue appears in the final line with all the finality of an inductive exposition: "Malheureux les états tombés dans cette erreur!" ("Unhappy are the States that have made [the tail's] mistake"). The fable is, moreover, written in conversational language with scattered vertical and horizontal modulations (e.g., ll. 5, 28, 36) and two thematically significant figures—the cause-effect parallel of physical and mental lucidity and blindness (l. 30), as well as the ambiguity of *erreur* (l. 37), signifying both a factual or logical mistake and its effects: mental aberration and physical wandering. Finally, the fable is problematic, requiring a reconstruction that inter alia might assert the dangers of allowing to rule freely those without talent, training, or experience in the arts of government.

Lack of explicit exposition is, of course, the most conspicuous variance from the norm of book 7. This omission causes a deviant, reconstructive relationship between the fable's parts: that is, the reader must infer an exposition from the apologue alone. The omitted exposition is but one aspect of the fable's formal incompleteness, because the second apologue—whose beginning, middle, and end are compressed into a single verse—requires much amplification to make explicit its point-by-point analogy with the first. Thematically the fable is also incomplete, for the narrator neglects to state whether leadership by the sighted part (the head of the serpent, the best-endowed member of the polity) is truly proof against disaster or merely reduces its risk to an acceptable level. This lacuna leaves the apologue partially unresolved or anticlosural, in addition to setting up an unstable irony that permits a series of mutually undercutting interpretations, so that the narrator's values are in some doubt. At the very least, however, it is plausible that he would affirm a conservative, potentially risk-averting solution to the problem of who should rule. Thus, the fable is less immediately resolvent than others discussed so far, and, in fact, than most fables in the book.

Resolution and Independence

Slightly less deviant than the preceding fable, "Le Rat qui s'est retiré du monde" (The rat who withdrew from the world) mockingly presents, without formal or thematic omission and in burlesque ecclesiastical terms, a narrative of choice. For reasons to be made clear below, contextual ambiguity makes the exposition (ll. 32–36) somewhat unreliable, thus requiring reconstruction. Finally, the fable conforms to the mode by its use in lines 6 and 7 of thematically significant images of roundness and interiority, which not only establishes a synechdochal relationship between the scene (here, a cheese) and the agent but suggests the fundamental egotism and the eventual ampleness of the rat.

In all other respects, the fable is at variance with the norm of the book: there is but one apologue, constructed on an intergeneric analogy and presented without vertical modulations of style. More importantly, the exposition—

> Que désignai-je, à votre avis,
> Par ce rat si peu secourable?
> Un moine? Non, mais un dervis:
> Je suppose qu'un moine est toujours secourable.

> In your opinion who is it I designate
> In this Rat of such little generosity?
> A monk? Oh, no: that's a dervish trait.
> I assume charity always defines a monk's religiosity.
> (ll. 32–35)

—is a coy puzzle that appears to condemn the freedom achieved by the rat and his human analogues through art or the adoption of constraints. This apparent contradiction with the values of book 7 stems from a lack of formal and thematic clarity that in turn contributes to thematic anti-closure. Specifically, there is a discrepancy between the plot form and the narrator's interpretation of it. As presented by scene and much of the summary, the rat is nothing more or less than an aspiring epicurean, who seeks security and untroubledness by withdrawal from the world into a perfect hermitage that provides both shelter and sustenance. His refusal to aid his brethren proves his devotion (cf. l. 13) to the creed, which frowns upon unnecessary social or political involvement because of its attendant risks. For these reasons, certainly, the rat is a saint (l. 31), albeit a pagan one in the style of Epicurus or Lucretius: that is, relatively unmindful of god or gods. (Hence, when he advises the beleaguered rats to pray for divine assistance [ll. 28–29], he seems to echo the cynical narrative comment of ll. 11–12, most accurately rendered by the saw "God helps those who help themselves.") Superimposed on this form is a systematic metaphor (culminating in the exposition) that likens the rat to a monk (ll. 7, 13, 15, 25–29) whose withdrawal from the world is less disciplined and self-denying than selfish, and whose refusal of aid to his congeners not only violates his vow of charity but smacks of rank hypocrisy. That the pagan and Christian perspectives intersect in several of the verses just cited results in ambiguity and anticlosure: How, in fact, does the narrator view the rat, and what is the reader to infer? I propose that the fable is an instance of double irony[23] comparable to that found in book 12, fable 1, "Les Compagnons d'Ulysse," in which mutually exclusive viewpoints are played off against one another not only in the apologue but in the narration itself. The difference between book 2, fable 1 and book 7, fable 3, however, is that the narrator is genuinely playful, showing through techniques of representation and language that the same action, its causes, and its effects, are subject to radically different interpretation and judgment, depending on moral perspective. If a final solution is anywhere implied to make this problematic fable resolvent, it may be sought in the total context of book 7, or even in the *Fables* as a whole, which—within human limits and practicality—affirm the epicurean, not the Christian, line.

Varieties of Intermediate Fable

Thirteen fables in book 7 fall between the extremes discussed above. Though limitations of space preclude full analysis of all such "intermediate" texts, it will be possible to discuss three, each of which is indicative of the mean in its various manifestations.

The Ironic Benediction

"Les Vautours et les pigeons" (The vultures and the pigeons, 7.8) is an uneven mix of modal and nonmodal features, slightly biased toward the former. The single, somberly narrated apologue, built on an intergeneric comparison, is a tragedy of temperament, for the pigeons pass from good to bad fortune, not by erroneous choice, but by well-meaning, unmindful surrender to impulse: they are, after all, the birds "que la mère d'Amour / Met à son char" ("which Love's mother each day / Has pull her chariot") (ll. 7–8). In essay format, the inductive exposition makes clear that for security and untroubledness, peaceable impulses cannot always be given free scope; indeed, they must at times be replaced by a discipline, namely, the art of promoting murderous dissension among enemies. An epicurean for whom virtue is a means, not an end, La Fontaine clearly suggests that the beatitudes should be recast: Blessed are the cunning mischief-makers, for they shall survive.

Formally and thematically complete, the fable is also formally, if not thematically, closural: if the thesis applies to the general run of creatures, there is clearly no solution for those, like the pigeons, who are absolutely incapable of acting in their own best interest when such action would conflict with temperament. Though there is no form-format discrepancy, the fable has at least two problems of relative clarity, both occurring in lines 14–24. First, if the narrator appears inexplicably sympathetic to the sanguinary vultures, writing with admiration of their epic efforts (e.g., ll. 19–21, 24) and with pity for the death of their great warriors (ll. 14, 18), he is actually showing—

through ironic use of free indirect style—the passions that accompany and reinforce the pigeons' moral disposition to reconcile the antagonists. Second, the reference to Prometheus's hopes for the abatement of his torture (ll. 15–16) is not merely decorative: it suggests symbolically that the pigeons' wrongheaded strategy may have extended deleterious effects. Combined with alliteration, the reference also establishes an analogy, for both Prometheus and the pigeons are grievously punished for a generous act, though in Prometheus's case generosity is accompanied by a certain canniness, a quality denied the pigeons. Finally, as suggested, apologue and exposition are correspondent.

Stylistically, the fable modulates widely from its conventional base, as seen in the epic, mythic, and erotic passages already noted, as well as in stretches of reportage (military and diplomatic, especially ll. 28–33). In addition, the text is especially rich in puns and metaphors that strongly support the fable's thesis. Typical is the play on the term *grâce* (l. 35) indicating not only the thanks due from the vultures to the pigeons but also the divine favor that the pigeons uselessly enjoy (cf. ll. 7–8), and their equally pleasing but unhelpful combination of physical beauty (l. 27) and sweet sounds, common to all birds (l. 5). Indeed, sound, taken both literally and figuratively, provides several thematic terms: *émute* ("riot and motion") (l. 1), *sons éclatants* ("brilliant song") (l. 5), *accorder* ("harmonize") (l. 29), and *chamailler* ("squabble") (l. 32): ideally, inner and outer worlds are harmonious—filled with melody, free of clangorous conflict—but in fact, as the apologue shows, inner harmony (the product of security and untroubledness) may paradoxically depend on the promotion of external disharmony, achieved by astute application of the vultures' own nonmusical arts of *adresse* ("skill"), *ruse,* and *surprise* (l. 19).

In sum, the fable is both didactic and resolvent, thus—in finality—deviant.[24]

Sheer Guesswork

Though "Les Devineresses" (The fortune-tellers, 7.15) is slightly less deviant than the preceding fable, its modal features are in the main technical, stylistic, and final. Formally, the fable contains only two typical traits: an essay-exposition and multiple apologues, one of which, that of the lawyers, is analogically, rather than causally or circumstantially, related to those of the fortune-tellers. The apologues combine narrative (in the accounts of the title characters) with description (in that of the lawyers). The apologues, moreover, have less to do with choice than circumstance, are not pervasively burlesque, and are in each case inductively constructed. For its part, the exposition deals, not with freedom, constraint, and artfulness, but with the role of uncontrollable extraneous factors—such as chance, preconception, dogma, stubbornness, error, and fancy—in the formation of public opinion. Finally, the relationship between apologue and exposition is purely and simply deductive; ironic reconstruction is unnecessary.

Formally and thematically complete and closural, the fable contains one form-format discrepancy: the apologue of the lawyers is embedded in what purports to be an integral part of the second expository section. On the other hand, there is complete correspondence between apologue and exposition. Fundamentally, the style is familiar, with local modulations: horizontally to the languages of commerce (e.g., ll. 19, 36, 46) and of witchcraft (ll. 39–40), and vertically to that of myth and popular superstition (vv. 9, 30). The latter involves thematically significant equivocations and figures. There is, in fact, a systematic, tongue-in-cheek antithesis between the *devins* ("seers") (cf. "*Devineuse*" ["fortune-teller"]) (l. 13); *la pythonisse* (the sorceress) (l. 8); and the Sibyl (l. 30) of classical antiquity—all celebrated in legend and literature, if not history, for their accuracy as well as art—and the vulgar tricksters of Paris, who depend more on temerity and chance (ll. 15–17), as well as on widespread misprison (willful and other) of their talents and achievements. The figural connection between the fortune-tellers and the lawyers is both metaphoric and metonynmic, playing on the perceived continuity of container and contained: just as "le meuble et l'équipage aidaient fort" ("furnishings and setting helped much") in the efforts of the successful fortune-teller (l. 38), so the narrator claims to have seen "une robe mal mise / Gagner gros: les gens l'avaient prise / Pour maître tel" ("rumpled robes win adherents / And big fees; on one such the people did rely") (ll. 47–49). Nowhere stated, but everywhere implied in this didactic, resolvent work is the client's need for an art of reading, interpreting, and valuing—or more frequently, discounting—signs of all types.

Nine-Tenths of the Law

"Le Chat, la belette, et le petit lapin" (The cat, the weasel, and the young rabbit, 7.16) represents a near-perfect balance of modal and nonmodal features. The fable contains two apologues, that of the title characters—a narrative constructed on an intergeneric analogy—and that of the "petits souverains se rapportants au rois" ("little lords bringing debates to heads of state") (l. 47), a description constructed on an intrageneric analogy. Dealing explicitly in the first case, and implicitly in the second, with the risks of submitting a dispute to arbitration by a powerful, self-interested authority, both are presented in a merry and, at times, mocking manner. Ellipsis of the exposition establishes a reconstructive relationship between apologue and principal part.

The fable is both formally and thematically incomplete: not only is the exposition omitted, but the second apologue, being descriptive, has no finale (implied, however, is a likelihood that the king will eventually annex—or devour—the petty sovereigns' territory). In addition, the narrator omits disclosure or evaluation of any choices other than inflexibility of negotiating stance and recourse to an inappropriate arbitrator. These incompletenesses entail anticlosure of form in the second apologue and of theme throughout. There is also a form-format discrepancy, with the second apologue appearing in the place of an inductive exposition and presented conclusively, as though it were indeed the principal part. Finally, authorial values are unclear, though possibly inferable from the total context of the book and the *Fables*. If so, narrator and implied author may imply the usefulness and prudence of a calculus concerning the relative risks and benefits of compromise, unilateral withdrawal, or violence, with preference going to the option that in the given situation poses the least long-term threat to physical security and mental untroubledness. On the other hand such a calculus may be out of the question because of circumstances or the antagonist's temperament.

Though composed predominantly in low style, the fable is rich in modulations. Horizontally, legalisms—*premier occupant* ["first tenant"] (l. 17), *l'octroi* ["pact"] (l. 22), *l'usage et la coutume* ["custom and usage"] (l. 25), and *arbitre expert sur tous les cas* ["a skilled referee in cases like these"] (l. 35)—are found almost side by side with military language: *déloge sans trompette* ["moves out without fanfare"] (l. 14) and *beau sujet de guerre* ["dignified cause for a fight"] (l. 18). Vertically, there is the mocking inflation of *palais* ["palace"] (l. 1), *Dame* ["milady"] (l. 2), *pénates* ["household gods"] (l. 5), *alle[r] faire à l'Aurore sa cour* ["going to pay Aurora her court"] (l. 6), *souterrains séjours* ["underground dwellings"] (l. 9), *royaume* ["kingdom"] (l. 20). These, and the sardonic pun *mit les plaideurs d'accord* ["put the litigants in accord"] (l. 45), are integral parts of a system that associates exteriority (exclusion, achieved or threatened, from one's lodgings) with antagonism and separation, while conciliation and union are linked with the interiorization of the devoured. Moreover, the transition from one pair of states to the other is ascribed, in part, to successful art: *faisant la chattemitte* ("conducting himself more unctuously than any cenobite") (l. 33), the violently acquisitive Raminarobis theatrically disguises himself as a *dévot hermite* ("pious recluse") (l. 32), a *saint homme de Chat* ("a saint of a cat") (l. 34), a *bon apôtre* ("good apostle") (l. 43).

Highly problematic, the fable is ultimately resolvent.

Ratios of Conformity and The Pattern of Distribution

The degree to which each successive fable conforms to the mode of book 7, as well as the arrangement of modal, deviant, and intermediate poems, is revealed by the following schematism.

1. "Les Animaux malades de la Peste" (The animals stricken by the plague) (80 percent conformity)

2. “Le Mal Marié” (The man who married badly) (76 percent)
3. “Le Rat qui s’est retiré du monde” (The rat who withdrew from the world) (42 percent)
4./5. “Le Héron et la fille” (The heron and the maiden) (96 percent)
6. “Les Souhaits” (The wishes) (50 percent)
7. “La Cour du lion” (The lion’s court) (75 percent)
8. “Les Vautours et les pigeons” (The vultures and the pigeons) (60 percent)
9. “Le Coche et la mouche” (The coach and the fly) (60 percent)
10. “La Laitière et le pot au lait” (The dairy woman and the crock of milk) (75 percent)
11. “Le Curé et la mort” (The curate and the deceased) (60 percent)
12. “L’Homme qui court après la Fortune et l’homme qui l’attend dans son lit” (The man chasing fortune and the man awaiting her in bed) (75 percent)
13. “Les Deux Coqs” (The two cocks) (75 percent)
14. “L’Ingratitude et l’injustice des hommes envers la Fortune” (Man’s ingratitude and unfairness to Fortune) (50 percent)
15. “Les Devineresses” (The fortune-tellers) (70 percent)
16. “Le Chat, la belette, et le petit lapin” (The cat, the weasel, and the young rabbit) (55 percent)
17. “La Tête et la queue du serpent” (The head and tail of the snake) (38 percent)
18. “Un Animal dans la lune” (An animal on the moon) (85 percent)

I conclude that 80–96 percent (i.e., approximately the highest quartile) represents the modal range, that 38–42 percent (approximately the lowest quartile) represents the deviant range, and that 50–76 percent (approximately the two median quartiles) represents the intermediate range. On that basis, the distribution pattern of the fables in book 7 is ternary. Section A (fables 1–5) opens with a statement of all three possibilities: a weak form of the modal (fable 1), a strong form of the intermediate (fable 2), as well as a weak form of the deviant (fable 3), and concludes with the strongest possible reassertion of the modal (fable[s] 4–5). Not only does the modal dominate the first section, but the final shift from deviant (in 3) to modal (in 4 and 5) announces the closural sequence. Section B (fables 6–16) consists entirely of intermediate fables, not only fluctuating in a narrow range but also containing some near-symmetries: e.g., a subgroup consisting of fables 6–14 opens and closes with texts registering 50 percent, peaks three times at 75 percent in fables 7, 10, and 14, and the doubling effect of the last two fables echoes that of 8–9 at the approximate midpoint of the intermediate range. Fables 15 and 16 constitute a kind of preclosural deviation from the intermediate movement of the rest of the section, introducing two new levels of intermediacy, 70 percent and

55 percent. Section A′ (fables 17 and 18) repeats the terminal movement of section A—namely, a passage from deviancy to conformity, although there is a slight, chiastic variation—whereas fable 3 is low-deviant and fables 4/5 are high modal, fable 17 is high deviant and fable 18 is low modal.[25]

Envoi

Book 7 is thus organized both formally and rhetorically not only in terms of a mode and degrees of variance from it, but also by the clustering of modal, intermediate, and deviant fables in an ABA′ pattern. To what extent La Fontaine consciously sought—or was even aware of—such coherence and precision cannot, of course, be known. Only future research, moreover, will show whether this order is unique to book 7 or resembles that of the other eleven divisions. The question cannot be discounted: along with a reassessment of the poet's complex relationship to the fable heritage and to epicureanism (both ancient and modern), the disposition of individual books is the major problem now facing the advanced student of La Fontaine's masterpiece.

Notes

1. For the notions of suite and potpourri, see Gemino A. Abad, *A Formal Approach to Lyric Poetry* (Quezon City: University of the Philippines Press, 1978), pp. 24–25, 380–81.

2. Leo Spitzer, "L'Art de la transition chez La Fontaine," reprinted in *Etudes de style* (Paris: Gallimard, 1970), pp. 166–207; Jean-Pierre Collinet, *Le Monde littéraire de La Fontaine* (Paris: Presses universitaires de France, 1970), pp. 163–226; René Jasinski, *La Fontaine et le premier recueil des* Fables (Paris: Nizet, 1966); Pierre Bornecque, *La Fontaine fabuliste* (Paris: Société d'édition d'enseignement supérieur, 1973), pp. 89–102; Philip A. Wadsworth, "Le Douzième livre des Fables," *Cahiers de l'association internationale des études françaises* 26 (May 1974): 103–15; Nathan Gross, "Order and Theme in La Fontaine's *Fables*, Book VI," *L'Esprit Créateur* 21 (1981): 78–89; Richard Danner, *Patterns of Irony in La Fontaine's* Fables (Athens: Ohio University Press, 1985), pp. 131–67.

3. For the theory of the lyric adopted here, see the writings of Elder Olson—especially "A Conspectus of Poetry," *Critical Inquiry* 4 (1977): 159–80, 373–96—as well as Abad. In both, lyric is formally independent speech or scene (an integrated series of speeches), by contrast with episode (an interrelated series of scenes) and plot (an interrelated series of episodes).

4. The concept of developmental structure in the lyric is elaborated by Barbara Herrnstein Smith in *Poetic Closure: A Study of How Poems End* (Chicago: University of Chicago Press, 1968), especially pp. 109–38. Among other things, my book *The Knot of Artifice* (Columbus: Ohio State University Press, 1981) adapts Smith's concepts to the study of early seventeenth-century French lyric.

5. Ben E. Perry, ed. and trans., *Babrius and Phaedrus*, Loeb Classical Library,

no. 436 (Cambridge, Mass.: Harvard University Press, London: William Heinemann, Ltd., 1975), pp. xi–lxxiii.

6. For the distinction between action and apologue, see Sheldon Sacks, *Fiction and the Shape of Belief* (Berkeley: University of California Press, 1964), pp. 1–69; David Richter, *Fable's End* (Chicago: University of Chicago Press, 1974), pp. 1–21; and Mary Doyle Springer, *Forms of the Modern Novella* (Chicago: University of Chicago Press, 1975), especially pp. 18–53.

7. A method for the classification of plot by cause and effect appears in Norman Friedman, *Form and Meaning in Fiction* (Athens: University of Georgia Press, 1975), pp. 79–101.

8. Elder Olson, *Tragedy and the Theory of Drama* (Detroit: Wayne State University Press, 1966), p. 71.

9. All citations of the La Fontaine that follow in text refer to volume 2 of Marc Fumaroli, ed., *Fables* (Paris: Imprimerie Nationale, 1985). (Book number appears first; fable number second. Thus, 1.15 in text means book 1, fable 15. Translations are quoted (or, in a few cases, adapted) from Norman B. Spector, trans., *The Complete Fables of Jean de La Fontaine* (Evanston, Ill.: Northwestern University Press, 1988).

10. Olson, "Conspectus," p. 394.

11. Wayne C. Booth, *The Rhetoric of Fiction* (Chicago: University of Chicago Press, 1961) and *The Rhetoric of Irony* (Chicago: University of Chicago Press, 1974). Also see Danner, *Patterns of Irony.*

12. Cf. Wolfgang Iser, *The Implied Reader* (Baltimore: Johns Hopkins University Press, 1974).

13. For a study of this fable see David Lee Rubin, "Four Modes of Double Irony in the *Fables* of La Fontaine," in *The Equilibrium of Wit: Essays for Odette de Mourgues* (Lexington, Ky.: French Forum Monographs, 1982), pp. 202–12.

14. Richter, *Fable's End*, pp. 3–4, 19–20.

15. Ibid., pp. 19–20.

16. Adapted from Abad, *Formal Approach*, pp. 292 ff.

17. See Richard Levin, *Multiple Plot in English Renaissance Drama* (Chicago: University of Chicago Press, 1971), especially pp. 1–20.

18. Booth, *Rhetoric of Fiction* and *Rhetoric of Irony.*

19. For the unifying use of allusion in early seventeenth-century French poetry, see Rubin, *The Knot of Artifice* and *Higher, Hidden Order: Design and Meaning in the Odes of Malherbe* (Chapel Hill: University of North Carolina Press, 1972), which also contains an analysis of allusion in "La Tortue et les deux canards" [The turtle and the two ducks], pp. 18–20.

20. John Porter Houston, *The Rhetoric of Poetry in the Renaissance and Seventeenth Century* (Baton Rouge: Louisiana State University Press, 1983), and Alastair Fowler, *Kinds of Literature* (Cambridge, Mass.: Harvard University Press, 1982), especially pp. 70–72, 145–46. For a more detailed treatment of the structure and functions of the poet's stylistic medleys, see my essay "*Fluctuat nec mergitur*: Polymodality in La Fontaine's *Fables*," forthcoming in the John Porter Houston memorial volume.

21. Cf. Cleanth Brooks, *The Well-Wrought Urn* (New York: Harcourt, Brace, 1947). For the structural use of puns and imagery in the early seventeenth-century French lyric, see Rubin, *The Knot of Artifice* and *Higher, Hidden Order.*

22. For certain details in this interpretation, I am indebted to my student Margaret Maryanne Murdock's M.A. thesis on La Fontaine's astronomical and astrological fables (University of Virginia, 1972); and to an unpublished paper by Professor Ellen Sugg. For the relationship of this fable to La Fontaine's political poetry, see my essay "Icon and Caricature: Poetic Images of a Sun King," in *Sun King: The Ascendancy of French Culture under Louis XIV*, ed. David Lee Rubin (Washington, D.C.: The Folger Shakespeare Library; Toronto and London: Associated University Presses, 1991).

23. See my "Four Modes of Double Irony."

24. For a contrasting analysis, see Jules Brody, "La Fontaine: 'Les Vautours et les pigeons'—an Intertextual Reading," in *Convergences: Rhetoric and Poetic in Seventeenth-Century France*, ed. David Lee Rubin and Mary B. McKinley (Columbus: Ohio State University Press, 1989).

25. For a detailed analysis of book 11, see my study *A Pact with Silence: Art and Thought in the Fables of Jean de La Fontaine* (Columbus: Ohio State University Press, 1991).

John Porter Houston

7. The Two Versions of *Les Fleurs du mal* and Ideas of Form

In 1857, upon the publication of the first edition, Barbey d'Aurevilly made his well-known reference to the "architecture secrète" of *Les Fleurs du mal*, and the phrase is often quoted, although it patently contains false associations. To begin with the adjective *secrète*, architecture is the most overt of arts; moreover, it is one that shows a pronounced fondness for symmetry, whether exemplified by a Gothic cathedral or a classical temple, the two architectural forms most likely to have occurred to a reader in Barbey's day. Symmetry, however, as the *Encyclopédie* had long before put it, risks being the ruin of other arts, despite its basic role in architecture. Nevertheless, we should be inclined to censure those who mindlessly repeat the phrase rather than Barbey himself, since the criticism of his period was notoriously lacking in adequate terms to describe literary forms.

The more common word applied to works of some complexity was *composition,* a not very old term in this sense, which supplemented the classical notion of dispositio, the latter referring to the arrangement of arguments in an oration. Since speeches were conceived of as both a logical (or pseudological) and a histrionic or emotive kind of persuasion, the idea was not difficult to transfer to poems, although classical rhetoric scarcely explored the arrangement of parts in a manner suitable for treating the range of Greek and Latin poetry.

Composition tended to bear with it the pedagogical association of a neat *plan* or outline, and it is obvious that even at the level of the individual poem, the ordinary notions of rational arrangement, associated in France with the name of Buffon, could not always apply to *Les Fleurs du mal*. While "Une Charogne" (A carrion), "L'Albatros" (The albatross), and "Obsession" (Obsession) might be reduced to the sort of *plan* in which order and conclusion are readily perceived, "Le Balcon" (The balcony) or the elliptical "Causerie" (Chat) represent patterns that ordinary rhetorical criteria could have less successfully explained. “La Chevelure” (The hair) occupies perhaps a middle ground between the traditional logic of development and a newer associational movement derived, in this case, from the process of involuntary memory. On the level of the individual line or sentence, which is what *compositio* referred to in Latin, some startling collocations appear in *Les Fleurs du mal* that also violate the customary organization of language:

> Fourmillante cité, cité pleine de rêves,
> Où le spectre en plein jour raccroche le passant!
> (p. 97)
>
> Swarming city, full of dreams, where the specter in broad daylight accosts the passerby![1]

The poetic *cité* and *raccroche*, a term of street commerce referring especially to hucksters and whores, demand, by their coexistence in one grammatical unit, a more elaborate theory of parts and wholes than was usual.

Baudelaire’s remark to the effect that his book, not being a pure “album,” had a beginning and an end, prudently avoids the question of what separates the opening and the closing, a matter he would probably have had as much difficulty conceptualizing as Flaubert would have had in explaining his fictional technique, even though he foresaw the creation of methods and terminologies for doing so. The critical faculties of the artist, to use a notion dear to Eliot and Valéry, tend generally to be more practical and directed to his own work than theoretical and disinterested. However, the peculiar balance between creative work and theorizing that Coleridge exemplifies makes his conception of literary structures, however flawed, worth considering in the study of romantic literature.

The idea of organic form, expounded by the German romantics, especially August Wilhelm Schlegel, and developed by Coleridge, offers a relevant historical term and theory for describing Baudelaire’s work, even though it found no obvious echo in France. Its analogy between a plant—whole and yet composed of quite varied elements—and a work of literature served to account for the diversity of literary forms, a diversity quite as conspicuous in French romantic literature as elsewhere. In the weakness of organic theory lies also its strength: the affirmation of the plant analogy in the absence of any serious knowledge of biochemistry betokens the faith the authors of *Faust*, *La Comédie humaine*, and *La Légende des siècles* had in the validity of the singular works they put together and that contemporary critical thought in France was hardly equipped to deal with.

I shall treat the ramifications of organic theory in regard to appropriate loci in *Les Fleurs du mal*, but I should like to make clear from the outset that I consider it primarily of historical value and not, as New Criticism did, an adequate account of literary forms in general. Biochemistry is better understood today, and the genetic mutations, cancerous growths, and other peculiar phenomena that are part of organic life suggest that romantic literary theory based on organicism is as fanciful and arbitrary as trying to explain plants in terms of poems (proceeding from the lower and more commonplace to the higher and rarer, in good Aristotelian fashion). I shall return to the insufficiencies of organic theory and suggest an alternative possibility.

Of the many allusions to the "architecture" of *Les Fleurs du mal*, most are, of course, somewhat vague, belletrist affirmations, but I shall refer to the two most elaborate accounts of it, which represent opposing points of view. Albert Feuillerat maintained that the 1857 edition of the work was superior in structure and power to the 1861 version, while, in a book-length demonstration, D. J. Mossop presented the second edition as a continuation and improvement on the first.[2] For him the general sense of the 1861 edition is implicit in the earlier one. Yet another point of view is possible: Antoine Adam, in his richly annotated edition of *Les Fleurs du mal*, rejected subtle attempts to see anything but the most obvious elements of organization in either edition.[3] The methods employed in discussing the work are not very elaborate in regard to theory. Thematic material tends to be considered as if a conventional *plan* or narrative were at stake. Mossop's arguments are more sophisticated than Feuillerat's, but his comparison of the volume to a "tragedy" with an "action" constrains him to a somewhat more linear and logical reading of Baudelaire than adepts of difficult or problematic literary forms may find appropriate. I believe still another approach to the problem has validity: the 1857 and 1861 versions of *Les Fleurs du mal* are essentially different works, with a somewhat different general sense, and each has a structure that is distinctive and reasonably satisfying in its own way. Organicism provides a useful perspective on both Baudelaire's poem cycles and their interrelations.

It is best to start with a brief analysis of how the 1857 *Fleurs du mal* was put together, since some of the problems commentators have found in it persist in the later edition, and several of the notions of structure that will emerge are relevant to the 1861 version. I shall discuss parts of the opening section, "Spleen et Idéal," in some detail, as a certain number of the greatest changes occurred there.

The relation of the "Au lecteur" to what follows presents us with a characteristic peculiarity: to speak of what will come to be identified as a "modern" state of mind or vice, Baudelaire uses a series of personifications culminating in the more fully developed image of Ennui smoking a water pipe. We have here an allusion to an allegorical convention that is usually traced back to Prudentius and in which abstractions are embodied in a more or less human shape. While Baudelaire uses some imagery that seems distinctly of his own day and renews the apostrophe ("Hypocrite lecteur"; [Hypocrite reader],

p. 6) by placing it at the end for maximum surprise and dissonance, he nonetheless reminds us that personification allegory had often been the vehicle for an orthodox moralizing, which contrasts sharply with the praise of a dark and sinister female to be found shortly afterwards in "Les Bijoux" (The jewels) or "Je te donne ces vers" (I give you these verses). Moreover, the antiquated air of the convention seems to represent some sort of significantly paradoxical taste in a volume that also contains the quite new genre of the dramatic monologue, such as we find it in "Tu mettrais l'univers entier" (You would put the entire universe) some twenty poems further on.

Allegory and exemplum are scarcely absent from romantic poetry, and the theoretical distinction between allegory (mechanical and bad) and symbolism (organic and good) formulated in Germany and England, if not in France, has been shown to be untenable.[4] At the same time, however, allegory as used, say, in *Les Contemplations* does not seem calculated to make us aware of a contrast between it and more recent modes of writing.[5] Thus Vigny's personification allegory in "Les Destinées" (The destinies) appears, in the aggregate of his later poetry, merely to conform to a certain Miltonic taste hardly surprising in a poet born more than twenty years before Baudelaire. The periodic recurrence of overtly old-fashioned conventions in *Les Fleurs du mal* suggests the generality of meaning that allegory is supposed to have—in opposition to the autobiographical and personal—as well as the self-conscious didacticism, at once serious and ironic in view of the book's frequently unedifying content.

Right at the beginning, we find an example of Baudelaire's peculiar ways of juxtaposing his poems. "Au lecteur," with its vision of Ennui, seems unrelated to "Bénédiction," the first numbered poem, which deals with the poet's ultimate redemption. However, the poet is said to be born into a "monde ennuyé" (bored world), and this tangential connection is one characteristic means of tying together poems that have no linear thematic movement between them. "Le Soleil" followed "Bénédiction" in 1857 ("L'Albatros" had not yet been written):

> Ce père nourricier, ennemi des chloroses,
> Eveille dans les champs les vers comme les roses;
> (p. 92)

> This foster father, enemy of anemic pallor, awakens in the fields verses [worms] as well as roses.

The double reference to the poet and to nature does introduce a linear grouping with "Élévation" (Elevation) ("Le langage des fleurs et des choses muettes": The language of flowers and mute things) and "Correspondances" (Correspondences):

> La Nature est un temple où de vivants piliers
> Laissent parfois sortir de confuses paroles.
>
> (p. 12)

> Nature is a temple where living pillars sometimes allow indistinct words to be uttered.

It is important to notice that the poet is not the only subject, but that nature—for which the sun is sometimes a synecdoche in *Les Fleurs du mal*—is amply evoked. Many commentators practice, instead of a purely esthetic analysis of *Les Fleurs du mal*, what I would call an archaeological investigation of the work. They are anxious to find the presumed date and circumstances of composition of each poem, and, as a result, they like to dismiss some poems as early and unrepresentative of the Baudelaire they have constructed. Such considerations lead almost always to the remark that Baudelaire detested nature, and therefore they ignore its important role in *Les Fleurs du mal*. However, it is the text of the book that generates meaning, not what Baudelaire said elsewhere or at a different time, and clearly the idea of nature is an essential one as we begin reading the 1857 volume.[6]

The sense of nature emerges more fully in "J'aime le souvenir de ces époques nues" (I love the memory of these naked eras), where we see that primordial beauty, that of the body, is related to nature, conceived as dominating an earlier period in the history of man:

> J'aime le souvenir de ces époques nues,
> Dont le soleil se plaît à dorer les statues.
> Alors l'homme et la femme en leur agilité
> Jouissaient sans mensonge et sans anxiété
> Et, le ciel amoureux leur caressant l'échine,
> Exerçaient la santé de leur noble machine.
>
> (p. 13)

> I love the memory of those naked ages, whose statues the sun is fond of gilding. Then, man and woman in their nimbleness loved without lies or anxiety, and, with the loving sky caressing their spines, made use of the health of their noble machine.

Thus, we have, along with poetic beauty and nature, a third notion introduced, that of history, and, in the course of the poem, the idea of the nineteenth century as a late and fallen age:

> Le Poète aujourd'hui, quand il veut concevoir
> Ces native grandeurs, aux lieux où se font voir
> La nudité de l'homme et celle de la femme,

> Sent un froid ténébreux envelopper son âme
> Devant ce noir tableau plein d'épouvantement.
> (p. 14)

> The Poet today, when he wants to conceive of these natural splendors, in those places where the nakedness of man and of woman are displayed, feels a shadowy cold envelop his soul before this black vision full of terror.

The somewhat neoclassical diction Baudelaire uses here may elude the modern reader unaccustomed to deciphering that particular version of periphrastic style: the *lieux* in question are public baths. One of the numerous paradoxical effects of *Les Fleurs du mal* derives from the way Baudelaire will at one time use decorous circumlocutions, at another introduce terms like *voirie* (in the sense of street sweepers) or *réverbère* (in the sense of street lamp).[7] Other forms of lexical disparateness in "J'aime le souvenir" include a reference to the chapped hands and lips of realist fiction (*gerçures*) just after a phrase on women and man that could have come from an eighteenth-century libretto: "les beautés qui le nommaient leur roi" (The beauties who named him their king). Later, figurative infant wraps (*langes,* the banal nursery term) are made of bronze, more poetically designated *airain*. The inelegant familiar locution *comme qui dirait,* "a sort of," and the rare *épouvantement* (terror)—sometimes considered stronger than *épouvante* (fright)—likewise seem to clash. This poem ostensibly in praise of lost natural beauty acquires, through odd juxtapositions of vocabulary, an effect of bemused irony, the generalized kind of irony we find in Flaubert, which does not so much have an object as represent qualified assertion, a submerged skepticism. Polarities in linguistic usage make one aware of at least potential contrary attitudes.

This oscillation between two conceptions of style that his contemporaries tended to find antithetical and mutually exclusive is paralleled by the increasing contrasts between past and present in the first twenty-five or so poems of the 1857 "Spleen et Idéal." Good weather and nature seem opposed to the city, which one inhabits in winter and which is also the characteristic background of modern life. This is not an invariable nexus of associations in the text, but one the reader tends to form almost unconsciously. From the city bathhouse we move to the main point of Baudelaire's gradually evolving chain of notions:

> Nous avons, il est vrai, nations corrompues,
> Aux peuples anciens des beautés inconnues:
> Des visages rongés par les chancres du coeur,
> Et comme qui dirait des beautés de langueur;
> (p. 14)

> We, corrupted nations, have, it is true, beauties unknown to ancient races: faces gnawed by chancres of the heart, and a sort of beauty of languor.

The historicizing character of romantic thought is so pronounced that it often makes one uncertain as to whether a writer's work is mythopoeic or documentary. When Baudelaire published a few poems in a review in 1851, he spoke of the historical basis of his work, which depicted "les agitations et les mélancolies de la jeunesse moderne" (The agitations and melancholies of modern youth). This pattern of temporal contrasts, represented sometimes in terms of city and country or sun and darkness, is stronger in the 1857 *Fleurs du mal* by virtue of the absence of certain imposing later additions that distract from it. The description of painters in "Les Phares" (The lighthouses), which follows "J'aime le souvenir" and runs from the exuberant healthiness of Rubens to the dark romanticism of Goya and Delacroix, might be taken as an implicit illustration of the changes in the conception of beauty.

"La Muse malade" (The sick muse) expresses a hope to return to the inspiration of Phoebus and Pan, but "La Muse vénale" (The venal muse) sees art as hopelessly debased. "Le Mauvais moine" (The bad monk) and "L'Ennemi" (The enemy) contemplate the danger of artistic impotence, and "Le Guignon" (Bad luck) considers the inaccessibility of beauty. So far Baudelaire has followed a thematic arrangement of poems that could be described as linear. The sequential relations between poems are fairly easy to grasp, so that the movement between the picture of nature and the poet through to his unfortunate modern situation is deftly accomplished. What follows, however, is a group of five poems that do not fit a linear interpretation.

In "La Vie antérieure" (The past life), "Bohémiens en voyage" (Bohemians traveling), "L'Homme et la mer" (The man and the sea), "Don Juan aux enfers" (Don Juan in Hell) and "Châtiment de l'orgueil" (Punishment and pride), Feuillerat finds Baudelaire's "qualités": love of liberty, independence, and limited pride. Mossop offers a similar explanation and adds the not unexpected archaeological comment that these are early poems that do not fit the "architecture." It is possible, however, especially in the light of later parts of "Spleen et Idéal," to consider that Baudelaire deliberately violated linear movement at times and that cross-references are as important in *Les Fleurs du mal* as the more smoothly sequential kind of order. Don Juan and the blasphemous theologian of "Châtiment de l'orgueil" seem related to later allusions to horrible modern beauty and Lady Macbeth; the story of the impious Don Juan, Shakespearean drama, and man's revolt against an orthodox God are quite characteristic preoccupations of the romantics in their search to define the modern. "La Vie antérieure" anticipates exotic references; "L'Homme et la mer" illustrates a correspondence, and "Bohémiens en voyage," with its mention of Cybele, recalls the poet's rapport with nature. I do not think I am indulging in any interpretive subtleties here; some familiarity with Baudelaire's contemporaries is perhaps by itself enough to suggest these far-from-recondite associations. Above all, I do not wish to imply that there are hidden keys to the patterns of Baudelaire's volume that I alone have uncovered. It seems to me that such strategies of reading are as unwarranted in regard to *Les Fleurs du mal* as are naive psychological speculations that imply that Baudelaire was somehow unique. Both simply betray unfamiliarity with the nineteenth century and its concerns.

Our awareness that a pseudonarrative linearity is frequently abandoned for an arrangement of cross-references increases when, after the superficially miscellaneous poems I have just mentioned, we encounter "La Beauté":

> Je trône dans l'azur comme un sphinx incompris;
> J'unis un coeur de neige à la blancheur des cygnes;
> Je hais le movement qui déplace les lignes,
> Et jamais je ne pleure et jamais je ne ris.
>
> (p. 24)
>
> I sit enthroned in the azure like an uncomprehended Sphinx; I unite a heart of snow to the whiteness of swans; I hate all movement that displaces lines, and never do I weep, never do I laugh.

This poem is sometimes explained as belonging to Baudelaire's art-for-art's-sake period and unrepresentative of his esthetics. However, this vision of a statue is again an evocation of an early form of art and beauty, one that is no longer available to the poet, and Baudelaire then, by contrast, evokes a more modern art in "L'Idéal":

> Ce qu'il faut à ce coeur profond comme un abîme,
> C'est vous, Lady Macbeth, âme puissante au crime,
> Rêve d'Eschyle éclos au climat des autans.
>
> (p. 25)
>
> What this heart, deep as an abyss, needs is you, Lady Macbeth, a soul powerful in crime, an Aeschylean dream born in the climate of boisterous winds.

This is not, however, the modern art of Gavarni's chlorotic girls but modernism in the sense in which Hugo and other romantics dated it from Shakespeare and the supposed split in conscience and dual sensibility that occurred with him. It is as if Baudelaire had changed his example of the modern in order to complicate matters for those who would eventually try to isolate his "critical theory" or his "doctrine" of modern beauty, to use a term once beloved of French academics. There are, as we shall see in regard to the 1861 *Fleurs du mal*, a few places where Baudelaire makes use of something like unambiguous statements and abstract propositions, but that should not encourage us to extract one simple idea from a range of attitudes.

From "La Géante," the primordial earth woman, to "Les Bijoux," which was placed after it in 1857 and was later suppressed by court order, we have yet another reminder of the strong historical theme present in the early part of *Les Fleurs du mal*:

> Du temps que la Nature en sa verve puissante
> Concevait chaque jour des enfants monstrueux,
> J'eusse aimé vivre auprès d'une jeune géante
> Comme aux pieds d'une reine un chat voluptueux.
> (p. 26)

> In the age when Nature, in her powerful energy, conceived every day monstrous children, I would have liked to live with a young giant, like a sensual cat at the feet of a queen.

and

> Je croyais voir unis par un nouveau dessin
> Les hanches de l'Antiope au buste d'un imberbe,
> Tant sa taille faisait ressortir son bassin.
> Sur ce teint fauve et brun, le fard était superbe!
> (p. 26)

> I thought I was seeing the hips of the Antiope united, by a new drawing, to the torso of a beardless youth, so much did her waist make her belly stand out. On that wild and brown skin the cosmetic was superb!

The contrast is rich: the beauty of nature, growth, and fecundity are set against a *new* beauty, suggestive of both the sterile sport and the hermaphrodite; outdoors and indoors, light and darkness are evoked. A reader who has never encountered the condemned poems in the 1857 volume can scarcely imagine how much was lost by their excision: "La Géante," perhaps a dull piece in itself, gains immeasurably by the abrupt movement to "Les Bijoux."

This last poem and the immediately following ones—those referred to as the "cycle" of Jeanne Duval—are resolutely poems of somber or exotic modern beauty. It is easy to regard the sequence from "Les Bijoux" to the envoi "Je te donne ces vers" as a coherent group (though one must remember certain poems were not in the 1857 edition); biographers have taught us that they all refer to Jeanne Duval. But what of the readers of 1857, who had no footnotes or introductions to tell them what to think about the origins of the poems? There are three poems on death, which are carefully separated ("Une Charogne," "Remords posthume" (Posthumous remorse), and "Je te donne ces vers"). Might not each of them have been seen as the conclusion of a group? Furthermore, Adam remarks that in "Le Balcon" and "Je te donne ces vers," for example, which were juxtaposed in 1857, the vision of the woman is very different. In "Le Balcon":

> Je sais l'art d'évoquer les minutes heureuses,
> Et revis mon passé blotti dans tes genoux.
> Car à quoi bon chercher tes beautés langoureuses
> Ailleurs qu'en ton cher corps et qu'en ton coeur si doux?
> (p. 40)

> I know the art of evoking happy minutes, and I relive my past huddled in your lap. For what use is there in seeking your languorous beauties elsewhere than in your dear body and sweet heart?

In the following poem the poet wishes that:

> Ta mémoire, pareille aux fables incertaines,
> Fatigue le lecteur ainsi qu'un tympanon,
> . . . . .
> Etre maudit à qui, de l'abîme profond
> Jusqu'au plus haut du ciel, rien, hors moi, ne répond!
> (p. 41)

> Your memory, like dubious fables, may tire the reader like a dulcimer . . . accursed being, whom nothing, from the deep abyss to the highest heaven, nothing except me answers.

Although the poems are not necessarily mutually exclusive, the contrast between the lyricism and the sweetness and gentleness of "Le Balcon" and the harsh envoi poem suggests the variety of attitudes that biographical information tends to smooth over in its attempt to epitomize the poet's relations with his Black Venus. Biographical criticism has had perhaps its most dismal success with Baudelaire, in that anyone who has read widely in studies of him finds it difficult to ignore distracting attributions of poems to the inspiration of this or that "Venus" and simply to read what Baudelaire wrote.

The foregoing complaint is especially relevant to the sense of subdivisions or changes in "Spleen et Idéal." As I have mentioned, Baudelaire's belated muse is much concerned with things past or coming to an end, so that temporary endings or false conclusions recur in "Spleen et Idéal." Indeed, the poems that follow the envoi to Jeanne Duval contain no suggestion of beginnings, and our accounts of Mme. Sabatier, to whom they were sent, seem sometimes to get in the way more than anything else. "Que diras-tu ce soir" and "Le Flambeau vivant" are a sequence related by the image of the torch. They both have an air of antiquated praise, a suggestion of medieval or renaissance poems of celebration:

"Je suis belle, et j'ordonne
Que pour l'amour de moi vous n'aimiez que le Beau;
Je suis l'Ange gardien, la Muse et la Madone."
Ils marchent devant moi, ces Yeux pleins de lumières,
Qu'un Ange très savant a sans doute aimantés;
Ils marchent, ces divins frères qui sont mes frères,
Secouant dans mes yeux leurs feux diamantés.
(p. 48)

"I am beautiful, and I order you, for love of me, to love only what is beautiful; I am the Guardian Angel, the Muse, and the Madonna." They walk before me, those Eyes full of light, which a very learned Angel has surely made magnetic; they walk, those divine brothers who are my brothers, shaking into my eyes their diamond-studded fires.

There followed in 1857 "A celle qui est trop gaie" (To one who is too gay), which some commentators want to assign to someone other than Mme. Sabatier. But the problem is not one of deciding what kind of poem Baudelaire should have sent her, but rather its place in "Spleen et Idéal":

Ta tête, ton geste, ton air
Sont beaux comme un beau paysage;
Le rire joue en ton visage
Comme un vent frais dans un ciel clair.
(p. 165)

Your head, your movements, your look are beautiful like a beautiful landscape; laughter plays in your face like a fresh breeze in a bright sky.

Clearly this refers back to the initial idea of nature, to which the poet's reaction has now changed:

Quelquefois dans un beau jardin
Où je traînais mon atonie,
J'ai senti, comme une ironie,
Le soleil déchirer mon sein,

Et le printemps et la verdure
Ont tant humilié mon coeur,
Que j'ai puni sur une fleur
L'insolence de la Nature.
(pp. 165–66)

Sometimes, in a beautiful garden where I was dragging my listlessness, I felt, like an irony, the sun tear my bosom, and

> the springtime and the greenery so humiliated my heart that I punished a flower for the insolence of Nature.

The poet then experiences a modern, nocturnal revolt against nature and threatens the woman with a sadistic nighttime assault, much as in the earlier "Je t'adore à l'égal" (I adore you equally), where, in a dramatic shift of style unparalleled in Baudelaire, antiquated adoration gives way to lurid romantic frenzy. In other words, there are analogous movements of tone quite independent of the woman addressed and very much related to Baudelaire's historical contrast between an older mood, beauty, and literary convention and those peculiar to his own time. (All this, of course, was lost with the poem's suppression.)

The violent contrast between "A celle qui est trop gaie" and the preceding poems leads to two confessions, that of the poet ("Réversibilité": Reversibility):

> Ange plein de gaieté, connaissez-vous l'angoisse,
> La honte, les remords, les sanglots, les ennuis,
> Et les vagues terreurs de ces affreuses nuits
> Qui compriment le coeur comme un papier qu'on froisse?
> (p. 48)

> Angel full of gaiety, do you know the anguish, the shame, the remorse, the sobs, the troubles, and the vague terrors of those frightful nights that squeeze the heart like a piece of paper being crumpled?

and that of the woman ("Confession"), who affirms:

> Que bâtir sur les coeurs est une chose sotte;
> Que tout craque, amour et beauté,
> Jusqu'à ce que l'Oubli les jette dans sa hotte
> Pour les rendre à l'Eternité!
> (p. 50)

> Building on hearts is a foolish thing to do, everything cracks, love and beauty, until Oblivion throws them into the basket on his back to return them to Eternity!

These two poems seem in a way to resolve the antithesis between "Le Flambeau vivant" and "A celle qui est trop gaie"; she is not an angel, and he is not a devil. But when we look a bit closer at the style, we notice that while his confession is eloquent in its anguish, hers contains, before the splendid Shakespearean image of Time with a basket at his back, lines that are a bit equivocal in implication:

Pauvre ange, elle chantait, votre note criarde:
    "Que rien ici-bas n'est certain,
Et que toujours, avec quelque soin qu'il se farde,
    Se trahit l'égoïsme humain;
Que c'est un dur métier que d'être belle femme."
(p. 50)

Poor angel, your shrill note was singing, "That nothing on this earth is certain and that, with whatever care it may disguise itself, human selfishness always betrays itself; . . . that it is a hard job being a beautiful woman."

This lament is not much superior in freshness to Emma Bovary's language. In fact, one might infer that, while the woman may be a nice enough object, her finest sentiments are trite and sound lifted from something she has read. The sense of cliché is sometimes difficult to establish in regard to French romantic verse because of its closeness in vocabulary to prose. As Louis Maigron demonstrated long ago, those of Baudelaire's contemporaries whose tastes were literary but who were not professional writers often wrote to one another in a kind of pastiche style that quickly depreciated poetic coinage.[8] Baudelaire's shifts of style elsewhere are frequently cunning, his sense of the hackneyed acute, for whatever reason he may use it. I suspect there is enough irony here to qualify the poem's value as a resolution of contraries. Moreover, to prevent too strong an effect of conclusion, Baudelaire returns to imagery suggestive of Dante and Petrarch in "L'Aube spirituelle" (Spiritual dawn), which follows.

Still another example of Baudelaire's avoiding a closure satisfying to biographical readings comes in "Le Flacon" (The flask), supposed to be the last of the poems addressed to Mme. Sabatier:

Je serai ton cercueil, aimable pestilence!
Le témoin de ta force et de ta virulence,
Cher poison préparé par les anges! Liqueur
Qui me ronge, ô la vie et la mort de mon coeur!
(p. 53)

I shall be your coffin, aimiable pestilence! The witness of your strength and virulence, dear poison prepared by the angels! Fluid which eats away at me, O life and death of my heart!

Now his love is a poison, which, by the principle of recurrence, recalls more the Jeanne Duval poems than the immediately preceding ones. Commentators consider this poem an envoi to the "cycle of the White Venus," but Baudelaire clearly intended no such break, for the following poem, "Le Poison," directly picks up the idea of a venomous bond between poet and lover:

> Tout cela ne vaut pas le poison qui découle
> De tes yeux, de tes yeux verts.
> (p. 54)

> All that is not worth the poison that flows from your eyes, from your green eyes.

The curious method of biographical commentary is to pretend that some rather varied poems make a coherent whole, but at the same time to break up the sequence of "Spleen et Idéal" into sections dealing with different women who are supposed to be treated quite differently. Baudelaire's complicated play of recurrence and cross-references is thereby suppressed, and we are left with the "album" he claimed not to have assembled.

What happens from this point on in "Spleen et Idéal" is that Baudelaire arranges his poems so that, while there are thematic sequences of two or more poems (notably the "Spleen" group), a good deal of contrast and cross-reference obtains. For example, "Le Poison" and "Ciel brouillé" (Uncertain sky) both depict, in sequence, a dangerous woman, but "Le Chat," which follows, is more reminiscent of the other cat poems than anything else. Next come poems of praise of beauty, "Le Beau Navire" and "L'Invitation au voyage" (Invitation to a voyage), but they are followed by "L'Irréparable" (The irreparable) (anticipating the later "L'Irrémédiable" [The irremediable]) and "Causerie," both poems of aging and pain concerning the past. If the bitterness of "Causerie" leads somewhat elliptically to "L'Héautontimorouménos," (The Self-executioner) the subsequent "Franciscae meae laudes" (My praises for Frances) could not be more contrastive.

The interplay between thematic linearity and cross-reference has bothered those commentators who note it. They show a distinct preference for the former. Thus the "Spleen" group, with which we can associate the preceding "Cloche fêlée" (Cracked bell) and the following "Brumes et pluies" (Mists and rains) and "L'Irrémédiable," seems a satisfactory conclusion to "Spleen et Idéal," while the real conclusion, with its very mixed series of poems, does not. However, the mild mood of some of these later poems, such as "Je n'ai pas oublié, voisine de la ville" (I have not forgotten, neighbor of the town), "Tristesses de la lune" (Sadness of the moon), or "La Musique," serves a perceptible structural function when we consider that Baudelaire, in 1857, placed the section "Fleurs du mal" directly after "Spleen et Idéal." "Fleurs du mal" is almost uniformly somber, and therefore some lightening of the tone at the end of the preceding section helps to set off, by a fairly vivid contrast, the series on eroticism and death.

Within "Fleurs du mal" we encounter one passage that contains the seed of the conclusion to the 1857 volume. In "Lesbos" the poet envisages some kind of redemptory value:

> Tu tires ton pardon de l'éternel martyre,
> Infligé sans relâche aux coeurs ambitieux,
> Qu'attire loin de nous le radieux sourire
> Entrevu vaguement au bord des autres cieux!
> (p. 26)

> You obtain your pardon from the eternal martyrdom inflicted unrelentingly on ambitious hearts, which the radiant smile, vaguely glimpsed at the edge of the other heavens, draws far away from us!

This notion of pardon stands out in the midst of so much imagery of deathly eroticism and points toward the final poem. Although making synthesizing generalities about sections of *Les Fleurs du mal* is a more delicate and risky matter than it is with even a complicated but structured collection like Hugo's *Les Contemplations*, we can characterize "Fleurs du mal" as the lowest point in the depiction of experience in the whole work. There is a kind of analogy in the 1857 *Fleurs du mal* to a harrowing of hell, with a certain feeling of ascent from the depths on the far side of evil. It is a common romantic idea that the nineteenth century was a sort of purgatory on earth, or even a temporary hell. Thus Baudelaire conveys carefully the idea of a fall from an earlier age at the beginning of *Les Fleurs du mal*, and he will complement it with a rising movement at the end. This cyclic pattern, which Northrop Frye would derive ultimately from the Bible, is, of course, characteristic of the romantic imagination to the point of obsessiveness.

"Révolte" (Revolt) which follows "Fleurs du mal," rejects Christianity and its tyrannical God in favor of man; the theme is a familiar romantic one, and it is idle to argue about Baudelaire's religious convictions in regard to it. Again, the text is the source of meaning, not Baudelaire's comments elsewhere. To say, as is done, that the verse belongs to Baudelaire's "socialist" period does not obviate the fact that it serves as an explosion of energy and decision after the often passive submission to destruction in "Fleurs du mal." We note that the pattern of fall, revolt, and ascension is the revolutionary variant, widespread in the nineteenth century, of the Christian cyclic myth. "Le Vin" (Wine), the penultimate section in 1857, also suggests escape from the wretched conditions of life. Its flaw, according to Feuillerat, who would otherwise defend the cheerful celebration of wine, lies in the somber "Vin de l'assassin" (Assassin's wine). However, the poem, with its depiction of a sordid crime, serves to qualify the praise of wine: wine is not the ultimate good but a step by which some of life's horror can be dispelled. Only death will constitute the final release. In this connection, we observe that to see wine in changing perspectives merely recapitulates a typical movement of "Spleen et Idéal" by which, as I have pointed out, occurs the juxtaposition, in the 1857

Fleurs du mal, of the female figures of "Le Balcon" and "Je te donne ces vers," who, if not quite antithetical, bear very different associations.

"La Mort" (Death) in 1857 consisted of only three sonnets. This has been seen as a great weakness in the "architecture" of the volume, too slim a conclusion for so much that precedes. Obviously, Barbey d'Aurevilly, whose impression of an edifice was based on the 1857 volume, was scarcely thinking of any real building when he made his remark. This asymmetrical ending is a tentative, suggestive one rather than a resounding conclusion, for reasons that emerge from the third and final poem. Death is presented as a consolation for lovers and for the poor in the first two sonnets; then comes "La Mort des artistes" (Artists' deaths):

> Combien faut-il de fois secouer mes grelots
> Et baiser ton front bas, morne caricature?
> Pour piquer dans le but, de mystique nature,
> Combien, ô mon carquois, perdre de javelots?
>
> (p. 152)

> How many times must I shake my bells and kiss your low forehead, gloomy caricature? To hit the target, mystic in nature, how many javelins must I lose, o my quiver?

The historical reference reaffirms itself here: the lines are reminiscent of "La Muse vénale," the depiction of the low estate to which art has fallen in modern times. A particularly apt word is *caricature;* Baudelaire, like his contemporaries, had observed that the romantic period saw an extraordinary flowering of this minor art. Beyond that, there is perhaps a certain ironic awareness of all the senses the word *artist* had acquired in the nineteenth century: aside from the neutral meaning of one who practices an art, such as sculpture; there was the artistic temperament of the pretentious dabbler or affected sensibilities; the artist like Jeanne Duval, who appeared on the stage as an adjunct to prostitution; jugglers or other popular entertainers, who were as much artists as Michelangelo; and all the other dubious applications of the word. The trivialization of the noun was almost simultaneous with its acquiring the most grandiose connotations.

Recalling the effect of allegory that Baudelaire explicitly created in "Au lecteur" and periodically reinforces with generalizing, third-person references like "L'Homme et la Mer" or "Le Crépuscule du matin" (Dawn), we should observe that the lovers, the poor, and the artists whose deaths are depicted in the concluding sonnets are neither the same persons nor different ones. A certain deliberate indeterminacy obtains, as in, say, the Seven Ages of Man speech in *As You Like It*: not every Elizabethan was necessarily and successively a soldier and a justice, any more than Baudelaire's modern youth necessarily and universally experienced alienation from God or morbid sexual tastes. The identification of modern youth with the artist, whom we see at the beginning of the work in "Bénédiction" and in the final poem, is more suggestive than definitive. We must simply refer to the romantic artist's tendency to see himself as the most perceptive, aware, and therefore historically distinctive member of society, a role earlier artists had claimed less publicly, whatever their private opinions may have been. Moreover, the notion of young men being poets before they settled down to being grocery storekeepers offers merely a parodic image of a common nineteenth-century idea, which no doubt had a kind of validity for romantic culture that it scarcely has today.

A further reference back to the earlier part of *Les Fleurs du mal* occurs in the tercets. Whereas in "Bénédiction" the poet will receive after death a crown of light, here the light imagery is qualified:

> Il en est qui n'ont jamais connu leur Idole,
> Et ces sculpteurs damnés et marqués d'un affront,
> Qui vont se martelant la poitrine et le front,
>
> N'ont qu'un espoir, étrange et sombre Capitole!
> C'est que la Mort, planant comme un soleil nouveau,
> Fera s'épanouir les fleurs de leur cerveau!
>
> (p. 153)

> There are those who have never known their Idol, and those sculptors, damned and marked by insult, who go about beating their chests and foreheads, have only one hope—strange and dark triumph! It is that death, hovering like a new sun, will make the flowers of their dream blossom!

Besides the key words of *soleil* and *fleurs,* we find the peculiar locution "strange and dark triumph" (the sense of *Capitole* here), suggestive of the curious role of language in connection with the past in the book. The old expression *monter au Capitole* ("to triumph") is adapted to a new kind of imagery, but we are conscious of the poet's intense awareness of the outmoded high style of neoclassicism, as we are at a number of points in the volume. Baudelaire's sense of the modern seems necessarily to involve reference to past ideals and ways of expression, but they are unlike the primarily parodic allusions to literary tradition we find in Laforgue. Neither the old nor the contemporary suffices in itself, whence the oddly mixed diction characteristic of *Les Fleurs du mal* and exemplified by the romantic-neoclassical "étrange et sombre Capitole."

Light and dark mingle in this redemption that is equivocal, limited, or uncertain. Here we find Baudelaire rejoining other romantics in the groping, hesitant way they envisaged some end of the purgatory of life. There is a certain analogy, for example, with the end of *Les Contemplations*, where Hugo represents the poet as sitting atop a huge volcano and staring into its dark depths that are God: flashes of light periodically illuminate this ambiguous deity, and the sense is that of a hoped-for but by no means absolute salvation. Baudelaire's imagery follows this pattern of conceiving a perhaps partial redemption, one not to be anticipated in traditional terms of glory. Here we see how the design of the 1857 *Fleurs du mal* reflects a modified and historicized version of the myth of primal innocence, fall, and salvation. Most of the volume deals with the earthly purgatory, since that is what is present and certain, but in the beginning and in the end we glimpse origins and a longed-for ultimate release.

If my necessarily partial account of the 1857 *Fleurs du mal* seems full of qualifications and rather less neat than a paraphrase of the *Discours de la méthode*, the reason is that the volume itself was not conceived in terms of "composition" but belongs rather to that group of romantic works for which the notion of organic form is peculiarly appropriate.[9] The ramifications of this theory correspond not only to certain effects we have observed but also to the general circumstances in which Baudelaire put together the two *Fleurs du mal*. While organic form is thought of as an indissoluble whole, it is not necessarily a static one, for, like a plant, the work of art grows. We are moderately well acquainted with this aspect of *Les Fleurs du mal*, since Baudelaire planned a volume of verse for many years before 1857. The titles chosen were first *Les Lesbiennes* (The lesbians) and then *Les Limbes* (Limbo), which clearly has connotations of an ill-defined, uncertain time or place—like the nineteenth century in romantic thought—before *Les Fleurs du mal* was settled on in the mid-1850s. We also know something of the dating of various poems. It is clear that at any given moment in its maturation the book would have been different from what it was to be in 1857, just as the second edition in 1861 is a different book from the first. However, in terms of organic form the work would not necessarily have been imperfect, all stages of growth, as in a plant, having a valid structure. In this sense any notion of the definitive seems to be eliminated, though at the same time the idea of a perfect whole forms a characteristic part of organic thinking. The fact of growth is, in other words, divorced from teleological considerations.

The opposite of the organic conception of form is the classicizing, mechanistic one, which emphasizes *plan* or outline. In organic terms, each work has its own structure, one that is not imposed from the outside like mechanical form or some preconceived "architecture." This means, of course, that such a thing as symmetry may or may not be present, symmetry being merely, in many cases, an automatic rhetorical pattern that does not grow out of the material but is forced onto it. We can see the implications of organic theory for the general shape of the 1857 *Fleurs du mal*: "Spleen et Idéal" is long and contains a great variety of poems; "La Mort" is extremely short. This is the way Baudelaire's material worked itself out. We may prefer the second edition because it contains more poems and other formal patterns, but this does not invalidate the 1857 one.

Another facet of the theory of organic form is assimilation of diverse and often opposing elements. This is reflected in the heterogeneity or antithetical relations in the movement from poem to poem that we often perceive. If Baudelaire had had a strictly logical conception of his work, he might well have refused to include many early poems, but whatever Baudelaire the man thought at any given moment, Baudelaire the artist had a comprehensive view of his work by which divergent attitudes and styles belonged together, a fact commentators tacitly avoid by labeling this or that poem early, as if it could thereby be ignored. The once-popular notion of Baudelaire as poetic modernist is an excellent example of the blinkered vision and selectivity from which general interpretations of his work have suffered: his taste for stiffly rhetorical forms like the analogy poem ("L'Albatros" or "Bénédiction") and various types of allegory was as pronounced as his interest in elliptic movement, submerged themes (the first "Spleen," of which Michael Riffaterre has said that the unstated key notion is "house," in a negative sense), and implicit plot ("La servante au grand coeur": The magnanimous servant). In fact, Baudelaire amused himself in "Le Cygne" (The swan) by writing the poem twice: the same material is first presented in a radically free-associative pattern and an irregular relation of verse to syntax, and is then reintroduced in part two, following a neat reverse chronological order that has a greater coincidence of grammatical and prosodic divisions. To my mind the range of poetic structures in *Les Fleurs du mal* constitutes a far more striking example of assimilation than of any thematic diversity.

Finally, the interdependence of all parts, as well as their subordination to the whole, is an important tenet of organic form that is especially relevant to *Les Fleurs du mal*. The principles of recurrence and cross-reference ensure such an interdependence, as does the reconciliation of the antithetical. Such relations are extremely dense in the work, so much so as to make the linearity prized by a commentator like Mossop seem but an intermittent feature of its organization. Again, the mechanistic conception of *plan* cannot deal with this aspect of the volume.

At the same time, we recognize obvious weaknesses in organic theory. Whether, for example, the last twenty-five or so poems in the "Spleen et Idéal" of 1857 are truly assimilated into the book might be contested. I have spoken of their fulfilling a certain contrastive function with regard to the somber "Fleurs du mal" that follow, but that is scarcely more than a loose relationship, and to speak of interdependence would be absurd. A plant's assimilation of carbon dioxide and soil nutrients through a chemical process has little to do with juxtaposing poems. Naturally, interpretive sophistication must choose its own limits, since organic theory does not set up any at all, and the temptation of wearisome overreading is a serious one.

With antithetical material a similar problem arises. Aside from the fact that all antithetical elements can be seen as logically necessary to one another, the reconciliation of contraries can take peculiar and debatable forms, such as the phrase "étrange et sombre Capitole," by which we might say that dualisms associated with the modern and the old are collapsed at the end of the 1857 *Fleurs du mal*. Yet we can also see this as merely the verbal device of oxymoron, which deconstructs itself without much critical help. Notions like limited or qualified salvation do not, perhaps, designate redemption at all, but merely play with words idly.

Finally, when the great English exponent of organic theory cut the original end off "Frost at Midnight," supposedly to make it a better poem, Coleridge's action was less consonant with his convictions than suggestive of a neoclassical gardener wielding a set of mechanical snippers according to a "plan." Nonetheless, organicism supplied a more supple approach to poems than the traditional idea of composition, and certainly a work of which two distinct versions exist can profit from this perspective.

Of the thirty-five new poems added to the 1861 edition of *Les Fleurs du mal*, some, like "La Chevelure" or "Chant d'automne," have certain similarities in imagery or theme to earlier poems; these take their place in the collection without conspicuously altering it, save that they enrich it with their own peculiar beauty. Certain other pieces, however, bring in new material, especially rich in theological implications, and they tend to color the volume in a special way, which makes it a distinctly new work. A first example is "Hymne à la beauté" with its query as to the moral status of beauty:

> Viens-tu du ciel profond ou sors-tu de l'abîme,
> O Beauté! ton regard, infernal et divin,
> Verse confusément le bienfait et le crime,
> Et l'on peut pour cela te comparer au vin.
>
> . . . . .
>
> Que tu viennes du ciel ou de l'enfer, qu'importe,
> O Beauté! monstre énorme, effrayant, ingénu!
> Si ton oeil, ton souris, ton pied, m'ouvrent la porte
> D'un infini que j'aime et n'ai jamais connu?
>
> (p. 28)

> Do you come from the farthest heaven or do you come out of the abyss, o Beauty? Your glance, infernal and divine, pours forth a mixture of blessing and crime, and in that you can be compared to wine. . . . Whether you come from Heaven or Hell, what does it matter, o Beauty! enormous, frightening, ingenuous monster! if your eye, your smile, your foot open for me the door of an infinity that I love and have never known?

The poem has been added at the head of the Jeanne Duval and other love poems. In a sense, it develops a question implied by the juxtaposition of love poems radically different in tone, but, by its explicitness, it invests everything that follows with a clearer sense of the opposition of good and evil. This illustrates the principle of interdependence of parts; what had been a suggestion we now read as an overt theme in the course of "Spleen et Idéal."

Moreover, we note that this "theme" takes the form of a proposition of an abstract and general character: "Whether beauty is good or evil makes no difference." It is rather more difficult and risky to devise so broad a statement subsuming poems as they appear in 1857. We might from the 1857 edition derive the idea that neither modern beauty nor the older kind is good or bad, but that involves more interpretation and the difficulty of deciding whether *bad* means "evil" or "unpleasant" or "monotonous" or whatever. However, to see a reasonably clear proposition in "Hymne à la beauté" demands no rash leap in ideas or elaborating a suggestion into a relatively fixed category of thought like "evil."

At the same time, we observe that the historical scheme, which is fairly pronounced in the 1857 volume, becomes less clear when the good or evil of modern experience is thrust forward as a dominant question demanding resolution. This new dilemma complicates the earlier antithesis between past and present by focusing on just one of its terms. Not only does the notion of whether modern beauty derives from good or evil distract us from the historical scheme; it also recalls to us that indifference to good and evil, such as is formulated by "Hymne à la beauté," is a well-developed theological concept. The connotations of the sin of acedia include both sloth and ennui, so that the end of "Au lecteur" now seems to have a different sense: ennui becomes connected, by the addition of "Hymne à la beauté," to another system of references in *Les Fleurs du mal*, one that acquires great significance because it reaches its culmination in the new ending of the 1861 volume, the final stanzas of "Le Voyage."

But before we reach Baudelaire's new concluding poem, still another antithetical relation is elaborated, which is at most only vaguely present in 1857, if at all. We first become aware of it near the end of "Spleen et Idéal," which was radically transformed. A number of poems of a somewhat restrained tone (such as "Je n'ai pas oublié, voisine de la ville") were removed, and Baudelaire added five poems consonant with the "Spleen" ones. "Le Goût du néant" (The taste for nothing) gives that last word new prominence and thematic status in *Les Fleurs du mal*; coupled with moral indifference ("Que tu viennes du ciel ou de l'enfer, qu'importe": What does it matter whether you come from heaven or hell?) it seems to commentators to mark a new stage in Baudelaire's sensibility and to cast a particular light on the whole second edition. But equally important is the imagery of nature in the new poems. Lloyd James Austin was the first to point out that in its new form the structure of "Spleen et Idéal" has a strong thematic contrast based on the idea of correspondences.[10] While the correspondences at the beginning of the section are traditional ones between the divine and earth, now nature reflects the infernal:

> L'un t'éclaire avec son ardeur,
> L'autre en toi met son deuil, Nature!
> Ce qui dit à l'un: Sépulture!
> Dit à l'autre: Vie et splendeur!
> ("Alchimie de la douleur," p. 83)
>
> One illumines you with his ardor, the other places his mourning in you, Nature! What says to one "Tomb," says to the other "Life and glory!" (Alchemy of pain)
>
> Cieux déchirés comme des grèves,
> En vous se mire mon orgueil,
> Vos vastes nuages en deuil
>
> Sont les corbillards de mes rêves,
> Et vos lueurs sont le reflet
> De l'Enfer où mon coeur se plaît.
> ("Horreur sympathique," p. 84)
>
> Skies torn like strands, my pride admires itself in you, your vast mourning clouds are the hearses of my dreams, and your gleams are the reflection of the Hell where my heart is happy. (Sympathetic horror)

Whereas the "Spleen" poems had dealt simply with bad weather, here nature is seen in a generalized way as a correspondence of hell, which does not suit the centuries-old function of correspondence as a form of theodicy. "Obsession" is even more specific, taking up the images of trees or "vivants piliers" (living pillars) and of the sea (as in "L'Homme et la Mer") and reinterpreting them in a demonic sense. This new idea tends, as do the 1861 additions in general, not only to submerge the historical theme of the 1857 volume but to differentiate strongly its theology from that of the earlier form of the work. Finally, the artist as the natural representative of romantic times becomes a less conspicuous feature than in 1857, where "Bénédiction" and the concluding poem both stressed his importance.

With such a massive thematic buildup at the end of the new "Spleen et Idéal," Baudelaire saw fit to begin the next section with peoms milder in tone, "Paysage" (Landscape) and "Le Soleil" (The Sun). They introduce an entirely new grouping, the "Tableaux parisiens" (Parisian tableaux) in which earlier and more recent poems intermingle. Baudelaire's critics seem unanimous in their praise of this new section, but their attempts to characterize it have not always been felicitous. Not all of these poems depict Paris, nor are they free from a *je* who participates as well as contemplates. However, this *je* is perceived as being rather different from that of many poems of "Spleen et Idéal," a fact that has encouraged critics to speak of impersonality. Ross Chambers has recently tried to study this *je* more searchingly, as well as to analyze the complex cyclicity of "Tableaux parisiens," which separates it from the preceding and following sections.[11] There is an intricate arrangement of daytime and nighttime poems, poems of the street and poems of enclosed spaces, which revolves on itself. Pieces that are in some respects heterogeneous are thus held together in a subtle structure.

If "Tableaux parisiens" pleases everyone, "Le Vin" is a much criticized episode. By placing it after "Tableaux" in the second edition, Baudelaire evidently modifies its meaning to suggest merely popular scenes rather than a joyous release from man's condition. The following "Fleurs du mal" section is unchanged, except for the elimination of the condemned pieces, which include the stanza on pardon and the glimpse of a redemption that I quoted earlier and that fits so well the thematic pattern of the 1857 edition. While the sense of "Fleurs du mal" seems relatively stable in its passage from one edition to another, "Révolte" in 1861 appears, in this totally new context, to be more highly theologized. The reaction against the Christian God no longer seems to be the affirmation of man's desire for social justice but rather the low point in the veering between God and Satan: "Enfer ou Ciel, qu'importe?" ("Le Voyage": The voyage, p. 143). A poem like "Le Possédé" (The possessed), added to "Spleen et Idéal" would appear to confirm this reading. Satanism may seem distastefully puerile, but it enters into the pattern of *Les Fleurs du mal* in order to form a contrast with the new version of "La Mort."

The order of the original three sonnets of "La Mort" remained unchanged, but Baudelaire added three more poems that move away from the 1857 ending and even nullify it. This is an interesting example of how context or the interdependence of parts can function. Erich Auerbach wrote a commentary on "La Mort des artistes"—based on its place in the second edition—in which he finds mockery, bitterness, and nothingness to be the import of the poem and uses the subsequent "Le Rêve d'un curieux" (A curious man's dream) as a gloss.[12] In the latter poem:

> J'étais mort sans surprise, et la terrible aurore
> M'enveloppait. —Eh quoi! n'est-ce donc que cela?
> La toile était levée et j'attendais encore.
>
> (p. 154)

> I had died without any surprise, and the terrible dawn was enveloping me. —Well! Is that all it is? The curtain had gone up and I was still waiting.

Clearly "La Mort des artistes" meant nothing of the sort in 1857, but by the principle of the interdependence of parts, one may reread it in another light according to its repositioning in 1861.

The most extraordinary example of growth in the whole second edition is the conclusion to "Le Voyage," a poem that begins by alluding to preceding sections of *Les Fleurs du mal* in a lengthy summary before an entirely new direction is taken in the end:

> O Mort, vieux capitaine, il est temps! levons l'ancre!
> Ce pays nous ennuie, ô Mort! Appareillons!
> Si le ciel et la mer sont noirs comme de l'encre,
> Nos coeurs que tu connais sont remplis de rayons!
>
> Verse-nous ton poison pour qu'il nous réconforte!
> Nous voulons, tant ce feu nous brûle le cerveau,
> Plonger au fond du gouffre, Enfer ou Ciel, qu'importe?
> Au fond de l'Inconnu pour trouver du *nouveau*!
>
> (p. 160)

> O Death, old captain, it is time! let's lift anchor! This country wearies us, o Death! Let's get under way! If the sky and the sea are black as ink, our hearts, which you know, are filled with light! Pour your poison for us so that it may comfort us! So much does this fire burn our brain, we want to plunge to the depths of the abyss, Hell or Heaven, what does it matter? Plunge to the depths of the unknown to find what is *new*!

The combination of light and darkness persists, but the burden of the poem is quite different from that of "La Mort des artistes," however it is read. As in "Hymne à la beauté," we find an almost abstractly and generally formulated idea: the poet is indifferent to the distinction between good and evil, the verb *ennuie* defining his state of mind. But here the negative notion of acedia impels him to anticipate a state beyond it, and so we have a succinctly dialectic movement, quite unlike anything in the 1857 *Fleurs du mal*. If there is any broad direction of thought in the earlier volume, it exists largely by implication, and one could maintain that the oxymoronic "sombre Capitole" is merely a version of one of those irreconcilable antitheses French romantic literature is rich in and that seem especially to inform Hugo's work. In "Le Voyage," however, Baudelaire steps beyond opposites in a clear logical move, whose formulation offers nothing especially ambiguous. Moreover, the last word, *nouveau,* creates a notable contrast to the liminary "Au lecteur," with its concluding vision of the sameness of ennui. By analogy we see that indifference to good and evil also involves collapsing the antithesis between divine and demonic correspondences, which constitutes the other prominent new feature of the 1861 *Fleurs du mal*.

However, there is perhaps more to the closing lines of "Le Voyage" than a logical movement of broad implication, since this structural function does not precisely define their emotive import, which has been variously interpreted. One of the more subtle readings of the poem takes them as an expression of pre-Nietzschean "tragic joy."[13] This gloss implies an entirely new tone at the end of the volume. If indeed we see Baudelaire as conveying a "joyous, though anxious, faith in the future," the ostensible conclusion to *Les Fleurs du mal* is somewhat open-ended, which, moreover, is a characteristic possibility of organic form.[14] The idea of growth implies further potentialities.

Finally, we notice that the *nous* of the last stanzas of "Le Voyage" has been defined in the course of the poem as one part of humanity, the "coureurs sans répit" (relentless runners) seeking various kinds of experience. Beauty is not their concern so much as the anguish of being caught by Time with his net, as Baudelaire expresses it, and they are not, by the end of the poem, particularly identified with the present moment. In fact, this psychological portrait replaces the general allegory of modern man of 1857, although the actual use of personifications and allegorical structures ("A une madone": To a madonna; "Les Sept Vieillards": The seven old men) increases somewhat. Thus, the 1861 *Fleurs du mal*, while necessarily more complicated because of its greater number of parts, is actually a more explicit work to the extent that "Le Voyage" retrospectively informs it.

Moreover, if we look at all the longer poems Baudelaire added to the second edition, a further aspect of his design becomes apparent. The movement of historical time—the fall from a higher original estate, as in "J'aime le souvenir . . ."—is transferred to personal time. This is the internalization of history, which was a dominant feature of European romantic thought and has been most relevantly treated perhaps by Meyer H. Abrams in *Natural Supernaturalism: Tradition and Revolution in Romantic Literature* (New York: Norton, 1971). The time that forms the subject of "Le Masque" (The mask), "Le Goût du néant," "Chant d'automne" (Autumn song), and "L'Horloge" (The clock) is that of the poet's life, as objective history recedes in importance. A most elegant illustration of the process can be found in "Le Cygne," where the sight of Haussmann's urban renewal project, a characteristic expression of modern life and taste, does not lead to historical reflections but reminds the poet of his and others' private histories and personal fall. "Les Petites Vieilles" (The little old women) deals again with personal time in the framework of modern life. Another kind of internalization occurs in "La Chevelure," where paradise is situated in the tropics rather than in primeval days and will be regained through the inner journey of involuntary memory. The mention of childhood at the beginning of "Le Voyage" completes this transference of the pattern of world history to psychological and individual history. The particular brilliance of all these poems has the effect of making the previously established references to world history seem secondary or merely complementary in the 1861 *Fleurs du mal*. While this thematic material is certainly present in the first edition of the work, by the principle of the interdependence of parts, it now assumes greater significance.

I have avoided discussing heretofore the notion of unity, which seems to me to be the weakest legacy of romantic organic theory. If we look, for example, in the *Princeton Encyclopedia of Poetry and Poetics*, we find, *sub verb*, a statement characteristic of organicism filtered through New Criticism: "Unity is the most fundamental and comprehensive aesthetic criterion, upon which all others depend." There follows a farrago of quotations, paraphrases, and allusions running from Plato to the present and which can be reduced to the same concept of unity only by total faith in unitary thinking, analogy run wild. Recently the notion of unity has been called a convention of reading,[15] and the fact that some deconstructionist criticism seems to imply a convention of unresolved conflicts tends to confirm to what extent we approach a work of art with certain expectations. There is little intellectual profit in making some leap of faith and affirming the existence of total unity—because it is absurd, if necessary. Actually, the most useful point of view, I think, is to distinguish various conventions of unity on the part of poets as well as on the part of readers, and as we do so, certain loose historical patterns seem to emerge. To take an obvious example, readers have become adept, since New Criticism, at detecting in a work seemingly secondary elements that create what one might call a submerged or half-concealed pattern, which passes for unity: the ambiguity of height and depth, up and down, in some of Hugo's poems is just such a unity, as is the way in which the characters in Racine's *Andromaque* use expressions that separate them, as it were, from their physical and psychological states and attributes ("Comment lui rendre un coeur que vous me retenez?": How can I give her my heart, which you retain?—1. 4. 344) The ultimate absurdity arises when a classicist, distraught at the seeming insufficiency of metaphoric chains in Homer, invents Homeric "fire symbolism" in order that Greek epic not seem too inferior to *The Waste Land*. It is a critically unsophisticated reader who cannot find unity when he puts his mind to it, and years of this practice have made the concept slightly disreputable. Jacques Derrida's strictures on the notion of perfect form, virtually a synonym of *unity*, are relevant: fervently to proclaim the unity of *Les Fleurs du mal* is a bit like declaring that one believes in God.[16]

While French criticism never absorbed organic theory, which could have been of great usefulness to it at times, Mallarmé formulated a notion of structure that, though scarcely elaborated on by most of his commentators, represents an interesting alternative.[17] He defined the work of art in terms of rapports or relations, his most succinct phrase being *rhythme de rapports*" ("rhythm of relations"). Analogies like the plant one are eliminated, as is any affirmation about unity or the interdependence of parts. The abstractness of Mallarmé's thinking constitutes its virtue, for he was searching for a concept that would embrace various structures with a temporal dimension: literature, music, dialectic thought. With this in mind, we can see, with whatever elaboration we care to indulge in, the patterns that inform *Les Fleurs du mal*: even heterogeneity, which in a sense is the contrary of unity, furnishes us with a richness of relationships, although their definition might elude us. Ultimately, one could probably, given the variety of these relationships, construct some system by which they would all somehow be at least indirectly connected, but I do not think that kind of demonstration is especially useful to write up or to try to memorize. I am reminded of the (to me) appalling suggestion that one proceed through all of Proust separating the metaphors from the metonymies.

The history of *Les Fleurs du mal* as organic form is incomplete, interrupted as it was by the death of Baudelaire—a nice reminder of the peculiar way literature and the life process are intertwined in such theory. There was to have been a third edition, incorporating poems written since 1861, but since Baudelaire did not live to put it together, the actual third edition was the work of two friends, who crammed the book with poems whose inclusion Baudelaire might not have approved. This edition is generally considered so unsatisfactory that at least one commentator was inspired to invent his own third edition of *Les Fleurs du mal*.[18] Of course, Baudelaire's intentions are not known, and only speculation, such as Feuillerat indulges in, is possible. In any case, none of the poems Baudelaire published after 1861 are so radically different from his preceding work as "Le Voyage." We are left, however, with the frustration of having the condemned pieces and a further group of "Nouvelles Fleurs du mal" forever consigned to the appendices of modern editions. Such are the problems implicit in the theory and practice of organic form.[19]

Notes

1. All citations of *Les Fleurs du mal* are to the Antoine Adam edition (Paris: Garnier, 1959). The translations have been provided by Mona Tobin Houston.

2. See Albert Feuillerat, "L'Architecture des *Fleurs du mal*," in *Studies by Members of the French Department of Yale University* (New Haven: Yale University Press, 1941), pp. 221–330, and D. J. Mossop, *Baudelaire's Tragic Hero: A Study of the Architecture of "Les Fleurs du mal"* (London: Oxford University Press, 1961).

3. The Adam edition of *Les Fleurs du mal* includes a comparative table of the 1857 and 1861 *Fleurs du mal*, as well as Baudelaire's statements about his work and other relevant material.

4. See Paul de Man, "The Rhetoric of Temporality," in *Interpretation, Theory and Practice*, ed. Charles S. Singleton (Baltimore: Johns Hopkins University Press, 1969).

5. See Suzanne Nash, *Les Contemplations of Victor Hugo: An Allegory of the Creative Process* (Princeton: Princeton University Press, 1976), and John Porter Houston, "Design in *Les Contemplations*," *French Forum* 5, no. 2 (May 1980): 122–40.

6. Weather has received some attention in itself. See Arden Reed, *Romantic Weather: The Climates of Coleridge and Baudelaire* (Hanover, N.H.: University Press of New England, 1983).

7. I have discussed at some length the mixture of old and new styles and structures in Baudelaire's poetry. See Houston, *The Demonic Imagination: Style and Theme in French Romantic Poetry* (Baton Rouge: Louisiana State University Press, 1969), pp. 86–117.

8. Louis Maigron, *Le Romantisme et les moeurs* (Paris: Champion, 1910).

9. I am following the summary of organic form in Meyer H. Abrams, *The Mirror and the Lamp: Romantic Theory and the Critical Tradition* (New York: Oxford University Press, 1953), pp. 171–75.

10. See Lloyd James Austin, *L'Univers poétique de Baudelaire* (Paris: Mercure de France, 1956), pp. 92–99.

11. See Ross Chambers, "'Je' dans les "Tableaux parisiens" de Baudelaire," *Nineteenth-Century French Studies* 7, no. 1, 2 (Fall-Winter 1980–81): 59–68, and Arden Reed, "Trois paysages urbains: Les Poèmes liminaires des "Tableaux parisiens," *Modern Philology* 80, no. 4 (May 1983): 372–89.

12. See Erich Auerbach, *Scenes from the Drama of European Literature* (New York: Meridian 1959), pp. 2–24.

13. See Edward K. Kaplan, "Baudelaire and the Battle with Finitude: 'La Mort,' Conclusion of *Les Fleurs du mal*," *French Forum* 4, no. 3 (September 1979): 219–31.

14. See Abrams, *The Mirror and the Lamp*, p. 220.

15. See Jonathan Culler, *The Pursuit of Signs* (Ithaca, N.Y.: Cornell University Press, 1981), pp. 68–70.

16. See Jacques Derrida, *L'Ecriture et la Différence* (Paris: Seuil, 1967), pp. 9–27.

17. See John Porter Houston, *Patterns of Thought in Rimbaud and Mallarmé* (Lexington, Ky.: French Forum Monographs, 1986), pp. 115–18.

18. See Robert-Benoît Chérix, *Commentaire des "Fleurs du mal"* (Geneva: Pierre Cailler, 1949).

19. Other works of interest are Colin Burns, "Notes on the First Edition of *Les Fleurs du mal*," *Nottingham French Studies* 2, no. 1 (May 1963): 14–24, and "Architecture secrète: Notes on the Second Edition of *Les Fleurs du mal*," *Nottingham French Studies* 5, no. 2 (October 1966): 67–79; Marcel A. Ruff, *Baudelaire*, tr. Agnes Kertesz (New York: New York University Press, 1966).

Sandra Daniel

8. *Hérodïade*: The Bound Book

The importance of *Hérodïade* in Stéphane Mallarmé's work cannot be overestimated. His creative existence from his early twenties to a note scribbled the day before his death was cadenced by the composition of this poem.[1] Even the conception of "Le Livre," perhaps the pinnacle of his poetic ambitions, begins with a reference to *Hérodïade*: "l'oeuvre qui sera l'image de ce développement. Trois poèmes en vers dont *Hérodïade* est l'Ouverture" ("the work that will be the image of this development. Three poems in verse, of which *Hérodïade* is the Overture"[2]) (*Correspondence* 1:240). Of the three existing parts of the poem, Mallarmé published only the "Scène" during his life.[3] Yet the fact that he devoted his last years to the composition of a "Prélude" and a "Finale," fragments of which were found among his notes, indicate that he viewed all five parts as forming a coherent whole.

It is this very notion of coherence that has so sharply divided the critics, a division that rests essentially on two main points. First, in spite of Mallarmé's letters to the contrary, the importance of the biblical myth and doctrinal Christianity is upheld by such noteworthy readers as Jean-Pierre Richard and Sylviane Huot and contested by Gardner Davies and Robert Greer Cohn. Second, the presence of opening and ending sections has reinforced the idea of a historical development, supported by Davies and Huot, but contested by Cohn and Derrida.[4] While all agree on the existence of an internal coherence, studies based on theater, phonostylistics (using the letters of "Hérodïade" as a basis), and depth psychology have failed to uncover the relation between the parts.

To these approaches I would like to add another by suggesting that the parts of *Hérodïade* are experimental texts in reading process and that the format of books, one of Mallarmé's favorite topics, may provide a textual means of assessing the coherence of the poem as well as exploring some aspects of Mallarmé's experimentation in the cultural and aesthetic process of reading, the assimilation of *livre* to *lire* or *lyre*.[5] When Mallarmé proposes himself as a "reader" of one of his favorite topics—music, theater, or dance—he consistently presents the problem of reading in terms of the production of a single mental image or representation from a multiplicity of signs. This may be done by reduction: "Un solitaire tacite concert se donne, par la lecture, à l'esprit qui regagne sur une sonorité moindre, la signification: aucun moyen mental exaltant la symphonie, ne manquera, raréfié, et c'est tout—du fait de la pensée" (*OC*, p. 380) ("A solitary concert is given, by reading, to the mind, which regains by means of the least sound, the meaning: no mental means exalting the symphony will be lacking, rarefied, and that's all—as a result of thought"). Or, one may read by the careful analysis of multiple details until an intuitive threshold is reached and one is able to read the whole: "à se demander devant tout pas, chaque attitude si étranges, ces points et taquetés, allongés ou ballons, 'Que peut signifier ceci' ou mieux, d'inspiration, le lire" (*OC*, p. 307) ("to ask oneself of each step, each pose so strange, these points and wedges, lengthened or inflated, 'What might this mean?' or better, by inspiration, to read it"). Or, one may read parts of a text by annotation or the doubling or paralleling of a single detail: "l'orage battant la plume délicieuse de sa toque, voilà le caractère peut-être et l'invention du jeu de ce contemporain qui tire l'instinct parfois indéchiffrable à lui-même des éclairs de scoliaste. Ainsi m'apparaît rendue la dualité morbide qui fait le cas d'Hamlet" (*OC*, p. 302) ("the storm battering the delicious plume of his hat, there is perhaps the character and invention of the strategy of this contemporary who draws the instinct, sometimes undecipherable to himself, from the flashes of the annotator. Thus appeared revealed to me the morbid duality that makes Hamlet's case"). Here, reading is not passive reception but active response resulting in the production of another sign.

This approach suggests that *écriture* and *lecture* are complementary activities involving analogous cognitive processes. There is even the suggestion that they are interactive or capable of modifying each other. Although Mallarmé often complains that his contemporaries do not know how to read (*OC*, p. 386), he views reading as a conditioned process, a set of habits (*OC*, p. 360), or a technique (*OC*, p. 387). As such, reading habits develop and persist because they are adequate to the texts on which they are used (*OC*, p. 360). If readers are to improve, texts must demand more of them; lazy writers make for lazy readers. By means of a subtext, or "miroitement en dessous," as well as the "jeu de correspondences qui confirme la fiction" (*OC*, p. 380) ("the play of interrelationships that confirms [the work's] fictionality"), Mallarmé requires that his reader decipher or decode the text, separating banal, surface intelligibility from meaning. This process he calls "divination," apparently a combination of analysis and intuition, and it applies equally to the reader decoding the text as to the poet, actor, and dancer mastering the means of representation (*OC*, pp. 300, 305).

In a rare schematic description of his own reading of books, Mallarmé wrote: "Par une mentale opération et point d'autre, lecteur je m'adonne à abstraire la physionomie, sans le déplaisir d'un visage exact penché, hors la rampe, sur ma source ou âme. Ses traits réduits à des mots, un maintien le cédant à l'identique disposition de phrase, tout ce pur résultat atteint pour ma délectation noble, s'effarouche d'une interprète" (*OC*, p. 318) ("By a mental operation and no other, reader, I give myself over to abstracting the physiognomy, without the displeasure of an exact face leaning, beyond the footlight, over my source or soul. Its traits reduced to words, a support ceding it to the identical arrangement of the sentence, all this pure result attained for my noble delight, takes offense at an interpreter."). As in the reading of theater, music, and ballet, we see the emphasis on abstraction from surface multiplicity and the subsequent reduction to words as preparation of a sign capable of further interpretation. Yet in terms of books, Mallarmé has added a third element, the disposition or place of the sign in the text. In fact, "divination" in books is also present in the language of printers as part of an internal format: "L'air ou chant sous le texte, conduisant à divination d'ici là, y applique son motif en fleuron et cul-de-lampe invisibles" (*OC*, p. 387) ("The air or song beneath the text, leading to divination in the meantime, places there its motif as an invisible floweret and tailpiece").

In all the arts Mallarmé emphasizes the relationship between reading or interpretation and physical format. The page, orchestra pit, footlight, and stage act as framing devices that set an activity apart as a privileged communication and shape its interpretative mystery. Although format may enter intermittently into the interpretation process of the performing arts, only in books does it appear to function consistently as both frame (*pliage*) and as internal, interpretative fold (*pli*). It is format, or rather the use made of it, that distinguishes different types of printed material. In "Le Livre, instrument spirituel," Mallarmé writes that both the newspaper, or *feuilleton,* and books share *le pliage* and the shadow of black ink on paper. But there the similarity ends, for the newspaper makes no use of its *pliage* and has, therefore, no composition or rhythm and no significant *ombre,* or shadow. The newspaper is classed among the *étalages,* those texts without thickness or depth, whose end-to-end composition is haphazard and incoherent (*OC*, p. 379). Its columnar format induces the reader to adopt a *va-et-vient* ("coming and going") reading technique that requires no interpretive effort.

In contrast to that of newspapers, the *pliage* of books has two functions. First, as the result of the actual folding and binding process, it is synonymous with the rhythm of the text and establishes the "jeu de correspondences" (*OC*, p. 379). It fixes the succession of reading and the place of the work's significant features, thus determining the reader's "divination" or assimilation of the sign's *ombre*. Mallarmé states that the basis of the poet's election is an "instinct des rythmes" ("instinct for rhythms") and that it is this rhythm or internal ordering that becomes the poet's stand-in in the text (*OC*, pp. 366–67). Second, the *pliage* guarantees the mystery or privileged nature of the text and forms the threshold between physical format and interpretation (*OC*, p. 381). The cutting of the folded page releases the text from the subjectivity of the writer, although the *plis* will always keep the original fold marks.

The word *pli* benefits from a double meaning in Mallarmé's work. It is the physical fold of books, fabrics, fans and also the figurative "habit" of the dictionary within Mallarmé's special context of a modification in the veil of the temple (*OC*, p. 360), where *temple* may be read as human consciousness and *fold* as a habit or cognitive crimp in the veils of attitudes or feelings (*OC*, pp. 382, 340, 321), or of surface sensations (*OC*, p. 335). If *pliage* is the physical juncture of writer and reader, *pli* is the point at which personal cognition or representation meets social habits or ingrained attitudes. And, as with *pliage*, both reader and writer meet and participate along the folds of the *pli*. The writer creates a fold from surface intelligibility and its significant subtext. The reader's assimilation begins with this *pli* moving from surface to subtext and then expands by the addition of a personal image or representation along this fold line. This three-dimensional construction of mental functions as temple-veil-fold provides flexibility, for one can read and write along the edge of the fold, within the cylinder of the fold, or around and within the fold. Thus, reading and writing rely on the combined function of *pliage,* placement, and *pli,* sign.

I suggest that *Hérodïade* offers a lesson in reading process that may be described as a progressive displacement of the distinctive feature of the book, the *pli,* and of its corollary, the *pliage*. Each part presents a different alignment of sign and placement. In the "Ouverture ancienne" the *pli* is the channel or conduit that permits reading past and present as an unfolding of similar sounds and image frames. In the "Scène" the prepositional tension between *dans* and *sous* (dans la glace / sous la glace, dans la chevelure / sous la chevelure, etc.) focuses on the intertwinings of identity as present reflection and identity as ancestry, and renders problematic the space, or *pliage,* necessary to accommodate both. In the "Cantique de Saint Jean" the *pli* and *pliage* exist within the allegorical relationship of the poem to its anecdotes, to which it stands as a sign.

In the "Ouverture ancienne," which begins the published version of *Hérodïade*, the reader follows a description of Hérodïade's room given by her nurse. One moves from the window to the tapestry on the wall, to the dress of the nurse, to the bed, to an analogy of the bed and the book, and then to the problem facing Hérodïade, her unwillingness to accept and conform to her roles as woman and priestess. The reader becomes accustomed to movement in space from far to near. This spatial progression is accompanied by a temporal progression: the dress of the nurse grows out of the tapestry, itself depicting an ancient sibyl, and the milk of the nurse has succored the "child," Hérodïade, in a seemingly unbroken ancestral line. Themes of nourishment, apprenticeship, and teaching combine to suggest the transmission of knowledge from one generation to the next. The constant movement from background to foreground and from past to present establishes the reader's impression of a series of rectangular, interlocking frames, each with an opening, or *ouverture,* into the next. Hérodïade's problem, however, is her inability to add to this pattern, in a word, to write:

> L'eau morne se résigne
> Que ne visite plus la plume ni le cygne
> Inoubliable:
>
> (*OC*, p. 41)

> The dismal water resigns itself
> That neither the pen [*or* the feather] nor the swan visit
> anymore
> Unforgettable:

The pertinent stylistic features are repetition of images, *plume, pli* (tapestry, dress, mind, shroud, bedsheets, dreams), and phonemic recalls, of which the most often noted is the presence of *v,* as in the lines "Le vieil éclat voilé du vermeil insolite / De la voix languissante, nulle, sans acolyte" (*OC*, p. 42) ("The old, veiled splendor of the rosy fleeting / Of the languishing voice, void, without [a] follower [*or* accomplice]"). Both emphasize the successiveness of reading and encourage the reader to turn spatial and temporal differences into similarities by reading each frame as a simple evolution of the *pli* or each *v* image as an unfolding of the letter. The overall effect is one of continuity. The interlocking qualities of both techniques give the sensation of a piling up of frames, of a certain thickness, admirably expressed in the last lines:

> Sur l'enfant exilée en son coeur précieux
> Comme un cygne cachant en sa plume ses yeux,
> Comme le mit le vieux cygne en sa plume, allée
> De la plume détresse, en l'éternelle allée
> De ses espoirs pour voir les diamants élus
> D'une étoile mourante, et qui ne brille plus.
>
> (*OC*, p. 43)

> On the exiled child in her precious heart
> Like a swan hiding its eyes in its feather [*or* pen],
> As did the old swan in its feather [pen], path
> Of the anguished feather [pen], in the eternal path
> Of her [its] hopes to see the chosen diamonds
> Of a dying star that shines no more.

The oral mode of transmission ("voix du passé," évocation," "incantation") and the similarity of technique between representation (repeated images) and placement (repeated phonemes) suggest a text that folds back upon itself in a series of *plis* and *replis* maintained by the "path of the feather [pen]" or the act of reading and teaching as simple transmission. The *pli* as a channel or conduit connects past to present, background to foreground, as an effect of memory or recall. The *pli-repli* metaphor encompasses both intelligence and instinct and suggests that the "Ouverture ancienne" is a genetic text or *grimoire* ("instinctual script") out of which other texts grow. As with music, the instrumentation of the text invites and challenges one to create; it "défie la civilisation négligeant de construire à son rêve, afin qu'elles aient lieu, la Salle prodigieuse et la Scène" (*OC*, p. 334) ("defies civilization neglecting to construct according to its dream in order that the wondrous Theater and Stage happen.")

Assimilation of such a text is based upon the assumption of a parallelism between writing and speaking. The repeated use of the *pli* image suggests the redundancy of speech and the phonemic recalls recreate the phonetic processing of the spoken word. Charles Fries,[6] following the studies of Bloomfield, offered a theory of reading which asserts that reading, like listening, is a primary activity and that the process is simply one of matching the graphic representation and the spoken word. If we are to take the priestess Hérodïade as an example, this technique is not entirely successful because it provides only for the reception of the text but not for a response. The "Ouverture ancienne" shows that coherence can be maintained by sound and tone alone, as in music. Yet, with the possible exception of Wagner, the only response in music is the silence of the audience. Although phonemic techniques appear in other works, nowhere are they present to the same extent as in the early pieces. I suggest that Mallarmé experimented with ever more complex and active notions of the assimilation of texts.

The second section of the poem, the "Scène," is a dialogue between the Nurse and Hérodïade, which probably accounts for its theatrical title. Textually, however, the drama of Hérodïade's desire for independence in the cold, metallic world of her ancestors is played against the backdrop of the "Ouverture ancienne." She has "read" the nurse's book, and in her response the same themes and questions of the "Ouverture ancienne" reappear in the "Scène." Hérodïade's mockery of the nurse is presented as a parody of the nurse's style with the same images and phonemic recalls:

selon qui, des calices
De mes robes, arôme aux farouches délices,
Sortirait le frisson blanc de ma nudité,
Prophétise que si le tiède azur d'été,
Vers lui nativement la femme se dévoile,

Me voit dans ma pudeur grelottante d'étoile,
Je meurs!

(*OC*, p. 47).

according to whom, from the calices
Of my robes, aroma of unsociable [*or* fierce] delights,
Would leave the white shudder of my nudity,
Prophesies that if the lukewarm dawn of summer,
Toward which naturally the woman unveils herself,
Sees me in my shivering, starry modesty,
I will die!

Even when Hérodïade ceases to mock the nurse and speaks of her own desires, she returns unconsciously to the phonemic recalls of the "Ouverture ancienne," including the insistence on the letter *v*:

Mais avant, si tu veux, clos les volets, l'azur
Séraphique sourit dans les vitres profondes,
Et je déteste, moi, le bel azur!

(*OC*, p. 48)

But, first, if you would, close the shutters, the seraphic dawn
Smiles in the profound windows
And I detest, I do, the beautiful dawn!

These intratextual references establish the "Ouverture ancienne" as a subtext of the "Scène." Unable to break with the earlier script or to erase it as a palimpsest, Hérodïade parodies and argues with it. The reader senses the tension between the surface commentary and the unvoiced poem just beneath it in the temporal and spatial shifts of perspective produced by the drawing in of a text that is external and anterior to the present drama.[7]

Early in the "Scène," Hérodïade explains her trips to the tombs of her ancestors: "Le sais-je? tu m'as vue, ô nourrice d'hiver, / Sous la lourde prison de pierres et de fer" (*OC*, p. 44) ("Do I know? you saw me, o winter nurse, / Under the heavy prison of stones and iron"). *Sous la lourde prison* is ungrammatical but may be understood by displacement. A reader who chooses the image may substitute *pierre tombale* ("tombstone") for *prison de pierres* but this substitution loses the sense of confinement. Or, a reader may choose to substitute *dans* for *sous* and, in so doing, lose the allusion to tomb and death. The attempt to analyze this line raises the problem of representation of a multifaceted image, Hérodïade-Nurse, "Ouverture ancienne"–"Scène," the "clair regard du diamant" ("the clear gaze of the diamond"), within the mime of language.

The textual center of this problem is Hérodïade's speech as she looks at herself in a basin of water. It begins with a metaphor for internal vision: the water "frozen" by ennui, the memories of her past as *feuilles,* or leaves, *sous la glace* ("under the ice or glass"). Yet the following lines shift the perspective from internal memory to external reflection: "des soirs, dans ta sévère fontaine, / J'ai de mon rêve épars connu la nudité!" (*OC*, p. 45) ("some evenings, in your severe fountain, / I have known the nudity of my scattered dream!"). If the reader chooses to resolve the images, assimilation is possible only by shifting the connotation of the nouns, "in your ice, under your ice; in your mirror, under your mirror; in your window, under your window. Satisfying as a resolution because such linguistic shifts reflect Hérodïade's psychological changes, the resulting partial images cannot be reduced to a unit. Bound to a common sign, *glace,* the connotations are mutually exclusive and thus create no *ombre,* no "silent object" (*OC*, p. 400), or illusion that equals the vision of the thing.

Barbara Johnson, in her discussion of referentiality in Mallarmé, writes: "Mallarmé's famous obscurity lies not in his devious defogging of the obvious but in his radical tranformation of intelligibility itself through the ceaseless production of seemingly mutually exclusive readings of the same piece of language. Reference is here not denied but suspended."[8] In the "Scène," language does not evoke Hérodïade, but mimes her inability to represent herself. As Hérodïade's parody of the nurse does not recreate the "Ouverture," but is rather a commentary on it, so Hérodïade's self-presentation does not represent her, but is an annotation to a text that remains in suspense beneath her words.

In her attempt to achieve perspective and to find a position from which to align both past and present conceptions of her identity, Hérodïade collapses time into space using isolated images to produce coherence and then reads the images as two-dimensional reflections. The hair reflects history as weapons and arms present in her bedchamber; her dress occasions the linguistic parody of the nurse's past language; the basin reflects both past and present images. The problem, however, is not the image as space, but the linguistic space of reading and writing, a plastic space in which *dans ta glace* and *sous ta glace* could exist. Here, format is critical, for if we are to follow Mallarmé and "read according to the page" (*OC*, p. 387), it makes a difference if "page" means the two-dimensional folio or the multidimensional folded sheet, or *feuillet.*

Opposed to the speaking and reading analogy of Charles Fries, Ignatius Mattingly asserts that reading is not a primary linguistic activity, but is a secondary activity based upon speaking and listening.[9] Processing occurs in two analysis-by-synthesis loops, one inside the other. The first loop analyzes and synthesizes the phonological and semantic levels of the written text in terms of the spoken language, while the second loop reworks this information in terms of the syntactical and contextual rules of the written language. Hérodïade has mastered the first loop, in that she can imitate and modify the nurse's script, but she is unable to complete the second loop and master the rules of syntax and context. Jacques Schérer, emphasizing the importance of the spoken word for Mallarmé, wrote: "le problème des rapports entre le parlé et l'écrit est fondamental pour la compréhension de son oeuvre" ("the problem of the relationship between the spoken word and the written one is fundamental for the comprehension of his work").[10] Hérodïade's error as a beginning writer is, not her reliance on the spoken word, but her incomplete linguistic awareness of the difference between speech and writing. She remains unaware that the act of speaking produces a multilevel space structured and contoured by voice control, physiological cues, and repetitions that background and foreground the words. In a written text, such a space must be created linguistically. Although bound to the nurse's text, Hérodïade is unaware of it as background and writes as if she were using a flat sheet rather than a folded page. She makes no use of the temporal and spatial functions of *pliage* either as the merger of text and subtext or as the internal dispersal of images throughout the reading sequence.[11]

In the "Cantique de Saint Jean" the text seems transparent in that the more obvious language signals are absent. And yet an action occurs almost visually on the page. The reader is faced with a balanced series of images describing ascension and descension that becomes a crescendo ending with the enigmatic verse "Penche un salut" (*OC*, p. 49) ("Bow your head [*or* Raise your glass]"). Its puzzling quality does not stem from an ungrammatical relationship but from conflicting intuitions that these words are semantically incompatible but entirely fitting given the preceding context of balanced ascending and descending images.

If the reader resolves the final verse as a variant of *pencher,* the line may evoke a movement of greeting, *incliner la tête*. Or, if a reader chooses *salut* as the starting point, the movement of a toast, *lever un verre,* may come forth. In either instance, the line is read as a unit, and the mental representation created is an image capable of generating a new reading of each of the preceding images. Language produces a sign and resembles the "corporeal writing" of the dancer: "alors, par un commerce dont paraît son sourire verser le secret, sans tarder, elle te livre à travers le voile dernier qui toujours reste, la nudité de tes concepts et silencieusement écrira ta vision à la façon d'un Signe qu'elle est" (*OC*, p. 307) ("thus, by means of a commerce of which her smile appears to reveal the secret, without tarrying, she gives you through the last veil that always remains, the nudity of your concepts and silently will write your vision in the manner of a Sign that she is"). The sign is a transparent simulation of the idea, but it is also a translation or transposition permitting the reader to act or write a new script. The poem-sign remains central but stands in allegorical relationship to the reader's text. "Quand s'isole pour le regard un signe de l'éparse beauté générale, fleur, onde, nuée et bijou etc. si, chez nous le seul moyen exclusif de le savoir consiste à en juxtaposer l'aspect à notre nudité spirituelle afin qu'elle le sente analogue et se l'adapte dans quelque confusion exquise d'elle avec cette forme envolée" (*OC*, p. 295) ("When a sign is isolated for our notice from the scattered general beauty, flower, wave, cloud and jewel, etc., if, within us, the only exclusive means to know it consists in juxtaposing an aspect of it to our spiritual nudity in order that we feel its similarity and adapt ourselves to it in some exquisite confusion with this vanished form").

At this point dance and language become capable of that magical act of transposition, or *translatio*[12] where incorporeal sounds become concrete fabrics, where fixed stage sets are replaced by "la mobilité choréographique" of the mind, where "la scène libre, au gré de fictions, exhalée du jeu d'un voile avec attitudes et gestes, devient le très pur résultat" (*OC*, p. 309) ("the free stage, following the will of fictions, exhaled from the play of a veil with attitudes and gestures, becomes the very pure result"). Here even the sign is erased and the poem has become *planche* ("stage"), or pure format. Reversed is our original conception of *pli* and *pliage* where the *pli,* or image, becomes sign as it is dispersed throughout the text by *pliage,* or structure. In the "Cantique de Saint Jean" the image is both sign and dispersion; it "deposits" itself as a sign capable of semiotic development. The *pliage,* or purified structure, remains as the poet's legacy or gift to the reader freed from habit or conditioning. The poet abandons the usual role of writer-interpreter for the liberating stance of writer-choreographer, the creator of a new *grimoire,* or book of initial rhythms.

With the title, the reader may consider the biblical anecdote as the text behind the poem and read this action as an allegory of decapitation. But without the title, there is no reason to even consider this anecdote and the "Cantique de Saint Jean" may equally refer to the change in the poet's vocation and to the "cutting off" and freeing of both writer and reader:

> Mais selon un baptême
> Illuminée au même
> Principe qui m'élut
> Penche un salut.
>
> (*OC*, p. 49)

> But according to a baptism
> Illuminated by the same
> Principle that elected me
> Bow your head [*or* Raise your glass].

We need only consider that the *principe* that elects the poet is an instinct for rhythms and that rhythm, the work's format, or *pliage,* permits the *disparîtion élocutoire du poète* ("the oratorical disappearance of the poet") in order to see in this last line the poet as he doffs his hat (bows her head) in greeting (health, victory) to the reader who has intuited the poem as both representation and performance, as *Scène et Salle*.

The treatment of *Hérodïade* as a study in the format of books suggests that as the *feuillet* tends toward the folio, the reading process is modified accordingly. Mallarmé never loses sight of the genetic script, the *gynetexte* of primary literary activity, speaking and listening. Yet reading is not an oral activity, and different linguistic strategies exist to induce even clever readers to frame the text in certain ways. A creature of many functions, the book often appears as a *volume quelconque* ("a nondescript book"), a cultural storehouse, or a didactic tool. When associated with learning or teaching, *lire* ("reading") suggests the existence of bindings, constraints, and the fixed frames of the book's covers. But as the *instrument mental par excellence* ("superior mental instrument"), as the theater for representing the world, as the *vol d'une flamme* ("flight of a flame"), the *parallélisme des feuilles* ("parallelism of the pages") becomes an invitation to reading as mobility, to the freedom of semiotic production, to the vibration of a multiplicity of signs and a challenge to the reader to assimilate, to interpret, and to write. *Lyre* (speaker and writer) is backed by its homonym *lire* (listener and reader). The ideal reader must "perform" at all levels: in the assimilation or reduction that shows comprehension of the text; in its interpretation or enactment; and in the internalization of its rhythm or structure so that the reader, joining the author, adds new signs to the universal rhythm that is The Book.

Notes

1. Stéphane Mallarmé, *Correspondence* in three volumes: vol. 1, ed. H. Mondor and J.-P. Richard (Paris: Gallimard, 1959); vols. 2 and 3, ed. H. Mondor and L. J. Austin (Paris: Gallimard, 1965, 1969). The first letter concerning *Hérodïade* is dated October 1864, *Correspondence*, 1:174. The last reference appears as the last text in *Correspondence*, vol. 3.

2. All translations are the author's.

3. The "Scène" ("Scene") appeared in the *Parnasse contemporain* in 1871. The "Ouverture ancienne" ("Former overture") and the "Cantique de Saint Jean" ("Canticle of Saint John") appeared in posthumous collections. See the publication history of the fragments in Stéphane Mallarmé, *Oeuvres complètes*, ed. H. Mondor and G. Jean-Aubry (Paris: Gallimard, 1945), pp. 1440–48. (All further citations will be to this edition and will appear in the text as *OC*, followed by the page number.)

4. Jean-Pierre Richard, *L'Univers imaginaire de Mallarmé* (Paris: Seuil, 1961); Sylviane Huot, *Le "Mythe d'Hérodïade" chez Mallarmé: Genèse et Evolution* (Paris: Nizet, 1977); Gardner Davies, *Les Noces d'Hérodïade: Mystère* (Paris: Gallimard, 1959); Robert Greer Cohn, "New Approaches to *Hérodïade*," *Romanic Review* 72, no. 4 (1981): 472–81. Cohn, "New Approaches," pp. 472–73. Jacques Derrida, "The Double Session," in *Dissemination*, translated with an introduction and additional notes by Barbara Johnson (Chicago: University of Chicago Press, 1981), pp. 270–71.

5. All of these questions come to the fore in Mallarmé's notes and fragments for *Le Livre*. This multivolume work was to have been presented to the elite as theatrical enactments by the poet, who would have interpreted the analogies between the parts and the multiple interpretations of the texts. The public, however, was to have received the bound volumes in which, without the presence of the poet, coherence and interpretation became problematic. See Jacques Schérer, *Le "Livre" de Mallarmé: Premières recherches sur des documents inédits* (Paris: Gallimard, 1957).

6. Charles C. Fries, *Linguistics and Reading* (New York: Holt, Rinehart and Winston, 1963), pp. 121–32. Although this theory of reading is generally doubted today, Mallarmé's interest in the symbolic value of letters, the poem as hieroglyph, and his view of the poem as the expansion of a letter indicate that he entertained a link between the word and its graphic representation.

7. In addition to context, the aroma of the dress, the basin, the candle opposed to the light of dawn, as well as actual echos of the "Ouverture ancienne" appear in the "Scène."

8. Barbara Johnson, "Poetry and Performative Language: Mallarmé and Austin," in her *The Critical Difference: Essays in the Contemporary Rhetoric of Reading* (Baltimore: Johns Hopkins University Press, 1980), p. 65.

9. Ignatius G. Mattingly, "Reading, the Linguistic Process, and Linguistic Awareness," in *Language by Ear and by Eye*, ed. J. F. Kavanaugh and I. G. Mattingly (Cambridge, Mass.: MIT Press, 1972), pp. 133–47.

10. Jacques Schérer, *Grammaire de Mallarmé* (Paris: Nizet, 1977), p. 65.

11. For discussions of the four-sided nature of the interpretive process from different points of view, see Cohn, "New Approaches," p. 472, and Derrida, "The Double Session," pp. 260 ff.

12. This section on reading as performance owes much to the article by Albert Sonnenfeld, "Mallarmé: The Poet as Actor as Reader," in *Yale French Studies*, 1976: pp. 159–72.

Suzanne Nash

9. Apollinaire's *Alcools* and the Disorder of Modernity

Many Apollinaire critics have looked for the underlying unity of *Alcools*, but without very satisfying results. Their failure to find a convincing argument for a logic governing the collection's architecture may be due to the fact that they have generally proceeded on the assumption that the poet himself, at the moment of ordering, had a coherent view of his own project. I am not at all certain this was the case for Apollinaire in 1913. In fact I believe the organization of *Alcools* into a collection can be seen as a destructive rather than a constructive gesture, in that it enacts a further subversion of the symbolist ideal of ultimate unity already only precariously in place in many of the individual poems written at an earlier date. As in the analytical phase of cubist painting, the collection's ironic juxtapositions multiply the perspective from which one can read individual poems, leaving the reader with the sense of being caught in a directionless vortex, rich in images of contradictory value. This breaking up of perspective does not, however, take place with the violence and coldhearted certainty other avant-gardists like the futurists or surrealists would show. In fact, the poet never breaks unequivocally with the past. One hears his hesitation in "Zone," when after proclaiming: "A la fin tu es las de ce monde ancien" (*OP*, p. 39) ("In the end you are weary of this ancient world—*A*, p. 3"),[1] he turns immediately to an ancient figure of pastoral and the nostalgia of apostrophe to characterize the achievements of technology: "Bergère ô tour Eiffel le troupeau des ponts bêle ce matin" (*OP*, p. 39) ("Shepherdess O Eiffel Tower your flock of bridges is bleating this morning"—*A*, p. 3). Even in "La Jolie rousse" (The pretty redhead) when he insists upon the brotherhood of contemporary artists as adventurers in rebellion against tradition, he begs for his public's indulgence in the language of Catholic liturgy, "Pitié pour nous qui combattons toujours aux frontières / De l'illimité et de l'avenir / Pitié pour nos erreurs pitié pour nos péchés"

(*OP*, p. 314) ("Pity us who fight always at the boundaries / of infinity and the future / Pity our errors pity our sins"—*Ca*, p. 345).

Apollinaire's "tradition" was not that of a previous aesthetics of discontinuity—as it would be for the avant-garde of the 1960s, for example, when surrealism was already constitutive of that tradition—but one that still drew on a learned past to reveal its resonances with the language of the present. Only a few outsiders, rare men—poets, artists, musicians—could still make that connection for a public increasingly attracted by the allure of mass culture. The iconoclasm of the cult of technology was that it glorified a worldview that could sweep away man's significance as an individual, and Apollinaire was never fully ready to make that gesture. If *Alcools* presents an anguished and confused leave-taking with the past, the poems written between 1914 and 1916, later to be published in *Calligrammes*, reflect a utopian effort to reconcile these past values with the techniques that threatened to make them obsolete. But my concern here is with *Alcools* and the compelling nature of its uncertainties, rather than with later reconciliations. Briefly put, I believe that Apollinaire's concept of "the new art" shifted significantly sometime between 1912 and 1914, and that the ambivalent feelings resulting from this change account for the emotional intensity and even incoherence that has caused *Alcools*, more than any of his other works, to survive beyond its particular high-modernist moment.

The shift in Apollinaire's concept of what constitutes the modernism of modern art can be clearly demonstrated through a comparison of the aesthetic values put forth in his art criticism written from 1902 to 1913 with certain key formulations in "L'Esprit nouveau et les poètes" (The new spirit and the poets), published in the *Mercure de France* in 1918.[2] But too stark a comparison would be misleading, since, as I hope to show, contradictions are already present in some of the articles written in 1913, contemporaneously with the publication of *Alcools*. This change corresponds to the shift from an aestheticist view of art as an autonomous model of an invisible and sacred world order to a materialist view of art as an open-ended, perhaps even transitory, expression of historical change—art as artillery—as Apollinaire saw it in the early years of the war.[3] Both of these views coexist in a more obviously unresolved way in *Alcools* than in the art essays, and place Apollinaire's poetic practice in 1913 ahead of, or at odds with, his theory at that time. I do not believe, however, that this change ever signalled Apollinaire's uncompromising adherence to a revolutionary position vis-à-vis the society of his time. Instead, it indicated his desire to be the bard of a wonderful new age, just begun, in a language appropriate to the particular beauty and force of that age.[4] If there is violence, it is in the clash between Apollinaire's attachment to mystical values inherited from a romantic and symbolist past, which he understood needed new forms of expression in the rapidly changing mechanized world of modern Europe, and his premonition that these new forms of expression might constitute the very means by which those values might be destroyed.

When Apollinaire first began writing his art criticism, he did so, not to break with official culture, but because he believed that acceptance by the liberal cultural institutions of his time would ensure his painter-friends' public acceptance. His avowed purpose as publicist of the cubist painters was to help them gain acceptance into the Salon des Indépendents, which had by then usurped the prestige of the official salon.[5] He would do this by explaining the seriousness of their purpose and vision to the contemporary public. For him these works confirm, in a new, properly contemporary light (the light of conceptualization rather than imitation), the essential order and meaningfulness—"purity, unity, truth"—of the human spirit. He sees their break with tradition as purely formal in nature, a break with an aesthetics of imitation and the convention of three-dimensional perspective that had achieved only an incomplete rendering of that spirit. The development of cubist art, he claimed in "Réalité, peinture pure" (Reality, pure painting), 1912, was toward a more complete embodiment of that spirit—indeed, toward the direct representation of reality, what he called *pure* expression, light on the canvas, unmediated by style. "La lumière n'est pas un procédé, elle glisse vers nous, elle nous est communiqué par notre sensibilité. . . . En effet, ce sont nos yeux qui transmettent à notre âme des sensations perçues dans la nature" (*Ch*, p. 268) ("Light is not a method, it slides towards us, it is communicated to us by our sensibility. . . . In fact, it is our eyes that transmit the sensations perceived in nature to our soul"—*AA*, p. 264). For this almost mysical ideal, represented by the work of Robert Delaunay, he coined the term *Orphic cubism*.

All of Apollinaire's pre–World War I essays claim for art a synoptic or totalizing function that bears witness to the apotheosis of the godlike subjectivity creating it: "le peintre doit avant tout se donner le spectacle de sa propre divinité et les tableaux qu'il offre à l'admiration des hommes leur conférèrent la gloire d'exercer aussi et momentanément leur propre divinité." ("Sur la peinture" [1912], (*ME*, p. 47) ("above all, the painter must contemplate his own divinity, and the pictures which he offers to the admiration of men will confer upon them, likewise, the glory of exercising their divinity—if only for a moment"—"On Painting," *CP*, p. 10). In the words cited by Apollinaire of Delaunay himself, "Le créateur tient compte de tout ce qui se trouve dans l'univers par entité, succession, imagination, et simultanéité. . . . le sujet est éternel dans l'oeuvre d'art . . . l'expression pure de la nature humaine" (*Ch*, p. 269) ("The creator takes note of everything that exists in the universe through entity, succession, imagination, and simultaneity. . . . The subject is eternal in the work of art . . . the pure expression of human nature"—(*AA*, pp. 264–65). In "La Peinture moderne" (Modern painting), 1913, Apollinaire claims that cubism is less fragmented, more complete, than realism or naturalism, because it includes a multiplicity of elements from ordinary life seen from many perspectives simultaneously and dignified by the presence of the creative subjectivity that has saved them from the chaos of contingency through his ordering consciousness: "Ces matériaux étranges, bruts et disparates devenaient nobles parce que l'artiste leur insufflait sa personnalité à la fois robuste et délicates" (*Ch*, p. 273) ("These strange, rough, and disparate materials became ennobled because the artist endowed them with his own strong and sensitive personality"—(*AA*, p. 269). The ideal new art of the "fourth dimension," he tells us in "Sur la peinture," is a figuration of the infinite: "Telle qu'elle s'offre à l'esprit, du point de vue plastique, la quatrième dimension serait engendrée par les trois mesures connues: elle figure l'immensité de l'espace s'éternisant dans toutes les directions à un moment déterminé. Elle est l'espace même, la dimension de l'infini; c'est elle qui doue de plasticité les objets. Elle leur donne les proportions qu'ils méritent dans l'oeuvre, tandis que, dans l'art grec par exemple, un rythme en quelque sorte mécanique détruit sans cesse les proportions" (*ME*, p. 52) ("Regarded from the plastic point of view, the fourth dimension appears to spring from the three known dimensions: it represents the immensity of space eternalizing itself in all directions at any given moment. It is space itself, the dimension of the infinite; the fourth dimension endows objects with plasticity. It gives the object its right proportions on the whole, whereas in Greek art, for instance, a somewhat mechanical rhythm constantly destroys the proportions"—*CP*, pp. 13–14). According to this description, the work of art functions in precisely the same way as the symbol did for Goethe or Coleridge—as "the translucence of the eternal through and in the temporal."[6] At this stage in Apollinaire's theorizing about art, collage is not a reminder of the arbitrary intrusion of life into art or of the way the dislodged debris of lowbrow culture challenge the comforting illusion of harmony that high art depicts, as later critics of cubism such as Clement Greenberg would claim. Rather, the juxtaposition of anomalous objects stands as a reminder of the secret unity of all things.[7] The artist in the Georges Braque essay of 1908 is seen as a self-enclosed mystic speaking or painting from a privileged perspective. The new art is not future-oriented, but representative of a permanent, essential order, and it is superior to life in its ordinary manifestations. In his 1912 essay on the futurists, Apollinaire even goes so far as to refute these artists' claim to a radical break with the institution of art in order to reintegrate them into a tradition of art history that extends back to the middle ages. He begins his article with the sentence, "M. Marinetti veut jouer de notre temps en Italie le rôle de restaurateur des arts que saint François d'Assise y joua autrefois" (*Ch*, p. 213) ("M. Marinetti wants to play for our time the same role of restorer of the arts in Italy that St. Francis of Assisi played in times gone by"—*AA*, p. 200). This is not just a playful thrust at the nationalistic, anti-Catholic Italian avant-garde who did not want to recognize their debt to the French cubists, but the sign of Apollinaire's deep-felt reverence for the traditions of the past. Many of his articles begin with an effort to place the cubist works in an art-historical rather than a social, economic, or political perspective.

Occasionally, but very rarely in these pre–World War I texts, Apollinaire seems to have an intuition that art may have a more immediate social function to fulfill. This is especially true for the essays written around the time of publication of *Alcools*. In his 1913 revision of the 1905 Picasso essay, for example, one finds a clear emphasis on the importance of the medium of expression for its own sake, and with that, a certain consciousness of the connection of production to social change. Consistent with this awareness, the artist is seen as *homo faber* rather than demigod.

> Les mosaïstes peignent avec des marbres ou des bois de couleur. On a mentionné un peintre italien qui peignait avec des matières fécales; sous la Revolution française, quelqu'un peignit avec du sang. On peut peindre avec ce qu'on voudra, avec des pipes, des timbres-poste, des cartes postales, ou à jouer, des candélabres, des morceaux de toile cirée, des faux cols.
>
> Il me suffit, à moi, de voir le travail, il faut qu'on voie le travail, c'est par la quantité de travail fournie par l'artiste que l'on mesure la valeur d'une oeuvre d'art. *Ch*, p. 291)

> Mosaicists paint with pieces of marble or colored wood. Mention has been made of an Italian painter who painted with fecal matter; at the time of the French Revolution, someone who painted with blood. They can paint with whatever they wish—pipes, postage stamps, postcards or playing cards, candelabras, pieces of oil cloth, starched collars.
>
> For me, it is enough to see the work, one must be able to see the work. It is the amount of work accomplished by the artist that determines the value of the work of art. (*AA*, p. 281)

Similarly, in the Georges Braque essay of 1913 he no longer sees Braque as an ivory-tower artist, but as a man of his time, whose training as housepainter taught him an appropriately contemporary use of materials: "Ce n'est pas le moindre mérite de l'art qui se manifesta, en 1908, dans une oeuvre de Georges Braque, que de s'accorder avec la société où il évolue. . . . le métier de l'artisan, du peintre en bâtiment devrait être pour l'artiste la plus vigoureuse expression matérielle de la peinture" (*ME*, pp. 69–70) ("And it is not the least merit of the work Braque showed in 1908, that it was in accord with the society in which the painter was evolving. . . . the means of the artisan, of the house painter, should be the most vigorous material expression of painting to the artist"—*CP*, pp. 24–25). In part 5 of "Sur la peinture" (1913) Apollinaire has the insight that will place in question in a much more fundamental way his premises regarding the function of modern art: "Les grands poètes et les grands artistes ont pour fonction sociale de renouveler sans cesse l'apparence que revêt la nature aux yeux des hommes. Sans les poètes, sans les artistes . . . l'ordre qui paraît dans la nature et qui n'est qu'un effet de l'art s'évanouirait aussitôt. Tout se déferait dans le chaos. . . . Les poètes et les artistes déterminent de concert la figure de leur époque et docilement l'avenir se range à leur avis" (*ME*, p. 53) ("It is the social function of great poets and artists to renew continually the appearance nature has for the eyes of men. Without poets, without artists . . . the order which we find in nature, and which is only an effect of art, would at once vanish. Everything would break up in chaos. . . . Poets and artists plot the characteristics of their epoch, and the future docilely falls in with their desires"—*CP*, pp. 14–15). Here "great" art no longer reflects a permanent order, but, through the power of its essentially "imperialistic" techniques, it creates the illusion of that permanence for a docile public.[8]

But it will not be until after his return to Paris from the war that we see a more fully articulated break with the aestheticizing art theory of the pre–World War I articles. In "L'Esprit nouveau et les poètes" Apollinaire demands in the declamatory tones of the manifesto, quite different from the descriptive and often highly poeticized style of the journalistic pieces, that art play a collaborative role with other disciplines in the reconstruction of society. "L'esprit nouveau est avant tout ennemi de l'esthétisme, des formules et de tout snobisme. Il ne lutte point contre quelque école que ce soit, car il ne veut pas être une école, mais un des grands courants de la littérature englobant toutes les écoles, depuis le symbolisme et le naturisme. Il lutte pour le rétablissement de l'esprit d'initiative, pour la claire compréhension de son temps et pour ouvrir des vues nouvelles sur l'univers extérieur et intérieur qui ne soient point inférieurs à celles que les savants de toutes catégories découvrent chaque jour et dont ils tirent des merveilles" ("EN," p. 395–96) ("The new spirit is above all the enemy of estheticism, of formulae, and of cultism. It attacks no school whatever, for it does not wish to be a school, but rather one of the great currents of literature encompassing all schools since symbolism and naturalism. It fights for the reestablishment of the spirit of initiative, for the clear understanding of its time, and for the opening of new vistas on the exterior and interior universes which are not inferior to those which scientists of all categories discover every day and from which they extract endless marvels"—"E," p. 237). The artist no longer inhabits a private realm of essential forms, but is asked to join forces with the practicing engineers of a new technological society.

> Déjà, la langue scientifique est en désaccord profond avec celle des poètes. C'est un état de choses insupportable. Les mathématiciens ont le droit de dire que leurs rêves, leurs préoccupations dépassent

> souvent de cent coudées les imaginations rampantes des poètes. C'est aux poètes à décider s'ils ne veulent point entrer résolument dans l'esprit nouveau, hors duquel il ne reste d'ouvertes que trois portes: celle des pastiches, celle de la satire et celle de la lamentation, si sublime soit-elle. Peut-on forcer la poésie à se cantonner hors de ce qui l'entoure, à méconnaître la magnifique exubérance de vie que les hommes par leur activité ajoutent à la nature et qui permet de machiner le monde de la façon la plus incroyable? ("EN," p. 396)

> Already, scientific language is out of tune with that of the poets. It is an intolerable state of affairs. Mathematicians have the right to say that their dreams, their preoccupations, often outdistance by a hundred cubits the crawling imaginations of poets. It is up to the poets to decide if they will not resolutely embrace the new spirit, outside of which only three doors remain open: that of pastiche, that of satire, and that of lamentation, however sublime it be. Can poetry be forced to establish itself outside of what surrounds it, to ignore the magnificent exuberance of life which the activities of men are adding to nature and which allow the world to be mechanized in an incredible fashion? (p. 237)

An authentically modernist art should bear self-conscious witness to its experimentation with available materials. Surprise will be its basic mechanism, and a relativistic, even practical concept of creativity will replace mystical formulations of the beautiful as the "true," the "one," and the "pure." "Les poètes modernes sont avant tout les poètes de la vérité toujours nouvelle" ("EN," p. 393) ("Modern poets are above all singers of a constantly new truth"—"E," p. 235). Rather than an art that looks back to tradition for its moorings, it will be an art aimed toward the future, and ready at all times to cut free of the past. Il suffit que l'on soit aventureur et que l'on aille à la découverte" ("EN," p. 392) ("It is enough that one be adventuresome and pursue any new discovery"—"E," p. 234). Finally, art must be ethnic, situated in its national, historical moment, rather than universalizing and abstract.

Peter Burger, following Marcuse, sees this shift away from aestheticism typical of much early twentieth-century art as crucial for the eventual politicization of the avant-garde. In isolating art from the praxis of daily life or the work of art from the institution of art, proponents of an aesthetics that claims autonomy for the art object protect from any effective questioning the bourgeois society they claim to reject. Principles of organicity, harmony, autonomy, subordination of part to whole provide an "imagined satisfaction of individual needs that are repressed in daily praxis" and "art thus stabilizes the very social conditions against which it protests" (pp. 11–12). When these aesthetic values are challenged, and "negation of synthesis becomes a compositional principle" (p. 79), when shock is introduced to break the illusion of a logic of cause and effect, or techniques such as collage and montage are exploited to remind us of the fragmented nature of real life, then we see the birth of an authentic, i.e., politicized, avant-garde.[9] Although Apollinaire perceived himself as a belated apologist rather than an enemy of the new production-oriented society of his time, it is not surprising that later, more radically revolutionary avant-garde movements would claim him as a predecessor. The new antiaestheticizing impulse to dislodge, interrupt, and challenge that can be heard in the excited tone of "L'Esprit nouveau et les poètes," or seen in the violently experimental lyric of *Calligrammes*, is present as well in the disorderly ordering of Apollinaire's first collection of poetry. But here the break with the forms of the past for an acceptance of the realities of contemporary experience has not yet been resolved or fully rationalized.

Alcools, as a collection of poems written between 1901 and 1912, is on the threshold of the new age, and it derives its lyrical and dramatic force from the erratic shifts in tone and attitude in which the sequence of poems reveals the poet as protagonist of contemporary life. The collection does not tell a coherent story about the birth and coming of age of the new poet, but registers with great affective intensity and range the poet's effort to identify and control what appear as fundamentally irreconcilable forces, both seductive and threatening, in his experience of this new age. Feelings of loss and obsolescence vie with curiosity about the future; self-awareness and solitude, with the impulse to connect with a still impersonal collectivity. Occasionally, as in the case of the "A La Santé" or the Rhineland texts, poetic sequences constitute islands of emotional coherence, but they float detached, as part of the debris of a past in the process of breaking up, rather than as cohering elements.

Alcools thus provides us with a moving testimony to the sacrifices involved in Apollinaire's advocacy of the "new spirit" precisely because most of it was written during the years when the young poet was still trying to find contemporary meaning in outdated nineteenth-century forms. Reverence for a past that he is not yet willing to relinquish is cut through by irony, humor, and a sense of frustration, which surround the effort to conserve old ideals. It was, perhaps, the gathering together of his poems for *Alcools* in 1913 that provided him with the insight for the sentence quoted earlier from "L'Esprit nouveau et les poètes:" "C'est aux poètes à décider s'ils ne veulent point entrer résolument dans l'esprit nouveau, hors duquel il ne reste d'ouvertes que trois portes: celle des pastiches, celle de la satire et celle de la lamentation, si sublime soit-elle" ("It is up to the poets to decide if they will not resolutely embrace the new spirit, outside of which only three doors remain open: that of pastiche, that of satire, and that of lamentation, however sublime it be"). A comparison of *Calligrammes* and *Alcools*—strikingly different in form and tone, yet each containing poems written in 1912—would suggest that Apollinaire saw himself undergoing a distinct shift in his attitude toward the uses of the lyric at the time of the publication of *Alcools*. Whereas *Calligrammes* follows a fairly straightforward chronological ordering and for the most part is an enthusiastic yea-saying to the poet's role as inventor of new forms, *Alcools*, which contains poems from Apollinaire's very earliest, antisymbolist phase (1901–05) as well as poems written later in response to his discovery of the new art of cubism, thoroughly obscures chronology as an ordering principle. The poems taken as a whole seem to constitute a complex, poeticized story of the postromantic crisis that necessitated a new lyric mode and that required of the poet a painful detachment from certain cherished moral and aesthetic certainties.

The Orpheus myth, clearly alluded to at key moments throughout the collection ("Une épouse me suit c'est mon ombre fatale"—"Signe," *OP*, p. 125; "A wife pursues me my fatal shadow"—"Sign," *A*, p. 179; "J'ai eu le courage de regarder en arrière"—"Les Fiançailles," *OP*, p. 131; "I have had the courage to look backward"—"The Betrothal," *A*, p. 187) organizes Apollinaire's peculiar backward-glancing and sacrificial view of his role as poet of the modern age. But a living Orpheus, tied to the memory of his living bride

> Au soleil parce que tu l'aimes
> Je t'ai menée souviens-t'en bien
> Ténébreuse épouse que j'aime
> Tu es à moi en n'étant rien
> O mon ombre en deuil de moi-même
> ("La Chanson du mal aimé," (*OP*, p. 54)
>
> Shadow-wife I led you where
> You like to walk in sun and air
> In being nothing you were mine
> O my dear shadow wearing black
> You mourn for me behind my back
> ("Song of the Poorly Loved," *A*, p. 31),

contrasts with the dismembered Orpheus floating down the river of time to sing with the depersonalized and collective voice of contemporary humanity ("Il vit décapité sa tête est le soleil / Et la lune son cou tranché"—"Les Fiançailles"—*OP*, p. 133); "It lives headless its head is the sun / And the moon cut off at the neck"—"The Betrothal" *A*, p. 189).[10] Thematic repetitions specifically evocative of the alienated modern condition and reminiscent of the fin de siècle lyric (exile, disappointed love, *faux semblant,* prostitution), as well as certain characteristic formal procedures (refrain, use of negation, intratextual and intertextual echoings) suggest, nevertheless, the collections' obscured integrity. One feels, somehow, that these poems belong together, between the same covers and within the frame of the two poems written in 1912, "Zone" and "Vendémiaire." On the other hand, one is hard put to describe what constitutes the unity of *Alcools* in any convincing way. There is a disorderly aspect to the collection—what Georges Duhamel described correctly, but without any insight into its aesthetic or philosophical significance, as reminiscent of a *boutique de brocanteur* ("secondhand shop"). It is worth quoting Duhamel's cruel, even racist review of 1913 because it reveals how unprepared the prewar reading public still was for this subversion of an aesthetics of wholeness, continuity, and originality rooted in romantic and symbolist theory.

> Je dis: boutique de brocanteur parce qu'il est venu échouer dans ce taudis une foule d'objets héteroclites dont certains ont de la valeur, mais dont aucun n'est le produit de l'industrie du marchand même. C'est bien là une des caractéristiques de la brocante: elle revend; elle ne fabrique pas. Elle revend d'ailleurs parfois de curieuses choses; il se peut qu'on trouve, dans ses étalages crasseux, une pierre de prix montée sur un clou. Tout cela vient de loin; mais la pierre est agréable à voir. Pour le reste, c'est un assemblage de faux tableaux, de vêtements exotiques et rapiécés, d'accéssoires pour bicyclettes et d'instruments d'hygiène privée. Une truculente et étourdissante variété tient lieu d'art, dans l'assemblage des objets. C'est à peine si, par les trous d'une chasuble miteuse, on aperçoit le regard ironique et candide du marchand, qui tient à la fois du juif levantin, de l'Américain du Sud, du gentilhomme polonais et du facchino. (*Mercure de France*, 15 June 1913)

> I say: secondhand shop because in this shack there is a collection of discarded, anomalous objects, some of value, but none of which is the product of the merchant's own effort. That is one of the characteristics of the secondhand trade: it does not make anything, it resells; occasionally it even resells some surprising things; one may actually find on the grimy display shelves a precious stone mounted on a nail. All the stuff comes from far away; but the stone is a pleasure to see. As for the rest, it is an assortment of phony pictures, exotic, patched clothes, accessories for bicycles, and implements for personal hygiene. A truculent and dizzying variety replaces art, in the amassing of things. Through the moth holes of an old chasuble one can just see the ironic and bold glance of the merchant, who has something of the Levantine Jew, the Latin American, the Polish gentleman, and the Italian railway porter. (My translation)

Rather than a secondhand shop, one might have called this collection the atelier of modern art, a term more relevant for the kinds of experimentation that Apollinaire was practicing and that link him eventually to later, more obviously political writers like the surrealists, Brecht, or Francis Ponge. If in

Alcools a melancholy tone and the psychological alienation of the lonely city dweller seem to dominate, potential sentimentality or despair are undercut by iconoclastic humor ("Mon verre s'est brisé comme un éclat de rire"—*OP*, p. 111; "My glass has shattered like a peal of laughter"—*A*, p. 151). Baudelairean spleen, moreover, gives way to a sacrifice of the remembering self for a collective dynamics that promises new forms of social and spiritual communion. I say promises because the collectivity with which the lyric voice allies itself in the more self-consciously revolutionary "Vendémiaire" is one that sums up in hymnlike tones rather than one that challenges the achievements of its age. Nevertheless, it is the move from personal to collective that disrupts what, in Apollinaire's view, had become a fetishistic attachment to a romantic vocabulary by the turn of the century. The shift in attitude that in part, at least, accounts for the drama of *Alcools* when read as a whole is reflected in the difference between the two poems that Apollinaire chose to frame his collection. The speaker of "Zone" stresses the already worn-out nature of the modern city and the exhaustion of the sacred, finding freshness only in the religion of his childhood and coded personal references to private experiences. The speaker of "Vendémiaire," on the other hand, while still consigning himself to the past for his future readers—

> Hommes de l'avenir souvenez-vous de moi
> Je vivais à l'époque où finissaient les rois
> (*OP*, p. 149)

> Men of the time to come remember
> Me I lived when the kings were finishing
> (*A*, p. 211)

—nevertheless proclaims himself the distilled voice of his time ("le gosier de Paris"—*OP*, p. 154; "the throat of Paris"—*A*, p. 221) drunk with the factory-made saints and barbarian monarchs who have replaced the sacred pope of Rome as spiritual leaders of an industrialized Europe. The divided, alienated self of "Zone"—

> Tu n'oses plus regarder tes mains et à tous moments je
> voudrais sangloter
> Sur toi sur celle que j'aime sur tout ce qui t'a épouvanté
> (*OP*, p. 43)

> You don't dare look at your hands any more and I am forever
> wanting to cry
> About you about her I love about all that has scared you
> (*A*, p. 11)

—becomes the voice of *universelle ivrognerie* (*OP*, p. 154) ("universal drunkenness"—*A*, p. 221) in "Vendémiaire." One might say that *Alcools* represents what Renato Poggioli has identified as the agonistic moment in the avant-garde experience, whereby "catastrophe is transformed into miracle and the self-immolation of the creative personality into an art of the future." The present is understood in "Vendémiaire" and in the ordering of the entire collection, as a "forge of history in continual metamorphosis." Poggioli's distinction between reverence for the past that ends in conservatism and appreciation of the uses of the past for future reconstruction seems appropriate for a reading of *Alcools*: "Tradition itself ought to be conceived not as a museum but as an atelier, as a continuous process of formation, a constant creation of new values, a crucible of new experiences."[11]

It cannot be denied, however, that *Alcools* has certain museum or antique shop characteristics—through its revival of old forms: *chanson de toile,* aubade, *complainte;* through the use of symbolist parody: "Clair de lune," "Palais," "Rosemonde," for example; and through the recurrence of fin-de-siècle themes and motifs: *saltimbanques, tziganes* (gypsies), *Salomé, voyage, naufrage* (drowning). This faded, nostalgic quality gives one the feeling of reliving something—not as truth, however, in the way a latter-day symbolist poet like Henri de Regnier might, but self-consciously and with a touch of cynicism, as reproduction, in the way a professional forger of antiquities would see it.

> J'ai vu travailler un faussaire à Honnef, au bord du Rhin. . . . Il m'avait pris en amitié et je le vis une fois agenouillé dans son jardinet et salissant avec de la terre humide des poteries neuves qu'il vendit quelques mois après à un pasteur protestant amateur d'antiquités rhénanes. Ce faussaire n'était parfaitement heureux que les jours où il avait maquillé quelque fausseté. Il l'admirait ensuite en souriant et disant: "J'ai fabriqué un dieu, un faux dieux, un vrai joli faux dieu." Puis il prenait sa guitare et chantait, en tordant sa bouche édentée, de vieilles chansons allemandes qui célébraient Kaëtchen de Heilbronn ou Schinderhannes. ("Des Faux" [1903], *Ch.*, pp. 26–27)

> I once saw a counterfeiter at work in Honnef, on the Rhine. . . . He had taken a liking to me, and I once saw him kneeling in his little garden, smudging some pieces of brand-new pottery with moist earth. A few months later, he sold those pieces to a Protestant minister who was a collector of Rhenish antiques. That old counterfeiter was completely happy only on the days he had disguised some forgery. He would then admire his work with a smile and say, "I have created a god, a false god, a real, pretty, false god." Then he would take his guitar, and screwing up his toothless mouth, he would sing some old German lieder celebrating Katchen of Heilbronn or Schinderhannes. ("Fakes," *AA*, p. 12)

It is Apollinaire's use of pastiche as a form of self-criticism that Duhamel did not grasp and that constitutes the off-key tone of *Alcools*.

The celebratory voice of "Vendémiaire," which concludes *Alcools* and announces the collective reader of *Calligrammes*, is not arrived at easily. The analogy of the poet to a new Orpheus is complemented and offset by another analogy—that of Lazarus pulled haggard out of his tomb ("Tu ressembles au Lazare affolé par le jour"—"Zone," *OP*, p. 42; "Looking like Lazarus unwitted by the daylight,"—*A*, p. 43)—and the promise of a new Coming is, more often than not, disappointed, as in the persistence of the theme of betrayal in "L'Ermite" (The hermit), "Un Soir" (One evening), "Les Fiançailles," or "A La Santé," for example. Loss of the sacred and loss of a true love are analogous and suggest the loss of those aestheticist values of "unity," "purity," and "truth" that Apollinaire wanted to believe were embodied in the cubist painting of the "fourth dimension." The theme of *faux semblant* is not only a romantic lament of betrayed love in "La Chanson du mal aimé," but a recognition that poetic language can never coincide with experience through symbolic figuration. Renaissance does not mean birth of the same, but the beginning of something else. The opening stanzas of "La Chanson du mal aimé," which suggest a hellish scene—Orpheus in search of his dead bride—stress, through the repetition of various forms of the word *sembler* ("to seem"), the impossibility of all adequate connection or coming to rest in fixed values. The speaker, his *voyou*-shadow self, his unfaithful lover, and all of her avatars in history from the sirens to the Danaides to Annie Pleyden at once resemble each other and seem to be forms of mutual betrayal.

Un soir de demi-brume à Londres
Un voyou qui ressemblait à
Mon amour vint à ma rencontre
Et le regard qu'il me jeta
Me fait baisser les yeux de honte
(*OP*, p. 46)

In London on a dismal night
I met a hoodlum in the street
Who might have been my love
He looked so much like her his gaze
Made me blush and drop my eyes
(*A*, p. 19)

The knowledge of this certain deception is the legacy of the modern poet and the source of his tormented humor. One can hear it in the furious rejection of the elaborate metaphor of the Red Sea (which cunningly turns him into the persecutor of his shadow self) for a return to the literal, concrete (brick) origins of his experience, and an exasperated declaration of eternal love, even as he tries to write that love out of existence:

Je suivis ce mauvais garçon
Qui sifflotait mains dans les poches

Nous semblions entre les maisons
Onde ouverte de la mer Rouge
Lui les Hébreux moi Pharaon

Que tombent ces vagues de briques
Si tu ne fus pas bien aimée
(*OP*, p. 46)

I trailed him as he slouched along
Hands in pockets whistling
The street became a trough
Two billows of the Red Sea rose
And I was Pharoah he the Jews
Oh if I have not loved you well
Let that brick ocean comb and fall
(*A*, p. 19)

It is there again in "Les Sept Epées" ("The Seven Swords"), where he resorts to coded language for the expression of his most private desires and hopes. One can see it as well in the dramatic development of certain poems such as "Palais" ("Palace"), "Clair de lune" ("Moonlight"), or "Les Fiançailles," which in allegorizing the poet's mission, begin optimistically and end in betrayal or uncertainty. In "Clair de lune" the poet perversely chooses the meretricious language of symbolic self-mystification to express his skepticism regarding the instrument of his vocation:

Lune mellifluente aux lèvres des déments
. . . . .
J'ai peur du dard de feu de cette abeille Arcture
Qui posa dans mes mains des rayons décevants
Et prit son miel lunaire à la rose des vents
(*OP*, p. 137)

The honeyflowing moon is on every madman's tongue
. . . . . .
But I fear the bee Arcturus and his fiery sting
Who having put these slippery beams in my hands
Took his lunar honey from the rose of the winds
(*A*, p. 193)

Like the pretty woman of "1909," the language is all too seductive, all too easily assimilated by the sentimental reader of his period. In "Palais," where the poet ends up dining on his own dead thoughts in the palace of the king's concubine, Apollinaire puns, through the word *palais* (meaning "palace" and "palate") on the relationship of corrupt language to corrupt values.

But even more depressing than the bland taste of his own thoughts and tongue is the sight of the other guests eating them with relish:

Or ces pensées mortes depuis des millénaires
Avaient le fade goût des grands mammouths gelés
Les os ou songe-creux venaient des ossuaires
En danse macabre aux plis de mon cervelet

Et tous ces mets criaient des choses nonpareilles
Mais nom de Dieu!
Ventre affamé n'a pas d'oreilles
Et les convives mastiquaient à qui mieux mieux
(*OP*, p. 62)

But these thoughts dead for thousands of years
Had the stale taste of huge frozen mammoths
Bones and dreams were coming from the charnel-houses
In a *danse macabre* in the folds of my cerebellum

And all those meats shouted unheard-of things
But god almighty
A famished belly has no ears
And the guests went on munching one outdoing the other
(*A*, p. 45)

To cling to this illusionary "rose world" ("Rosemonde") is a form of sickness: "L'amour dont je souffre est une maladie honteuse," ("Zone," *OP*, p. 41) ("The love I suffer from is a shameful sickness"—*A*, p. 9) or even worse, necrophilia, as when the corpses in "La Maison des morts" (The house of the dead) declare eternal fidelity to one another in the clichéd language of old love lyrics. At rare moments, as in "Le Brasier" or at the beginning of "Les Fiançailles," a genuine hope for renewal is expressed, and the poet imagines himself a new Prometheus, a modern version of Rimbaud, fueling himself on the sacrifice of his former beliefs for a kind of cosmic rebirth in a world of radically altered forms. At these moments he can say:

Il n'y a plus rien de commun entre moi
Et ceux qui craignent les brûlures
("Le Brasier," *OP*, p. 169)

There is no longer anything in common between me
And those who fear burning
("The Brazier," *A*, p. 147)

But more often the lyric speaker presents himself behind the smile of the toothless forger, singing old folk songs to the tourists to give them the impression that they are getting the real thing. The modern poet of "L'Emigrant de Landor Road," who sets out ahead of everyone else to found a new country, experiences his vocation as that of a leave-taking and a departure for an unknown future, dressed in the used clothes of a dead past:

Mon bateau partira demain pour l'Amérique
Et je ne reviendrai jamais
Avec l'argent gagné dans les prairies lyriques
Guider mon ombre aveugle en ces rues que j'aimais
(*OP*, p. 105)

My boat will leave for America tomorrow
And I'll never come back
With the money I've earned on the lyric prairies
To lead my blind shade through these streets that I have
loved.
(My translation)

He is something of a clown rather than a Christ figure ("L'Ermite")—the betrayed prisoner of "A La Santé" poems, who turns like a bear in his cage and sees rays of light dance in the form of *pitres* ("buffoons") on his verses. The muse of the modern world is neither corrupt nor beautiful and is not especially seductive. She is a tired workingwoman, marked by time and disappointed hopes.

Ces femmes ne sont pas méchantes elles ont des soucis
cependant
Toutes même la plus laide a fait souffrir son amant
Elle est la fille d'un servent de ville de Jersey
Ses mains que je n'avais pas vues sont dures et gercées
J'ai une pitié immense pour les coutures de son ventre
("Zone," *OP*, p. 43)

These are not bad women but they have their troubles
And even the ugliest one has made her lover suffer
She is the daughter of a policeman from the Isle of Jersey
Her hands which I hadn't seen are hard and raw
I feel an immense pity for the scars on her stomach
(*A*, p. 13)

J'aimais les femmes atroces dans les quartiers énormes
Où naissaient chaque jour quelques êtres nouveaux
Le fer était leur sang la flamme leur cerveau
J'aimais j'aimais le peuple habile des machines
Le luxe et la beauté ne sont que son écume
("1909," *OP*, p. 139)

I have loved atrocious women in monstrous places
Where new creatures came to birth daily
Iron was their blood and flame their brain

I loved I loved the people expert with machines
Luxury and beauty are only their dross
(*A*, p. 197)

The new music that will accompany her appearance in the mechanized urban world is a strident one that grates on the spine as it voices the death cry of the old lyric:

Les dimanches s'y éternisent
Et les orgues de Barbarie
Y sanglotent dans les cours grises
. . . . .
Soirs de Paris ivres du gin,
Flambant de l'éléctricité
Les tramways feux verts sur l'échine
Musiquent au long des portées
De rails leur folie de machines
("La Chanson du mal aimé," *OP*, p. 59)

A barrel-organ sobs below
Eternity instead of hours
Is Sundays like this in a row

The nights in Paris all drink gin
And fall asleep with their streetlights on
Trolley-cars are mad machines
To make green sparks and scream like queens
("Song of the poorly loved," *A*, p. 39)

The basic tension of *Alcools*, one that is supported by the ordering of the individual works within a single collection, is expressed by two of the most lyrically powerful and haunting stanzas of "La Chanson du mal aimé." The first voices the struggle to preserve a sacred but naive memory of the past against oblivion, in words that, like flowers pressed under glass, maintain their antique beauty.

Je ne veux jamais l'oublier
Ma colombe ma blanche rade
O marguerite exfoliée
Mon île au loin ma Désirade
Ma rose mon giroflier.
(*OP*, p. 54)

Oh let me not be cured of her
My pretty dove my calm harbor
Still let memory see

That argosy that isle of spice
The petalled flower of her face
(*A*, p. 29)

The second stanza expresses a recognition that loyalty to the past can end in a thralldom that may kill the lyric voice altogether, poisoned by the tears of its salty lament:

Mon beau navire ô ma mémoire
Avons-nous assez navigué
Dans une onde mauvaise à boire
Avons-nous assez divagué
De la belle aube au triste soir
(*OP*, p. 47)

O pretty ship my memory
Isn't this far enough to sea
And the sea not fit to drink
Haven't we drifted far and lost
From fair dawn to dreary dusk
(*A*, p. 23)

But if this tension over the past ends in a deadlock, the ironic and skewed versions of familiar nineteenth-century forms inaugurate the spirit that will inform Apollinaire's work after 1914. Discontinuity is used as a conscious strategy for the (dis)ordering of this collection that means to break with an aesthetics of autonomy. Just as there is no clear-cut chronological progression from early to late poems or autobiographical development from young to old poet, there is no clear-cut evolution from old to new forms. Orpheus is both yearning for union with his bride and alternatively ready to scatter notions of unity to the four winds—"la rose des vents." When in one fell swoop Apollinaire removed all of the punctuation from the poems on the proofs of *Alcools*, he dislodged individual words and lines from their fixed positions, making the elements of his poems free-floating entities. This gesture was his leave-taking of the aestheticist principles of his symbolist heritage.

Adieu faux amour confondu
Avec la femme qui s'éloigne
Avec celle que j'ai perdue
L'année dernière en Allemagne
Et que je ne reverrai plus
(*OP*, p. 48)

Farewell false love I took you for
The woman that I lost last year
Forever as I think

I loved her but I will not see
Her any more in Germany
(*A*, p. 23)

Significance is no longer preordained; there is no longer any neat subordination of part to whole. The collection becomes a workshop rather than a finished form as one poem borrows parts from another to make up new configurations that may even bring the original poem's meaning into question. What Duhamel saw as tricky imitation, Apollinaire presents as contemporary recovery of the debris of the past. He is purposely disrespectful of his own work, imitating himself as pastiche in "Rosemonde" (Rosamond), "Signe," or "Palais" (Palace) for example, presenting a kitsch version of "Zone" or "La Chanson du mal aimé" in "Hôtel," or using lines from rejected poems to patch up new ones in "Le Voyageur," "L'Adieu," or "Les Fiançailles." Apollinaire's own offhand accounts of the genesis of many of his poems ("Le Voyageur" improvised while humming to himself in the street or "Le Mariage d'André Salmon" written on the top of the bus on his way to his friend's civil ceremony) bear out his impulse to desacralize the image of the creator as demigod and replace it with tinkerer, mechanic, or inventor, thus anticipating the rhetorical question of "L'Esprit nouveau et les poètes" of 1918: "Peut-on forcer la poésie à se cantonner hors de ce qui l'entoure, à méconnaître la magnifique exubérance de vie que les hommes par leur activité ajoutent à la nature et qui permet de machiner le monde de la façon la plus incroyable?" ("EN," p. 396) ("Can poetry be forced to establish itself outside of what surrounds it, to ignore the magnificent exuberance of life which the activities of men are adding to nature and which allow the world to be mechanized in an incredible fashion?"—"E," p. 237).

Apollinaire's well-known preference within individual poems for the isolated and shocking image, for the free-floating line ("Chantre" [singer]), or the word or even letter for its own sake ("Pâline," "Noubousse," "Malourène," "Podolie," "Salonique," "Zaporogue," or the illuminated letters of *Les Bestiaires*) is reflected in the discontinuous, often disorienting arrangement of the poems in the collection as a whole. They do not tell a coherent story, but give unexpected meaning to fickle moments of creative activity by their surprising juxtapositions. Nevertheless, it is only by reading the poems of *Alcools* together rather than separately that the reader can begin to understand that this is a poetry that takes itself seriously in a new way—as a "continuous process of formation." *Calligrammes*, many of which were written in the trenches, would be Apollinaire's most heroic acceptance of such a view, because there each poem-experiment offers itself to the reader as such—ready to be thrown away, impossible to collect or recite or remember except as a visual image—a sky rocket that requires a temporary but intense collaboration between reader and writer.[12] These are inventions that will not carry over into a tradition and that are never in danger of becoming a style—pure "coonskinism" or "potshots taken at the Redcoats," as Harold Rosenberg puts it in "Parable of American Painting."[13] In fact Rosenberg's comments on the American Action painters are entirely appropriate for Apollinaire's most experimental work: "In this gesturing with materials the aesthetic, too, has been subordinated." These are moments "when the modern artist feels himself released from value"; "acts of risk and will."[14] But what Apollinaire learned about the uses of the past in the "agonistic" phase of *Alcools* is not lost in the "activistic" stage of his understanding of the present in *Calligrammes*.[15] He does not mistake this revolutionary art for an ultimate act either. There is no dream of permanence in revolt here, as seems to be the case for the futurists and the surrealists. Intratextual echoings and repetitions are as present in *Calligrammes* as they are in *Alcools*, and a more traditional narrative poetry dialogues with the explosive visual shapes in a way reminiscent of "La Chanson du mal aimé," written in 1903. The frame poems—"Liens" and "La Jolie rousse"—insist on connections of a new sort that do not bind or strangle, although the exaltation of these modern forms of communication is always accompanied by a yearning for what is being let go:

> D'autres liens plus ténus
> Blancs rayons de lumière
> Cordes et Concorde
>
> J'écris seulement pour vous exalter
> O sens ô sens chéris
> Ennemis du souvenir
> Ennemis du désir
>
> Ennemis du regret
> Ennemis des larmes
> Ennemis de tout ce que j'aime encore
> ("Liens," *OP*, p. 167)

> Other more tenuous chains
> White rays of light
> Cords and Concord
>
> I write only to exalt you
> Oh senses oh cherished senses
> Enemies of memory
> Enemies of desire
>
> Enemies of regret
> Enemies of tears
> Enemies of all I still love
> ("Chains," *Ca*, p. 25)

> Ayez pitié de moi
> ("La Jolie Rousse," *OP*, p. 314)
>
> Have pity on me
> ("The Pretty Redhead," *Ca*, p. 345)

Apollinaire's poetry continues to move us because it does not throw away the past easily—it enters the deconstructive phase of modernism in full awareness that the force of the new art will be in the strength of its sacrifices.

Notes

1. All quotations from Apollinaire's poetry are from Guillaume Apollinaire, *Oeuvres poétiques*, ed. Marcel Adéma and Michel Décaudin (Paris: Gallimard, éditions de la Pléiade, 1965). (This work is cited in text as *OP*.) Unless otherwise stated, translations from *Alcools* are from *Alcools*, trans. William Meredith (New York: Anchor Books, Doubleday and Co., 1964). (Hereafter cited as *A*.) I have taken the liberty of removing his punctuation so as to remain true to Apollinaire's own practice, but have otherwise left his often rather free translation as is. Translations from *Calligrammes* are by Anne Hyde Greet in *Calligrammes: Poems of Peace and War (1913–1916)* (Berkeley: University of California Press, 1980). (Hereafter cited as *Ca*.)

2. Guillaume Apollinaire, *Chroniques d'art: 1902–1908*, textes réunis par L. C. Breunig (Paris: Gallimard, 1960), and Apollinaire, *Méditations esthétiques: Les Peintres cubistes*, ed. L. C. Breunig and J.-Cl. Chevalier (Paris: Hermann, 1965)—hereafter cited as *Ch* and *ME*). Apollinaire, "L'Esprit nouveau et les poètes," *Mercure de France*, 1 December 1918, pp. 385–96—hereafter cited as "EN." Translations from the *Chroniques* are by Susan Suleiman in *Apollinaire on Art: Essays and Reviews, 1902–1918* (New York: Viking Press, 1982)—hereafter cited as *AA*; those from *Méditations* are by Lionel Abel in *The Cubist Painters, Aesthetic Meditations, 1913* (New York: Wittenborn, Schultz, 1949)—hereafter cited as *CP*; and those from "L'Esprit nouveau et les poètes" by Roger Shattuck in *Selected Writings by Guillaume Apollinaire*, ed. and trans. Shattuck (New York: New Directions, 1950)—hereafter cited as "E."

3. I have borrowed the expression from John Updike's review, "Art and Artillery," of Ron Padgett's translation of Apollinaire's *Le Poète assassiné*, in the *New Yorker*, July 9, 1984, pp. 89–93.

4. See Emerson's declaration, "For the experience of each new age requires a new confession, and the world seems always waiting for its poet." (Quoted by M. L. Rosenthal and Sally Gall in *The Modern Poetic Sequence: The Genius of Modern Poetry* (New York and Oxford: Oxford University Press, 1983), p. 8.)

5. See Roger Shattuck, "Apollinaire's Great Wheel," in his *The Innocent Eye: On Modern Literature and the Arts* (New York: Washington Square Press, 1984), p. 294.

6. Samuel Taylor Coleridge, *The Statesman's Manual*, ed. W. G. T. Shedd (New York, 1875), p. 438. Georges Longrée makes a very strong case for the tight and continuing connection between symbolist thought and Apollinaire's application of cubism in his scrupulously documented study of the *Calligrammes—L'Expérience Idéo-Calligrammatique d'Apollinaire* (Paris: Librairie Jean Touzot, 1983). Longrée seems,

nevertheless, to detect a countertendency around 1912–13 to "abandon the old Symbolist dream of a union of all the arts" for an acceptance of a role as witness and recorder of the ever-changing forms of contemporary life. (See pp. 145, 149, 1153, for example.) Longrée and Shattuck both see this contradiction brought back into balance in the *Calligrammes*, although Shattuck does not see it resolved: "Apollinaire juggled two modes of meaning at once, verbal and visual. In combination these modes convey complementary messages—nostalgia and separation in contingent time, and individual consciousness surpassing collective consciousness in arrested time. They coexist yet cannot fuse" (Shattuck, "Apollinaire's Great Wheel," p. 315).

7. See Thomas Crow's excellent article, "Modernism and Modernity," in *The Vancouver Conference Papers*, ed. Benjamin H. D. Bucklok, Serge Guilbout, and David Solkin (Halifax: Press of the Nova Scotia College of Art and Design, 1983), and Clement Greenberg, "Avant-Garde and Kitsch," in *Art and Culture* (Boston: Beacon Press, 1961).

8. Shattuck uses the word *imperialist* to describe the poet's stance in "Lettre-Océan": "In 'Lettre-Océan,' . . . the heroism of modern life announced by Baudelaire in 1846 is hubristically affirmed in one of the most extreme experiments of modernism. The painter-poet climbs to the summit of his own universal experience and traces magic symbols on a piece of paper to re-create for the eye an instant or cross-section of collective consciousness. At the same time, the poetic intent expressed by the headlines and the circles is imperialist—the expanding ego striving to conquer the universe and surpass the collective rather than submit to it" ("Apollinaire's Great Wheel," pp. 311–12).

9. Peter Burger, *Theory of the Avant-Garde*, trans. Michael Shaw (Minneapolis: University of Minnesota Press, 1984), pp. 11–12, 79.

10. See Philippe Renaud, *Lecture d'Apollinaire* (Lausanne: Edition de l'homme, 1969), for a more exhaustive reading of the Orpheus myth in *Alcools*. His book remains one of the best studies of the themes, images, and prosodic structures of this collection written to date.

11. Renato Poggioli, *The Theory of the Avant-Garde*, trans. Gerald Fitzgerald (Cambridge: The Belknap Press of Harvard University Press, 1968), pp. 66–68, 73, 159.

12. Shattuck argues very imaginatively for the possibility of a reading-performance of "Lettre-Océan" whereby spatial designations and relationships are made audible ("Apollinaire's Great Wheel").

13. Harold Rosenberg, "Parable of American Painting," in *The Tradition of the New* (New York: McGraw-Hill Book Company, 1965), pp. 14–15.

14. Rosenberg, "The American Action Painters," in *The Tradition of the New*, pp. 26, 31, 34.

15. I have borrowed the terms *agonistic* and *activistic* from Poggioli.

Sarah Lawall

10. Bonnefoy's *Pierre écrite*: Progressive Ambiguity as the Many in the One

How can a poet mistrustful of closure, of fixed images, or of any manner of architectural whole bring himself to compose a lyric book? No one knows better than Yves Bonnefoy that writing a "book of poems" codifies a metaphysical perspective, and is thus a self-defeating enterprise for a poet of incompletion. Yet *Pierre écrite* (literally, "written stone") is the third collection in which Bonnefoy uses lyric form to challenge conventional concepts of aesthetic wholeness and symmetry, and moreover to deny that consummate technique has any value as an expression of human experience.[1] These attacks are embodied internally, however, in a calculated incompleteness of theme, image, perspective, and even meter that together subvert closure by openly seeking what is transitory and flawed. "Que saisir sinon qui s'échappe?" ("What is there to grasp at, if not that which flees?") he wonders in *Du mouvement et de l'immobilité de Douve* (*On the Motion and Immobility of Douve*—*P*, p. 44/66), and "l'imperfection est la cime" ("imperfection is the highest point") in *Hier régnant désert* (*Yesterday's Desert Reign*—*P*, p. 117/139). Bonnefoy's numerous essays on poetry and the visual arts reject the nineteenth-century notion of "well-made" art and formal beauty because it only "ruins being" ("celle qui ruine l'être," *P*, p. 114/136). Closure-oriented concepts of formal beauty and architectural perfection are in fact not adequate to explain the shape of this modern lyric book. Instead, *Pierre écrite* sets into play two complementary notions of unity: a formal unity that is demonstrated only to be denied, and the vision of a proximate One whose definition accumulates substance but not fixity throughout an expanding series of associations.

Bonnefoy's systematic evasion of perfect form marks him as a poet of the mid-to-late twentieth century. He has the existentialist writer's suspicion of closed options and the reifying essence (as F. C. St. Aubyn suggested in 1964, calling Bonnefoy the "first existentialist poet"),[2] and the New Novelists' distrust of symmetrical plots and integrated characters. His insistence on the changing and incomplete nature of perception, on a fragmented awareness of existence that incorporates both life and death, recalls the Heideggerian notion of an always-approximated reality in which we create intersecting networks of perception as a tentative intuition of the world. The literary pursuit of *near*-perfection is to be equated with the *ap*presentation of reality: a representation *to* the self that evokes something always aimed at, and never fully represented or possessed. This deferral of full communication relates, in turn, to modern linguistic refutations of language's ability to reproduce objective reality, a tradition running from Ferdinand de Saussure to Roland Barthes, whose chair Bonnefoy inherited at the Collège de France. Nonetheless, and although Bonnefoy welcomes the demystification of "transparent" language,[3] he maintains his fascination with the possibility of wholeness and authentic meaning, with the idea of an all-encompassing One whose relationship to the many has occupied philosophers from ancient Greece to the present. (Bonnefoy specialized in mathematics and philosophy for his baccalaureate degree in 1941, and continued studies in mathematics before devoting himself to poetry.) In "La Poésie française et le principe d'identité" (French poetry and the principle of identity), an essay published in the same year as *Pierre écrite*, he turns to Coleridge and cites approvingly the English poet's words that "the Beautiful is that in which the many still seen as many becomes one" (*I*, p. 256). Bonnefoy's notion of the relationship between the many and the one is more open-ended than Coleridge's organic model, with its suggestion of transcendent wholes. His intuited or proximate One makes itself known as a coordinating principle evolving through expanding relationships of similarity and difference.

What is the literary strategy that emerges from this desire to seek the One while maintaining the irreducible status of the many? Bonnefoy chooses a rhetoric of expanding ambiguity: an increasing density and multiplicity of textual and referential signs, themselves situated within frameworks that are constantly exceeded. Themes and tentative contexts are introduced, and larger symbolic horizons implied—but never established as a final frame, a single horizon against which we are to read the rest of the book. Instead, each glimpse of a potential framework is altered, developed, or exceeded in subsequent poems. The result is a network that stresses, not a single integrating structure, but the ability to remain *within* the linkage while extending a perspectivist unity: a many of constantly moving, multidimensional, and referential layers. Bonnefoy's favorite poet, Charles Baudelaire, attributes the profoundly "human" fascination of a moving ship to the same continuous generation of forms based in reality: "à la multiplication successive et à la génération de toutes les courbes et figures imaginaires opérées dans l'espace par les éléments réels de l'objet" ("to the successive multiplication—and to the generation—of all these curves and imaginary figures produced in space by the object's real elements").[4]

Throughout his work (and *Pierre écrite* is but one step in a career that later includes the extended and incantatory verse of *Dans le leurre du seuil* (*In the Lure of the Threshold*) and the poetic prose of *Rue Traversière* (Traversière Street),[5] Bonnefoy explores the possibility of poetic language as a way to name but not to fix, a way to exploit the "dream" of artistic imagination in full awareness of its negative, absenting aspects, and to drive language as a mediating wedge—a bridge of the imaginary—between dream and reality. Paradoxical as it may sound, this world forever out of reach is not a mere figment of the solipsistic imagination, but the real and inexhaustible basis of our apperceptions. We do not create the world: "au contraire, le monde est cela que nous percevons" ("on the contrary, the world is what we perceive"), states the philosopher Maurice Merleau-Ponty. Nonetheless, he continues, this perception of the world is visibly an approximation: "Chercher l'essence de la perception, c'est déclarer que la perception est non pas présumée vraie, mais définie pour nous comme accès à la vérité" ("In seeking the essence of perception, we are saying that we do not accept perception as true, but rather as the access to truth").[6] The One the poet seeks is never fully grasped, but always sensed as close, nearby in essence, approximate: brought nearer our horizon through a tactic of allusive ambiguity used as an instrument of increasing density and self-reference. "Pourquoi, d'abord, ne pas s'établir dans l'ambiguïté, la prenant comme donnée d'expérience . . . ce qui sera travailler sur soi, et donc sur le rêve même, qui . . . rendra l'écriture plus transparente" ("Why, then, should we not reside permanently in ambiguity, taking it as the data of experience . . . which will mean working on oneself, and therefore on the dream itself, which . . . will make writing more transparent"). Words used in this way are not transparent in the positivist sense of an immediately delivered referent, but transparent inside a mediated relationship, a self-conscious perception that evokes "le contact avec l'un, ce que j'appelle *présence*" (*E*, pp. 126, 141) ("the contact with the one, which I call *presence*").

Du mouvement et de l'immobilité de Douve is generally recognized as Bonnefoy's most "unified" book; indeed, a great deal has been written on its development and theatrical unity. John E. Jackson describes *Douve* as a "play in five acts"; Richard Vernier calls it "the most finished" of Bonnefoy's collections, "une suite de textes agencés de manière à former un poème continu et fini, qui progresse selon son argument métaphysique" ("a series of texts organized so as to make a continuous finished poem that develops according to its metaphysical argument"). Vernier continues by calling the second two collections "des recuils, non pas certes hétérocites, mais du moins formés de groupes indépendants les uns des autres" ("not really mixed books, but at least composed of independent groups"). We need not agree. Although Vernier is certainly right that *Douve* is more "finished" than the later books, and he describes in fascinating fashion its construction according to an "esthétique du manque" ("aesthetics of lack"), the question of unity has moved onto another plane by the time of *Pierre écrite*.[7]

Bonnefoy himself, in the autobiographical *L'Arrière-Pays*, describes his discontentment with the aesthetic vision of the early book, and accuses himself of having given in to "le plaisir de créer artistiquement, la préférence accordée sur l'expérience vécue à la beauté propre d'une oeuvre" (*AP*, p. 120) ("the pleasure of artistic creation, preferring a work's own beauty to lived experience"). *Hier régnant désert*, with its bitter attacks on the illusory nature of artistic perfection, is the result of this disillusionment. Only later does the poet (who has in the meantime discovered the mysterious "presence" of baroque art in its flight from fixed form) realize that there is a further role for poetry that need not exclude existential authenticity. "C'est dans mon devenir, que je puis garder ouvert, et non dans le texte clos, que doit s'inscrire et fleurir . . . cette vision" (*AP*, p. 149) ("It is in my evolving experience, which I can keep open, and not in the closed text, that . . . this vision . . . must be inscribed and flourish." He may change the poetic style that corresponds to his constantly open vision: *Dans le leurre du seuil*, written thirteen years after *Pierre écrite*, is almost epic in its sweep and extended stanzaic form, while the *Récits en rêve* of 1987 offer prose poems.[8] By 1965, however, Bonnefoy has discovered a poetic ontology that will allow him to write, and that he reaffirms in his inaugural lecture at the Collège de France, *La Présence et l'image* (*Presence and Image*).

Pierre écrite is the fruit of this moment of discovery, the last of these early lyric books, and the most visibly dedicated to the exploration of the role of art and the nature of textuality. The book concludes with a poem, "Art de la poésie," that is derived both in themes and images from the preceding poems; it thus differs from the endings of the first two volumes, which are primarily metaphysical summations. Bonnefoy's poetics restructure the ancient quest for essences inside two antiessentializing philosophies: modern materialist theories of language and a phenomenological perspectivism (Merleau-Ponty rather than Nietzsche) that focuses on the access routes to reality. He welcomes the demystification of language, refuses to believe in artificial wholes, recognizes the absence or loss in any act of naming, and accepts the cultural shaping inherent in words and artistic structures, but at the same time passionately denies any displacement of poetry onto the plane of psychological or sociological explanation—even more, of a quantitative semiotics. Instead, as Gérard Gasarian shows in another context, Bonnefoy uses this Barthesian "jeu de l'autre et du même, cette différence qui apparaît avec l'institution du signe" ("play of self and other, this difference that appears with the institution of the sign")[9] as a way of capturing a heightened sense of being through consciousness of illusion. Using strategies of deplacement and deferral, he rediscovers a poetic "origine du sens" ("origin of meaning").[10]

The superficial form of *Pierre écrite* is easy to describe, and provides a basic, if somewhat static, picture of themes and correspondences. The book is divided into four parts, of which the first is "L'Eté de nuit" (Summer of night), a cluster of seventeen poems with an initial nine-poem sequence also titled "L'Eté de nuit." According to Mary Ann Caws, this initial sequence is a "nine-part symphony" whose musical organization introduces the tensions of life and death, motion and stillness, that reappear throughout the book.[11] The same sequence offers a vision of the Garden of Eden that will be developed differently in various scenes, and that anticipates a corresponding sequence of six poems near the end of the book. The framing correspondence of two sequences is the clearest example of architectural organization in the volume, although it is—predictably—not perfectly symmetrical. The second and title section, "Pierre écrite," was first published separately in 1959 with lithographs by Raoul Ubac.[12] (Since lithography is a technique of etching in stone—the Greek word means "written stone"—this first edition offers a material analogy (or a bilingual edition?) for the poems of *Pierre écrite.*) The section contains seventeen poems, nine of them titled "Une Pierre" (A stone) and given the visual form of a gravestone epitaph with its centered lines (correspondingly, the first section contains two such epitaph-poems and the third has three). The third section, titled "Un Feu va devant nous" (A fire goes before us) contains nineteen poems and (postponing fuller discussion) develops the theme of reawakened light, life, and increased awareness through a new experience of love. Bonnefoy's second marriage is often mentioned to explain the stress on *nous* and the increased sensuality of this section, as well as the book's generally more positive tone or suddenly "transitive" speech.[13] The final section, "Le Dialogue d'angoisse et de désir" (The dialogue between anguish and desire), is divided between an initial six-poem sequence that transforms—with growing intensity—the beginning picture of recaptured Eden into a terrestrial *dire simple* ("simple speech"), and three ending poems that express this resolution in terms of the visual arts ("Sur une pietà de Tintoret": On a pietà by Tintoretto), the role of the poet ("Une Voix": A voice), and the summarizing "Art de la poésie" (Art of poetry).

Pierre écrite, like Bonnefoy's preceding two volumes, is not a collection of previously scattered poems but a coordination of clusters or groups. Inside each group, individual poems are self-sufficient, so much so that some have been anthologized. However, these poems also stop short of complete definition, as though the interpretation of certain images depends on a larger horizon to be supplied by the reader or by a poem still to come. Jean-Pierre Richard, in an essay on Bonnefoy that precedes *Pierre écrite* but is still relevant, remarks that the poet's organization recalls the symphonic or group-oriented structures of sixteenth-century poets in their development of archetypal images and mythologies of resurrection.[14] To such implied (though fragmented) structures the twentieth-century poet adds his own private mythology, which includes a meditation on the nature of poetic language and on the moral responsibility of the writer. It is useful to examine this private mythology (itself shaped by tradition and current culture, as the poet says), since it plays such a large part in coordinating different aspects of his poetry.

The overriding element in Bonnefoy's mythology is his preoccupation with unity: not the false unity of superficial form, but a sense of coherence and participation in life that is close to Joycean epiphany. The descriptions of this suddenly glimpsed unity are indeed epiphanic: it is "l'instant remplaçant l'éternel" (*E*, p. 124) ("The instant replacing the eternal"), occurring as the human being "participe de l'unité de cet Univers qui lui est alors immanent" (*E*, p. 133) ("participates in the unity of this Universe which is then immanent for him"), or a sympathetic awareness that reintegrates the universe and makes it "le fondement de l'être" (*E*, p. 123) ("the foundation of being" [Bonnefoy cites Plotinus], or a moment of illumination in which "le sens . . . peut se reformer dans les choses simples, assurant à chacune une place, une raison d'être, dans l'unité qui est plus que l'être, qui est en soi la lumière" (*E*, p. 117) ("meaning . . . can take on new shape in simple things, guaranteeing each one a place, a reason for being, in that unity that is more than being, which is in itself light"). Such a desire for transcendent unity could risk the charge of isolated subjectivity, even of that narcissism that Bonnefoy abhors (and whose temptation, in the form of the Gnostic yearning for a more perfect region *beyond,* he repeatedly describes). Yet unlike Joyce's epiphany, which is firmly based in the subject's own visionary perspective, Bonnefoy's proximity to the One requires a strong sense of the viewer's own finitude, and the recognition that material objects and human thought have shared existence in a common "site" so that what is realized is "*le corps de l'indissociable*" (*I*, p. 248) ("*the body of the indissociable*") rather than any privileged subjective vision.

Contact with the One comes in a variety of ways, all implying the simultaneous recognition of perfection *and* its lack. As Bonnefoy has asserted from *Douve* on, and as he reiterates under the sign of aesthetic integration in *Pierre écrite*, any apparently positive manifestation (life, light, symmetry) needs to be completed by its corresponding negative state (death, darkness, rupture). An exemplary image is the torn ivy leaf. "La feuille entière, bâtissant son essence immuable de toutes ses nervures, serait déjà le concept. Mais cette feuille brisée, verte et noire, salie, cette feuille qui montre dans sa blessure toute la profondeur de ce qui est, cette feuille infinie est présence pure, et par conséquent mon salut" (*I*, p. 24) ("The entire leaf, constructing its unchanging essence in all its veins, would already be the concept. But this leaf once broken, green and black, soiled, this leaf that shows in its wound all the depth of what is, this infinite leaf is pure presence, and consequently my salvation").

Correspondingly, the plan of a lyric book should also envisage wholes only to destroy them. Responding to Mario Maurin's suggestion that Bonnefoy should have written two more poems in *Douve* to complete a latent pattern of threes and sevens, Richard Vernier describes *Douve*'s asymmetrical pattern as a way of deceiving easy parallelisms through a shortfall of numerical sets, a *numérologie déçue* ("disappointed numerology").[15] Frédéric Deloffre has shown that *Pierre écrite* constantly proposes traditional classical meters, but then undermines them by interpolating hendecasyllables and unexpected metrical patterns. Moreover, Bonnefoy's hendecasyllable is irregular in its irregularity: instead of the expected nineteenth-century pattern, with its 5/6 meter, the poet suggests and then retracts the 6/6 alexandrine form by using a 6/5 meter. Similarly, he prefers to the habitual 4/6 decasyllable another suggestion of "fallen" alexandrine by employing a 6/4 meter. Deloffre explains these "limping" meters by citing Bonnefoy on the metaphysical implications of fixed form: "N'est-il pas vrai que la forme *a priori* de l'alexandrin . . . cette forme *donnée,* et qui tend par son inertie à une poésie close, c'est la suggestion qu'une idée—mythe ou suprême réalité—commande au monde sensible et doit à notre esprit imposer son cadre? Alors, la vie des mots en son sein, c'est l'acte même de la conscience, acceptant ou récusant cette loi"[16] ("Isn't it true that the *a priori* form of the alexandrine . . . this *given* form, which tends in its inertia towards a closed poetry, suggests that an idea—myth or supreme reality—governs the world of the senses and ought similarly to impose its frame on our mind? Well then, the vital core of words is the very act of consciousness, accepting or rejecting this law").

Sonorous qualities, as well as visual and metrical patterns, imply a governing structure and its related worldview. In an essay on Paul Valéry that rejects the older poet's use of closed forms, Bonnefoy singles out the mute *e* (the silent vowel that is heard as a syllable in traditional poetic form) as "cette faille entre les concepts, cette intuition de la substance" (*I*, p. 103) ("this fissure between concepts, this intuition of substance"). Another essay describes the mute *e* as "la lumière qui vient de l'Un" (*I*, p. 261) ("the light that comes from the One"). In each case, it is the simultaneous presence of a form and its negation that allows the One to exist.

The ambivalent richness of the One emerges most clearly in the discussions of imagery. Bonnefoy's early attraction to surrealism may derive from the movement's experimentation with startling, paradoxical images that transform habitual perception. Images carry most clearly Bonnefoy's definition of good and bad values, and display the moral/metaphysical choice that a poet (or any human being) makes between different ways of conceiving reality. "Bad" images are those that are purely conceptual, intellectual versions of experience in formal and idealist structures that often serve as a way to avoid the anguish and ambivalence of mortal consciousness. These are the images of aesthetic perfection, symbolist (and Gnostic) signs pointing away from this world to a higher beauty: images of "excarnation" as opposed to "incarnation."[17] They may arise from the poet's dream of a projected (Mallarméan or Oedipal) universe—the poet writ large, or a grander narcissism—or from any yielding to fixed states of being, including the extinction of self that is sought in some of the epitaph poems. This harmful conceptualism is often described as a *mirror image* (recalling Mallarmé's *Hérodïade*) for its flat reflection of experience. Words compose a "bad image" when language is accepted as the only reality, and bring about a deceptively fixed or "bad presence" (a concept Bonnefoy also personalizes as "the demon"—*I*, p. 247). Bonnefoy's passionate criticism of the Saussurean legacy centers on its infinite networks of empty relationships, its insistence that a word only "signifies" a particular concept and has no ontological capacity. In art (and Bonnefoy's discussion of Ubac brings up similar arguments related to the visual arts), the equivalent of this semiotic abstractionism is the art that reaches for "une sorte de perfection fille des rapports et des nombres" ("a sort of perfection derived from relationships and numbers"), or gives itself up to blind chance (*I*, p. 58).[18] Artists yield to the negative side of the image when they accept perfecting their medium as an end in itself: a dilemma for poets who, like Bonnefoy, are drawn to create beauty, but who fear destroying their vision in the process.

By the end of *Pierre écrite*, however, Bonnefoy has worked his way through the temptations of closed or perfect form, and found a positive or more open use of the image that will allow it to evoke full being. The metaphysical dialectics at work in this proper use of imagery are described in an essay of 1966, "Proximité du visage" (Nearness of the visage), that takes as its point of departure an exposition of Ubac's lithographs. Two major images of stone and inscription, materiality and dream, are developed in a way that illuminates the correspondence of these elements throughout *Pierre écrite*. The first image is that of an ancient Roman statue, the Venus of Paestum, whose belly is furrowed by the marks of a plow driven over the field in which she was buried. Simultaneously stone, a human (or divine) figure, and a work of art—sculpted by the artist and inscribed by the plow—she embodies a related series of realities: "Plus elle était rayée par le soc, plus elle semblait une pierre" ("The more she was scored by the plow blade, the more she seemed a stone"). After centuries, she is uncovered and it is then that "ce rocher se dénude et devienne figure" (*I*, p. 309) ("this rock is laid bare and becomes a human figure"). The second image in the essay reverses the movement of the first, in that it starts with everyday reality and gradually superimposes on it human consciousness and the artistic impulse toward unity. Bonnefoy describes here inscribed stones (part of local walls) that are covered with farmers' records of having brought part of their harvest in tithe to the local monastery. "Ces belles encoches" ("These fine notches") are first of all quantitative records of payment, but they begin to assume individual human character through the name, home, and handwriting traits visible in each inscription. In addition, some inscriptions finish off the record by enclosing the whole account with a boundary line, thus displaying a further "intention d'unité" ("drive towards unity") that introduces other nonquantitative values. "Ainsi le compte devient présence, le grain n'est plus un avoir" (*I*, p. 314) ("Thus the account becomes presence, the grain is no longer merely a possession"). Poetry and painting rise to this level of true presence, Bonnefoy suggests, when they combine the levels of knowledge, perceptions, and value. When poetry makes use of referential networks that reach into mundane reality and beyond the conceptualism of art, it expands into a larger dimension and triumphs "*dans* l'image même" (*E*, p. 148) ("*in* the image itself").

To attain this goal is to attain the *dire simple, langage clair,* and *universel langage* ("simple speech," "transparent/bright language," and "universal language" (*P* pp. 220/242, 226/248, 224/246; *WS* pp. 117, 129, 125) that Bonnefoy desires. Extending imagery into various dimensions of reference is one means; another, which the poet examines in "La Poésie française et le principe d'identité," is the choice of elemental or essential images. Not all words are equally useful in this enterprise, suggests Bonnefoy. Best are those that correspond to our sensuous experience of the world, where "il suffit que nous ayons tant soit peu vécu avec ces réalités notre attachement à la terre" ("we have to some degree lived, through these realities, our attachment to earth"). In addition, a more intense effect is created if the words express "essences"—understood here as "ces choses ou créatures qui semblent exister par soi pour notre conscience naïve dans notre expérience ordinaire" ("those things or creatures who seem to exist in themselves, for our naive awareness, in our ordinary experience"). Examples given are "wind, stone, fire"; *pierre* (stone) as opposed to the more fabricated *brique* (brick); *crier, rire,* or *boire* (crying out, laughing, or drinking) as opposed to the more specific—or specifically human—*grimacer, ricaner* (grimacing, sneering); (*I*, pp. 253–54). It might be objected that some of these choices reflect the author's personal experience of the country, and that a city poet might have different essential attachments. In Bonnefoy's universe, however, these are the archetypal images of nature that, combined with other elements of his personal mythology, compose an imaginary horizon of doubled reality that is tested in a multitude of associations.

We have seen some of these associations: the crumpled ivy leaf that signifies pure presence; the Garden of Eden; the demon of bad presence (complemented by the salamander as "*l'ange,* qui a chassé les démons . . . c'est l'Un"—*I*, p. 248; "the *angel,* who drove out the demons" and is "the One"); stone that, in its deep and ashen gray, is "l'entrée du réel" (*I*, p. 21) ("the entrance into the real") *I*, p. 21) or in Ubac "la chose méditée . . . une métaphore de l'être" (*I*, p. 59) ("the thing, meditated . . . a metaphor of being"); the mirror of conceptual vision; the image of a special site (*lieu, pays,* or *jardin;* place, country, or garden). We may add *fer* (iron) in its various meanings, *lumière* (light), whether lamp, dawn, or unspecified illumination; the tree with its foliage and fruit; summer; a ship; the sky and stars; water (especially as river);

and the frequent opposition of the colors red and gray. Several settings recur and metamorphose throughout *Pierre écrite*: the summer night, moving into dawn; the ship traversing space; the starry sky bending toward earth; the garden with its tree; the cemetery where tombstones recall another life.

Mingled with personal images are those drawn from the culture itself, for Bonnefoy—who has written on the dominant images and implications of medieval literature and baroque art—is well aware that a work of art expresses the cultural matrix in which it is produced. Thus *Pierre écrite* extends the network of consciousness into Judeo-Christian culture with the pattern of biblical references; into Greco-Roman culture with the frequent references to ancient art, mythology, and funerary rites; into aesthetic history with references to Mozart, Tintoretto, and Poussin's painting *Et in Arcadia Ego* (another *written stone*); and into a romantic-modern preoccupation with the ontological status of the writer. Bonnefoy once wrote that T. S. Eliot's *The Waste Land* had formulated the true myth of modern culture, except that the English poet underestimated the redemptive potential of interrogating the barren land itself (*I*, pp. 120–21). *Pierre écrite* recalls *The Waste Land* in its development by thematic groups, and in the interwoven strands of cultural experience, but its horizon opens on the inner experience of artistic and personal renewal rather than on Eliot's acid indictment of a sterile society.

The first grouping of poems begins with a sequence that moves from an idealized night scene to the promise of a new day created through words that divide—yet share the nature of—the sky above: "Un langage se fait, qui partage le clair / Buissonnement d'étoiles" (*P*, p. 171/193) ("Words emerge, divide the glowing / Foliage: stars"—*WS*, p. 19). This night scene can be read for itself, as a poetic evocation in which earth, on a summer evening, is transfigured into the recaptured Garden of Eden, but it also launches many of the themes and images of the rest of the book. The metrics of the first poem illustrate, in addition, Bonnefoy's tendency to present and curtail traditional forms: the sketch of an unfinished sonnet (two quatrains and a tercet) employs a mixture of alexandrines, hemistich, and five decasyllables (the 6/4 "fallen alexandrine").

> Il me semble, ce soir,
> Que le ciel étoilé, s'élargissant,
> Se rapproche de nous; et que la nuit,
> Derrière tant de feux, est moins obscure.
>
> Et le feuillage aussi brille sous le feuillage,
> Le vert, et l'orangé des fruits mûrs, s'est accru,
> Lampe d'un ange proche; un battement
> De lumière cachée prend l'arbre universel.

Il me semble, ce soir,
Que nous sommes entrés dans le jardin, dont l'ange
A refermé les portes sans retour.

(*P*, p. 163/185)

This evening it seems to me
that the starlit sky grows larger
And draws near us; that behind so many fires
The night is less dark.

And the foliage burns beneath the foliage; the green
swells, and the orange of the ripe fruit:
Lamp in the hand of a near-by angel;
A beating of hidden light overtakes the one tree.

This evening it seems to me
that we have entered that garden whose doors
The unreturning angel closed.

(*WS*, p. 3)

Part of the excitement of the poem lies in the poet's own incredulous anticipation of the miracle: "Il me semble . . ." that the sky is pressing closer, that the orchard's fruit and foliage are becoming more luminous, that a still-hidden, pulsating angelic light draws close. The poet seems to recognize the Tree of Life and the very garden from which humanity was excluded after the Fall. It is a brilliant evocation in its own right, but it is also recognized *as* an evocation ("Il me semble . . .") under the expanding pressure of the starry sky (which usually represents the idealizing dream, as opposed to the rough stone of earth), and finally it is a transfiguration, an old dream recaptured. It is, after all, the summer of night (as opposed to the "summer of day" appearing later), an illusory moment that will give way to dawn and a colder daylight. Many of the images will recur—the layering of leaves, or the doubling of images into deepened transparency, the movement of the sky toward earth, the change of light, the angel itself, and the "we" whose progress toward greater intimacy appears throughout—but the role of these images will vary according to context.

In subsequent poems, summer has become a ship with the beloved as the prow figure, the ship of a May dream unfurling the painted canvases of art. It is an ideal dream, an immobile perfection in which motion itself appears a flaw, and moreover, it is recognized as a beautiful reifying dream in which the poet creates or "speaks" the image of his beloved as half-asleep, her face recalling a carved figure or mask (a mask that will be set aside in the third section). "Navire d'un été, / Et toi comme à la proue, comme le temps s'achève, / Dépliant des étoffes peintes, parlant bas" (*P*, p. 164/186) ("Ship of a summer, /

And you as if at the prow, as time fails, / Unfolding painted cloths, talking softly"—*WS*, p. 5).

> Le mouvement
> Nous était apparu la faute. . . .
>
> Je te disais ma figure de proue
> Heureuse, indifférente, qui conduit,
> Les yeux à demi-clos, le navire de vivre
> Et rêve comme il rêve.
>
> (*P*, p. 165/187)
>
> Movement
> Seemed to us a sin. . . .
>
> I called you my figurehead:
> Halcyon, indifferent, who leads
> With half-closed eyes the ship of living,
> Who dreams as the ship dreams.
>
> (*WS*, p. 7)

Different combinations of the same and similar images explore the validity of these concepts: earth is fitted out as a ship, and her figurehead described as marked with red—the red that will later be associated with the red clay of the dead (p. 174/196), or with the lamp's fire, a red robe, and the light of existence. In one of the later poems in this section, the poet speaks of his need for her company in his ideal quest:

> Je ne savais dormir sans toi, je n'osais pas
> Risquer sans toi les marches descendantes. . . .
> Alors je t'ai voulue au chevet de ma fièvre
> D'inexister.
>
> (*P*, p. 176/198)
>
> I did not know how to sleep without you, I did not dare
> Risk without you the descending steps. . . .
> Then I wanted you at the bedside of my fever
> To not be.
>
> (*WS*, p. 29)

She becomes not only his beloved companion but an admonishing example of the way that the artist tends to use everything and everyone he encounters as part of his dream: his manner of envisaging reality colors not only broad perspectives but also the possibility of an authentic relationship with the woman he loves. This theme will be developed further in poems of the fourth section: "ai-je su t'aimer, / Ne sachant mourir?" (*P*, p. 214/236) ("Did

I know to love you, / Not knowing enough to die?"—*WS* 105); "O moins à contre-jour, ô mieux aimée, / Qui ne m'es plus étrangère" (*P*, p. 222/244) ("And in this light you are less obscure, my more truly / Loved, you are no longer strange to me"—*WS*, p. 121). "L'Ete de nuit" concludes with "Une Pierre" (A stone), a quatrain of dialogue between the two lovers that is set in the form of an epitaph, and leads appropriately into the next section, "Pierre écrite."

Most of the poems in the title section were published in 1959 with lithographs by Raoul Ubac, an artist whom Bonnefoy has discussed on many occasions and with whom he published a limited edition of "La Poésie française et le principe d'identité" with two etchings in 1967.[19] John E. Jackson speaks of this section as the "negative" section of the book, the demon of a temptation to seek immortality in death that will be exorcised in the more positive statement of the last section.[20] Six years after the publication of this separate section, Bonnefoy retained its title for the full volume, as if the range of issues raised by the earlier imagery were still valid for the entire poetic quest. The first association with these "written stones" is clearly the fact that they are tombstones, and the voices heard are either those of the dead speaking their own epitaphs, or of the poet, speaking to his companion in the cemetery. A poem in the third section suggests that the stone may also be the tombstone of *Et in Arcadia Ego*, a painting by Bonnefoy's favorite painter, Poussin, that depicts the Arcadian shepherds reading the sign of death in their midst (*P*, p. 217; *WS*, p. 111). Finally, the implications of the lithographer's art are also strong for this poet, who repeatedly speaks of the necessary interaction of concept and stone, dream and reality, imagination and brute matter, as the complementary materials of the act of presence.

Voices in "Pierre écrite" move back and forth between the poet's voice questioning the significance of this *lieu des morts* (*P*, p. 183, 185) ("place of the dead"—*WS*, 43, 47), and a cluster of tombstone voices that present different human perspectives on death from the vantage point of the grave. It is a peculiar mixture of life and death, consciousness persisting in the tomb in a way that seems more appropriate for a Homeric or Virgilian trip to the underworld, or for the Sartrean *Huis clos* (No exit) where the state of death is actually everyday life, than for the absorption into earth that is implied by accepting death as part of the life cycle. These voices have not accepted the reality of death, and almost invariably compare their former lives with the surprising fact of the tomb. A function of this section, therefore, is to illustrate, not death, but a series of human ideas about death: especially the temptation to seek any kind of immortality. Measuring life by concepts, avoiding ambiguity, or seeking the security of otherworldly "immortal" values is, for Bonnefoy, a form of death itself, the fatal attraction of the ideal. In "Pierre écrite," he interrogates the meaning of death in several ways, and receives a series of answers that include oblivion, the blind continuation of past habits, the disillusionment of religious hopes, and the wish for awakening in the dawn.

Two poems that offer questions or tentative answers are found toward the beginning of the section, both titled "Le Lieu des morts" and spoken in the poet's own voice.

> Quel est le lieu des morts,
> Ont-ils droit comme nous à des chemins,
> Parlent-ils, plus réels étant leurs mots,
> Sont-ils l'esprit des feuillages ou des feuillages plus hauts?
>
> What is the place of the dead—
> do they have a right, as we do, to roads—
> Do they speak—are their words more real—
> Are they the spirit of these leaves, or of a higher foliage?
> (*WS*, p. 43)

To the question of whether the dead have their own world, a higher reality, and truer, oracular speech, the poet suggests tentatively that they may also be simply the other side of existence as we know it, the fulfilling tear in the ivy leaf ("Peut-être gisent-ils dans la feuille du lierre, / Leur parole défaite / Etant le port de la déchirure des feuilles, où la nuit vient"—*P*, p. 183/205; "Here the dead may lie, in the ivy leaf / —Their ruined word / The harbor, the torn leaf, where the night comes in"—*WS*, p. 43). Or, adducing again the color red that was associated with the clay of the dead and seems to be associated with authentic existence as opposed to conceptual idealism: "Le lieu des morts. / C'est peut-être le pli de l'étoffe rouge" ("The place of the dead— / Perhaps it is a fold in the red cloth"). But the red cloth suggests a wearer, which leads indirectly to the figure of woman or angel, here associated with true earth and stone: "Peut-être tombent-ils / Dans ses mains rocailleuses . . ." (*P*, p. 185/207) ("Perhaps the dead fall / Into the rough [rocky] hands of the cloth"—*WS*, p. 47). It remains for the stones themselves to speak, which they do.

Between the two "Lieu des morts" poems there is a striking epitaph whose combination of psychological portraiture and subtly interconnected imagery makes it an excellent example of the tendency to seek security in concepts: "la belle mort" ("beautiful death") as Bonnefoy has said.

Une Pierre

> Je fus assez belle.
> Il se peut qu'un jour comme celui-ci me ressemble.
> Mais la ronce l'emporte sur mon visage,
> La pierre accable mon corps.

Approche-toi,
Servante verticale rayée de noir,
Et ton visage court.

Répands le lait ténébreux, qui exalte
Ma force simple.
Sois-moi fidèle,
Nourrice encore, mais d'immortalité.
(*P*, p. 184/206)

A Stone

I was pretty enough.
A day like this could resemble me.
But thorns cover my face,
And stone crushes my body.

Come closer
Straight-backed servant, you who are streaked with black,
and your short face—

Pour out the night's milk, it exalts
My simple force.
Stay with me,
Wetnurse still, but feeding me immortality.
(*WS*, p. 45)

The speaker's vanity persists in the grave, to the point that she imagines—in a comparison pathetically emphasizing her separation from life—that the beautiful day is to be measured by her own image. The sensuality of her attitude in this and succeeding lines is reminiscent of Phaedra in her illness, complaining of the weight of her hair and constantly aware of her body. Here, the dead woman's beautiful face and body are overcome by the briar and stone of the grave, and she must seek another guarantee: this time, by becoming part of an immortal and unchanging order. Speaking in regal tones that once more remind one of Phaedra commanding her nurse, she commands the gravestone as her servant and orders it to pour out the milk of ancient funeral rites: a libation that exalts her strength into immortality, and seals the bond between herself and the grave. (In the following poem, the second "Lieu des morts," the libation gesture is idealized as the goddess in the trees pours from a golden ewer.) Words of domination, power, and absolute order combine with the speaker's determination to control her fate, and enclose a scene of unquestioned beauty but also an image of conceptual death.

Other voices are not so commanding. A speaker who was satisfied to have left behind the cries of the living, and reached a transcendence beyond nature, now admits the nightmare of this isolation: "Des bêtes de nuit hurlent, c'est mon chemin, / Des portes noires se ferment" (*P*, p. 186/208) ("Night-beasts howl, and that is my road now; / And black doors close"—*WS*, p. 49). Another, decomposing, regrets love and lost identity, and finds religion no resource against nothingness as he falls "Sans dieu, sans voix audible, sans péché, / Bête trinitaire criante" (*P*, p. 187/209) ("Godless, voiceless, sinless— / A shouting three-headed beast"—*WS*, p. 51). There is hope toward the end of the section: "La face la plus sombre a crié / Que le jour est proche" ("The darkest face cried / That day is near") but in vain: "Mais la lune se couvre et l'ombre / Emplit la bouche des morts" (*P*, p. 195/217) ("But the moon is clouded and shadow / fills the mouth of the dead"—*WS*, p. 67). The impulse is not entirely frustrated, however, for in the next poem the image of tombstone is replaced by a bronze statue of Eros so that the image of blind materiality is given new life by art and love. Finally, the last poem is a happier dream—although it *is* a dream—of shared love inside the recognition of mortality: "J'aimais . . . que mourir ne fût en obscure fontaine / Que troubler l'eau sans fond que le lierre buvait. / J'aimais, j'étais debout dans le songe éternel" (*P*, p. 197/219) ("I loved . . . that death did no more than trouble the soundless water / In the dark fountain where the ivy drank. / I loved, I stood upright in the eternal dream"—*WS*, p. 71). It is an ending that leads directly into the third section, "Un Feu va devant nous," which presents the lovers' gradual awakening to real time and a daylight reality.

"Un Feu va devant nous" marks a complex development of parallel themes: the awakening of the lovers to a fuller reality, the rejection of mask or dream, and (impelled by two epitaph poems) a gradual renewal of faith in the power of words after the intuition of silence has been achieved. Of all the sections, this one is most directly focused on the two lovers: it begins in their bedroom where "la main pure dormait près de la main soucieuse" (*P*, p. 199/221) ("the pure hand slept by the careworn"—*WS*, p. 75) and, as the image of pure-conceptual and anxious-earthbound hand shows, the correspondence of the lovers is often used to convey the relationship of other parallel elements. At this point, the dependence on dream—the "masque aux yeux clos du rêve" (*P*, p. 200/222) ("the shut-eye mask of the dream"—*WS*, p. 77)—is to be dropped, the time of mortality enters the garden ("L'arbre vieillit dans l'arbre"; "The tree grows old within the tree"), and daylight invades the scene of previous nocturnal obscurity. "Toi aussi tu aimes l'instant où la lumière des lampes / se décolore et rêve dans le jour" (*P*, p. 201/223) ("You too, you love the moment when the lamps' light / Discolors, and dreams in the day" (*WS*, p. 79). The quality of light has changed, and with it the lovers' vision: "Nous ne nous voyons plus dans la même lumière" (*P*, p. 211/233) ("We no longer see each other in the same light" *WS*, p. 99). An epitaph-voice anticipates the angel of presence in a combination of light and darkness, crying

Un feu va devant nous.
J'aperçois par instants ta nuque, ton visage,
. . . . .
Cendre qui te détaches de la flamme
Dans la lumière du soir,
O présence
(*P,* p. 210/232)

A fire goes before us.
For a moment I glimpsed your name, your face,
. . . . .
Ember, you who fall away from the flame
In the evening light,
O presence
(*WS,* p. 97)

The poet himself, having learned to blend two lights—"Clarté de proche nuit et clarté de parole" (*P,* p. 215/237) ("Clarity of near-night, clarity of the word"—*WS,* p. 107)—is prepared to enter a reduced, irregular but simple world where he has the perfect understanding of one who is part of earth in soul as well as in body.

Le Livre, Pour Vieillir

Etoiles transhumantes; et le berger
Voûté sur le bonheur terrestre; et tant de paix
Comme ce cri d'insecte, irrégulier,
Qu'un dieu pauvre façonne. Le silence
Est monté de ton livre vers ton coeur. . . .

Tu vieilliras
Et, te décolorant dans la couleur des arbres,
Faisant ombre plus lente sur le mur,
Etant, et d'âme enfin, la terre menacée,
Tu reprendras le livre à la page laissée,
Tu diras, C'étaient donc les derniers mots obscurs.
(*P,* p. 217/239)

The Book To Grow Old With

Transhumant stars; and the shepherd
Arched over all earthly joy; and such peace
As this insect's uneven cry
Fashioned by an impoverished god. Silence
Rose from your book to your heart. . . .

You will grow old
And, facing against the color of the trees,
Casting a slower shadow on the wall,
Yourself the menaced earth: body and, at long last, soul;
You will take up the book where you had left it,
and say, "So those were the last difficult words."
(*WS*, p. 111)

With the end of "Un Feu va devant nous," the poet has achieved the awakened understanding that allows him to take up his book again, and in "Le Dialogue d'angoisse et de désir" (The dialogue between anguish and desire) that follows he is able to speak from the point of view of this acquired "dire simple," "langage clair," and "universel langage" to refashion the garden of the beginning, and to reinterpret the role of art. In the six-poem sequence that responds to the nine poems at the beginning of *Pierre écrite,* there is a gradual transformation of the first, idealized, and anticipatory experience. Here the poet is in charge of his dream ("I imagine" rather than "It seems to me"), and the god he imagines with a "sacrificial face" draws energy from the poet's own command: "Je lui dis: Sois ma force, et sa lumière augmente" (*P,* p. 219/241) ("I say 'Be my force;' and his light grows"—*WS,* p. 115). It is a cyclical movement in which the poet composes his own vision of the ideal within the real, a hard-won recognition of the immanent divinity of his own earth ("Car les fruits / Régnaient déjà dans l'arbre"; "For the fruit / Already reigned in the tree") that returns to illuminate him and offer a site where he can live: "les haut plateaux où je puis vivre" (*P,* p. 219/241) ("the high plains where I can live"—*WS,* p. 115).

The discovery entails two crowning achievements that reach toward the future. First is the capacity for a shared, unmediated love that does not need to project narcissistic images of its companion ("Nous n'avons plus besoin / D'images déchirantes pour aimer"—*P,* p. 221/243; "ô mieux aimée / Qui ne m'es plus étrangère. Nous avons grandi, je le sais"—*P,* p. 222/244) ("We can love now / Without the rending images"—*WS,* p. 119;) "my more truly / Loved, you are no longer strange to me. Yes, we have grown"—*WS,* p. 121). Following this near-abandonment of the image comes the redemptive use of art to fashion—in full consciousness—a real earthly paradise. The angel that awakens them at this apocalypse is the earth itself ("O de ton aile de terre et d'ombre éveille-nous"; "O wake us with your wing of earth and shadow")—pulsating clarity, the solid residue of light and life that can now reveal itself since their struggle between two realities has taught understanding:

Ici, où nous allons,
Où nous avons appris l'universel langage,

Ouvre-toi, parle-nous, déchire-toi,
Couronne incendiée, battement clair,
Ambre du coeur solaire.

(*P*, p. 224/246)

Here, where we walk,
Where we have learned the universal language,

Open up, speak to us, tear yourself apart:
Gutted crown, clear amber
Beating in the solar heart.

(*WS*, p. 125)

Appropriately, this final poem of the sequence has culminated in a metaphorical or artistic presentation of the recovered earthly paradise. The last three poems focus on the status of art itself, and the central one recaptures fragments of the new Eden imagery to present the scene from the point of view of the writer, qua writer. An exchange of voices in "Une Voix" questions the poet's ability to seize this reality, to drink the "almost absent" water that perpetually escapes our grasp. His response is not a description of grasping but one of depersonalization, of an inability to distinguish between facets of experience that leads to a sense of undifferentiated experience in which (as Rimbaud once claimed) everything speaks in and through him. The poet has been consumed by the language he speaks, but in a new dawn that brings the unsealing of the Book—or rather, of the stones, since they are the book of this earthly revelation. "Je suis cet autel vide, et ce gouffre, et ces arches / Et toi-même peut-être, et le doute: mais l'aube / Et le rayonnement de pierres descellées" (*P*, p. 226/248) ("I am the empty altar, and this pit, and these arches / And maybe you, too, and the doubt: cut certainly the dawn / And the resplendence of the unsealed stones"—*WS*, p. 129).

The final poem, "Art de la poésie," is more than a manifesto or even a personal statement: it is a composite trace of earlier poems, a network of themes and images that have been introduced in the course of the book. This poem effectively depends on the previous poems for much of its meaning. Its series of images, taken in sequence and without knowledge of the rest of the book, have only thin extratextual significance and compose in fact the most hermetic of poems. The publicly shared reality and common tradition that ground *Pierre écrite*'s first poem in natural landscape and biblical themes gradually move into the background as Bonnefoy's personal mythological patterns are superimposed. Consequently, the horizons of the last poem are narrowed in reference to the world *outside* the text, and greatly expanded in their *inner* textual dimensions.

Art De La Poesie

Dragué fut le regard hors de cette nuit.
Immobilisées et séchées les mains.
On a réconcilié la fièvre. On a dit au coeur
D'être le coeur. Il y avait un démon dans ces veines
Qui s'est enfui en criant.
Il y avait dans la bouche une voix morne sanglante
Qui a été lavée et rappelée.

(*P*, p. 227/249)

The Art Of Poetry

The eyes outside this night were dredged.
The hands, immobilized and warmed.
The fever was reconciled, and the heart told
To be the heart. There was a demon in these veins
Who fled, screaming.
There was a bloody disconsolate voice in the mouth,
It was washed and called forth.

(*WS*, p. 131)

Neither angel nor demon dominates in the reconciliation between dream and reality that is effected here. The demon is expelled, and the angel, earlier defined as presence, has disappeared into the act of poetry. (According to Bonnefoy, the task of French poetry is to create an "ordre profond, infraconceptuel, au sein duquel le poète pourra se vivre comme présence"—*I*, p. 266; (a "profound, infraconceptual order, at whose core the poet can live as presence"). In this new order, the poetic glance has been netted or dredged from the depths of the night—night in its many qualities as the idealizing dream of the summer night; the conceptual "nuit d'une phrase courbée" (*P*, p. 177/199) ("night of a vaulted phrase"—*WS*, p. 31), the existential darkness of existence ("l'obscurité propre de l'homme" (*P*, p. 181/203) ("man's own darkness"—*WS*, p. 39) contrasted with the stars at the beginning of "Pierre écrite"; the world of the dead (seen as isolation and terror—*P*, p. 186/208); the darkness of evening that intimates sleep, illusion, and error (and precedes dawn); the night of the poet's struggle ("tu sauvais / Nuit après nuit mes pas du gouffre qui m'obsède"—*P*, p. 176/198; "night after night / You saved me from the pit which obsesses me"—*WS*, p. 29), but also the night that makes the stars more beautiful ("astres, demeures, / Rivière plus brillante avec le soir"—*P*, p. 216/238; "stars, houses of heaven, / and you, river more brilliant with evening"—*WS*, p. 109). It is a night capable of its own illumination ("nuit claire"—*P*, p. 209/231; "clear night,"—*WS*, p. 95; and "Clarté de proche nuit"—*P,* p. 215/237; "Clarity of near-night"—*WS,* p. 107), and a night whose waters are finally baptismal.

Hands are now tranquil and warm: the hands associated with artistic creation, the joined "pure" and "anxious" hands, and certainly hands of a triumphant simplicity ("Et que tes mains sont nues, ô seules éclairées!"—*P,* p. 177/199; "And how your hands are bare: in the only light!"—*WS,* p. 31). *Séchées* for hands is primarily *dry* rather than *warm,* especially after the earlier *dragué* or *dredged,* which implies water; however, a note by the poet on the manuscript used by Susanna Lang for her translation proposes "warmed"—foreshadowing the following line's "fever." The fever, now appeased, is that same "fièvre / d'inexister" (fever / to not be—*WS,* p. 29) that tormented the poet at night in the first section (*P,* p. 176/198), and whose demon is now expelled from the veins "en criant" ("shouting")—a phrase that coordinates the demon with other flames and the perfect starry night of "le ciel criant son feu" (*P,* p. 181/203) ("the sky shouting its fire"—*WS,* p. 38) at the beginning of the section "Pierre écrite." In addition to the biblical overtones of angel driving out the devil, or Jesus the demons in Mark 5:1–13, there is a further connection with demonic negativity in "La Poésie française et le principe d'identité" published the same year: "J'appellerai *mauvaise présence* ce mutisme latent du monde. Et je suis même tenté de l'appeler le démon . . . tapi au fond de ce vide" (*In* p. 247) ("I will name *bad presence* this latent muteness of the world. And I am even tempted to call it the demon . . . lurking at the bottom of this emptiness").

Salvation from the demon comes through invoking the "principle of identity" in poetic language, thus creating the full analogy in which "le feu soit notre feu" (*P,* p. 224/246) ("May this fire be our fire—*WS,* p. 125). At the center of "Art de la poésie" is the identity of the heart with itself: "On a dit au coeur / D'être le coeur" ("the heart told to be the heart"). If there is an essential identity between the structure of the language and the concepts it names ("le langage lui-même, dans sa structure, reflète avec précision cet Intelligible"; "the language itself, in its structure, precisely reflects this Intelligible"; *I,* p. 258), then poetic language, when freed from artifice, may express presence. The "parole d'identité" ("speech of identity") in *Pierre écrite* is the heart partly to recapitulate the theme of love, but also because more abstract analogies must be illuminated by "le sens mystérieux de ce qui n'est que simple / Et fût tombé sans feu dans des mots sans amour" *P,* p. 211/233) ("the mysterious sense of what is only simple, / Or what would have fallen without fire, had words been without love"—*WS* 99). The culminating voice of this ars poetica is earthly, dull, and bloody, penetrated with reality: dull as the renewed angel of earth has a "dull forehead" ("le front est morne" *P,* p. 219/241) in contrast to the divine brilliance of his earlier, Edenic incarnation (*P,* p. 185/207). This dull voice has been washed and, in effect, baptized in the darkly ambiguous water of the beginning: *rappelée* in the sense of "recall to new life—to summon" ("appeler à revivre—to summon," according to another of the poet's notes on the manuscript used by Lang for her translation. The juxtaposition of bloodred color and night-dark water is prepared by a much earlier image placing "sur l'eau plus noire d'une table, / La robe rouge éclairante" (*P,* p. 199/221) "on the blacker waters of a table / The red robe in its own light"—*WS,* p. 75), but *dragué* at the beginning of the poem already implies an almost-absent water "cette eau presque absente"—(*P,* p. 226/248) as part of the washing at the end. This washing is more than baptism; it is also the physical washing of a new birth, of blood from the poetic voice newborn.

Reading "Art de la poésie" in this way is actually a reading *into* the poem of many associations set up earlier in the book; insofar as it pins down associations to clarify a theme, it sins (apologetically) against the multireferential structure of the ars poetica itself. Any "meaning" in the poem—and *sens,* or meaning, is very important to Bonnefoy—is a multidimensional construction that depends on a range of expanding associations. It does not exclude the logic of a developing plot (e.g., the quest for identity in *Douve*), or the coherence that comes from systematic reference to myth, but is in addition a technique for establishing a subterranean unity of metaphysical and moral implications. This second unity is expressed through a pattern of expanding images and overlapping references that challenge or complete each other, and that establish an overall proximate "unity" coordinated by their constant, though changing, relationship to the idea of an ungraspable, immanent One. It is the principle of the Supreme Analogy, derived from Baudelaire, Rimbaud, and the surrealists, but given new impetus under the impulse of semiotic studies of language.

Some of the expanding and ambiguous relationships have appeared across examples presented here, such as the varying associations of night. It is not difficult to take any major image—the ship, summer, light, enclosed and open spaces, the sky, water—and follow ways in which it is cast differently in the course of the book. *Fer* (iron), for example, metamorphoses through a number of incarnations, most of them making use of its resistant materiality (like stone), and some (like the Arthurian sword) already available in literary tradition. In its elemental materiality and implied shape as sword, *fer* wounds the heart of the image and that wound is light (*P,* p. 170/192); in its incarnation as *glaive* (sword; parallel to the previous use), it reverses the symbolic background to represent the indifference of the stars wounding earth (*P,* p. 175/197); as a rusty plowshare found in the grass, its earthy quality catches the light that is then able to "consumer le sel du doute et de la mort" (*P,* p. 202/224) ("consume there the salt of doubt and of death"—(*WS,* p. 81). "Le fer / Rouillé, parmi les hautes herbes—*P,* p. 202/224" is [the "rusty / Iron in the high grass"] identified as a plowshare ["*soc de charrue*] by a note on the Lang manuscript.) In the next poem, it appears as chains (Bonnefoy's gloss) from which we are liberated; in the last section, it suggests aggressive, warlike qualities as "le fer des mots de guerre se dissipe / Dans l'heureuse matière sans retour" (*P,* p. 220/242) "The iron of the words of war / dissolves in the joy of what is earth" (*WS,* p. 116). A final transformation is governed by the *shape* of the sword, which becomes "le fer, blé absolu / Ayant germé dans la jachère de nos gestes" (*P,* p. 224/246) ("Iron, the perfect wheat, / Having seeded in the fallow-land of our gestures"—*WS,* p. 125) before scattering its imperfections in eternity to prepare the final apotheosis of light. It may be useful to push beyond individual images, however, to see how the dimension of ambiguity is expanded past objects to changes in relationships themselves.

Any reader of *Pierre écrite* (or of *Dans le leurre du seuil,* Bonnefoy's next book)[21] will notice the great use made of parallel imagery: imagery whose potentially narrow binarism is opened out by inner changes such as the contextual shifts we have seen for *fer,* then by a larger parallelism that questions the bases of the first, and then by a functional relationship of both parallelisms to the nature of the proximate One. A useful example in this respect is the image of reflection, which occurs in so many forms but especially as a mirror, glass, or watery surface that gives a flat (conceptual) image of the reality it represents. There are developments beyond this limited existence: the reflection of the stars in water becomes a mediating force, and provides a way for their light to be absorbed if the speaker drinks the water (*P,* p. 164/186); and the poet's creating an idealized image of his beloved is indicated by her description as "le reflet d'une étoile immobile / Dans le geste mortel" (*P,* p. 165/187) (the reflected "image of an unmoving star / In our mortal gestures"—*WS,* p. 7). In each case, however, the mention of reflection suggests an absence of full life. Bonnefoy's response is, not to eliminate reflection, but to counter it with images of layering: multiple or parallel layers of reality, and the invoked division that opens up closure. Together, they add up to the layered transparency of presence. The tree has double branches and layered leaves (*P,* p. 170/192, 163/185, 183/192, 185/207, 205/227; *WS,* pp. 17, 3, 43, 47, 87), and there are two lights that must be mingled (*P,* p. 191/213, 215/213; *WS,* pp. 59, 107) in, presumably, "le jour au fond du jour" (*P,* p. 212/234) ("the day underlying the day"—(*WS,* p. 101) or "le boire éternel du jour plus bas que jour" (*P,* p. 179/201) (the "endless flow of the day below all days"—*WS,* p. 35). At the end, imagining has literally split in the mirror ("Imaginer / S'est déchiré dans le miroir" [*P,* p. 223/245; *WS,* p. 123, responding to an earlier plea, "Divise-toi": "divide yourself"—*P,* p. 170/192; *WS,* p. 17), and the advent of the angel of presence is heralded by the call "Ouvre-toi, parle-nous, déchire-toi" (*P,* p. 224/246) ("Open up, speak to us, tear yourself apart"—*WS,* p. 125). Together, division and the replications add up to the layered transparency of Presence, of a cumulative One that is not quite *there,* but (in an image that repeats this same parallelism writ large) always *proche* (*P,* p. 221/43, "close by" *WS,* p. 119). This proximate One is a dialectic image of ungraspable unity, a composite trace signified by reciprocal images of presence and absence.

Finally, there is a third and complementary use of ambiguity in the postponing of a defining framework for approximately the same set of relational characteristics: in our example, references to a ship and a clothed figure that recur in different contexts and amplify the boundaries of their initial implied identity. At the beginning of *Pierre écrite,* the poet describes his companion as a "figurehead" unfurling the painted canvas, eyes half-closed and smiling. Their ship is the "Navire d'un été" . . . "le navire de vivre" (*P,* pp. 164–65/186–87) (the "ship of a summer," or later, "the ship of living"—*WS,* pp. 5, 7). In the next poem of the sequence, the ship is absorbed into an image of the "terre comme gréée" *P,* p. 166/188 ("Earth / rigged like a ship"—*WS,* p. 9), and the figurehead is spotted with red. "L'étoile, l'eau, le sommeil / Ont usé cette épaule nue" (*P,* p. 166/188). ("The star, the sea, sleep / Have worn bare this shoulder"—*WS,* p. 9), part of a shadowed body and neck bent toward mortality. The figure's human or earthly nature is reinforced by the promise that "Ces frêles mains terrestres dénoueront / Le noeud triste des rêves" ("These frail hands of earth will / untie this knot, our dreams"—*WS,* p. 11), but in the same poem a complementary personification is initiated, that of the star in its "robe grise" (*P,* p. 167/189) ("gray robe" (*WS,* p. 11). While both earth and sky are linked in the sea's reflection, the ship metamorphoses to a more inclusive identity: "Tout ce qui est bougeait comme un vaisseau qui tourne / Et glisse" (*P,* p. 168/190) ("All that is, moved like a ship that turns / And glides"—*WS,* p. 13), which will allow for still further expansion. The eighth poem of the sequence begins with another evocation of a single figure that turns out not to be the previous woman and ship of life but the starry sky that bends, still like the woman, toward earth ("Mais ton épaule se déchire dans les arbres, / Ciel étoilé"; "the trees tear your shoulder, sky"). The next stanza reunites both figures under the sign of the imagination—"O notre image encore" ("Our image still")—but imagination wounded by materiality, subsequently called upon to divide itself into a dual reality as the "arbre aux rameaux de nuit doubles, doubles toujours" (*P,* p. 170/192) (tree "whose limbs are the night, branched, and branched again"—*WS,* p. 17). The scene begins to dissolve in the final poem of the sequence, where it takes on the quality of dream, but not before that dream has grown and gathered significance by multiplying its frames of reference.

Pierre écrite marks the intersection of stone and the artistic imagination. Over and over again, the poet brings up the "empty graphism" of modern art and linguistic theory as a problem that the artist must transcend. The answer is not to pretend that polysemy does not exist, or to evade the problem by returning to the false unity of symmetrical form and classical aesthetics: instead, we must accept "rencontrer là dans leur formation toujours récurrente nos ambiguïtés, nos polysémies" (*E,* p. 147) ("meeting our ambiguities, our polysemies, there where they recurrently take shape"). Bonnefoy's way of bringing polysemy into his work is to extend and transform associations from one moment to the next, creating an ambiguity that hints at the infinite regress of semiotic networks.[22] This ambiguity is brought within the realm of art only to be organized by artistic consciousness: Bonnefoy's use of parallelism, reversals, metonymic development, and subtle coordination of expanding references from one framework to the next offers multiplicity, not as raw data, but as patterns of experience. Here is the real role of the "dream" that has been interrogated so severely: as a waking dream, a self-aware use of the imagination, it allows the dreamer to be more than a passive recorder of chance relationships. In an essay on Raoul Ubac, Bonnefoy describes a stone bas-relief in terms that are close to the concerns and even chief images of *Pierre écrite* (published a year after the essay). He notes "les enchevêtrements au hasard, à l'infini du grain . . . de la pierre se prêter à la croissance du signe, étant interprétés comme feuilles d'arbres, comme entrelacements de leurs branches, et se laisser même gagner . . . par une beauté du simple . . . grâce à laquelle c'est l'arbre aussi, l'effrayant arbre réel, qui s'ouvre à notre venue" (*I,* p. 302) ("the random tangles, endlessly along the grain . . . of the stone, lending themselves to the growth of the sign, being interpreted as leaves on trees and as their entwined branches, and being overwhelmed . . . by a beauty made of what is simple . . . thanks to which it is also the tree, the frightening real tree, which opens out upon our arrival"). The stone's cracks and grain carry out the artist's conception of entwined leaves and branches (the sculpture is titled *Arbre*) and both—illustrating the ramifications of the sign—make possible a sudden presence ("notre venue"). In *Pierre écrite,* Bonnefoy displays a similar pattern of dense and polysemous internal references that overlay the multiplicity of the real, and inscribe the shifts of personal consciousness in the plurisignificance of language. It is a tactic of expanding, accumulating, coordinated but always open ramification that catches *presence* in its net, and establishes a proximate unity seized always from within; as such, it gives direction to the moral and aesthetic quest of *Pierre écrite,* and definition to its concluding "Art de la poésie."

Notes

1. Books by Yves Bonnefoy referred to here include the poetry collections *Du mouvement et de l'immobilité de Douve* (Paris: Mercure de France, 1953), *Hier régnant désert* (Paris: Mercure de France, 1958), *Pierre écrite* (Paris: Mercure de France, 1965), *Dans le leurre du seuil* (Paris: Mercure de France, 1975), *Poèmes* (Paris: Mercure de France, 1978), *Poèmes,* with an introduction by Jean Starobinski (Paris: Gallimard, 1982), and *Ce qui fut sans lumière* (Paris: Mercure de France, 1987). Prose works include *L'Improbable et autres essais* (Paris: Mercure de France, 1980), a revised and augmented edition that combines four texts: *L'Improbable* (1959), *Quatre notes* (1953–59), *La Seconde Simplicité* (1961), and *Un Rêve fait à Mantoue* (1967); *Rome 1630: L'Horizon du premier baroque* (Paris: Flammarion, 1970); *L'Arrière-Pays* (Geneva: Skira, 1972); *Le Nuage rouge* (Paris: Mercure de France, 1977); *Rue Traversière* (prose poems) (Paris: Mercure de France, 1977); *Entretiens sur la poésie* (Paris: Payot; Neuchâtel: A la Ba-

connière, 1981); *La Présence et l'image* (Paris: Mercure de France, 1983); and *Récits en rêve* (Paris: Mercure de France, 1987), which combines *L'Arrière-Pays, Rue Traversière, Remarques sur la couleur,* and *L'Origine de la parole.*

References to the separate collections *Du mouvement et de l'immobilité de Douve, Hier régnant désert,* and *Pierre écrite* are taken from the collected *Poèmes* (abbreviated *P* in the textual citations that follow), of which there are two chief editions: one by the Mercure de France in 1978, and one by Gallimard in the "Poésie" series in 1982. Permission to quote the French text of the poems has been granted by *Le Mercure de France.* Page references (to *P*) are double-cited, with the page number of the Mercure de France edition given first. A series of references to a poem will omit the title after the first citation. Other abbreviations are as follows: *L'Improbable* (*The Improbable*): *I; L'Arrière-Pays: AP; Le Nuage rouge: NR; Entretiens sur la poésie: E; La Présence et l'image: PI.*

Translations in the body of the text are my own, except for individual poems or sections of poems from *Pierre écrite,* where I use *Words in Stone,* translated by Susanna Lang in collaboration with Bonnefoy (Amherst: University of Massachusetts Press, 1976), cited as *WS* in text. Permission to quote the translated texts has been given by Ms. Lang.

English translations of Bonnefoy's poetry are also available in *On the Motion and Immobility of Douve,* trans. Galway Kinnell (Athens: Ohio University Press, 1968), *Poems, 1959–1975* (*Pierre écrite* and *Dans le leurre du seuil*), trans. Richard Pevear (New York: Random House, 1985), *Selected Poems* (selections from *Du mouvement et de l'immobilité de Douve, Hier régnant désert,* and *Pierre écrite*), trans. Anthony Rudolf (London: Jonathan Cape, 1968).

The following special issues on Bonnefoy are also of interest: *L'Arc* 66 (October 1976); *World Literature Today* (Summer 1979); and the proceedings of the Colloquium on Bonnefoy held at Cerisg la Salle, *Colloque Yves Bonnefoy* (Marseilles: Sud, 1983).

2. F. C. St. Aubyn, "Yves Bonnefoy: First Existentialist Poet." *Chicago Review* 17 (1964): 118–29.

3. "Un des grands apports de notre époque a été la mise en valeur de ce qu'on appelle le travail du signifiant, et correlativement la dénonciation de certains aspects illusoires de notre conscience de nous-mêmes" (*PI,* p. 15) ("One of the great contributions of our era has been to bring out what is called the working of the signifier, and accordingly to expose certain illusory aspects of our consciousness of ourselves").

4. Charles Baudelaire, *Fusées 22,* cited in Ian W. Alexander, *French Literature and the Philosophy of Consciousness* (New York: St. Martins, 1985), p. 73. (My translation.)

5. Michael Bishop, editor of the Rodopi series, has an interesting short chapter on Bonnefoy in his *The Contemporary Poetry of France: Eight Studies* (Amsterdam: Rodopi, 1985), pp. 117–36.

6. Maurice Merleau-Ponty, *Phénoménologie de la perception* (Paris: Gallimard [Bibliothèque des idées], 1945), p. xi.

7. John E. Jackson, in *Yves Bonnefoy* (Paris: Seghers, collection "Poètes d'aujourd'hui," 1976), p. 14, and Richard Vernier, "Prosodie et silence dans un recueil d'Yves Bonnefoy," *Studia Neophilologica* 16 (1973): 289, 93. See also the short chapter on Bonnefoy by Michael Bishop in his *The Contemporary Poetry of France.* pp. 117–36.

8. In a recent short monograph, Daniel Leuwers shows how the experience of loss and forgetting impels Bonnefoy to complicate his description of "presence,"

especially in work after *Pierre écrite*. See Daniel Leuwers, *Yves Bonnefoy* (Amsterdam: Rodopi, 1988).

9. Gérard Gasarian, "La 'rhétorique négative' dans la poésie d'Yves Bonnefoy," *Critique* 420 (May 1982): 376.

10. Gérard Gasarian later suggests a Freudian thematics of maternal origins to explain this deferred original meaning. See his *Yves Bonnefoy: La poésie, la présence* (Seyssel: Champ Vallon, collection "Champ Poétique," 1986).

11. Mary Ann Caws, *Yves Bonnefoy* (Boston: Twayne, World Authors Series, 1984), p. 20.

12. Yves Bonnefoy, *Pierre écrite* (Paris: Maeght, 1959). Eight poems accompany the lithographs in this volume, which was devoted to the artist's work and published as *Ubac* in the collection *Derrière le miroir* (Paris: Maeght, 1958). There are some minor changes between the poems printed in 1958–59 and those in the title section as published in 1965.

13. John E. Jackson, *La Question du moi: T. S. Eliot, Paul Celan, Yves Bonnefoy* (Neuchâtel: La Baconnière, 1978), p. 292.

14. Jean-Pierre Richard, *Onze Etudes sur la poésie moderne* (Paris: Seuil, 1964), p. 222.

15. Maurin's argument is based on the fact that the first section of *Douve* contains only nineteen poems, two short of twenty-one, whereas the middle sections consist of three sets of fourteen poems and the last section contains seven poems. Vernier's response occurs in "Prosodie et silence," p. 289; he continues his discussion of Bonnefoy's style and its relation to point of view in *Yves Bonnefoy ou les mots comme le ciel* (Tübingen: Gunter Narr Verlag, 1985).

16. Frédéric Deloffre, "Versification traditionnelle et versification libérée d'après un recueil d'Yves Bonnefoy," in *Le Vers français au XXième siècle,* ed. Monique Parent (Paris: Klincksieck, 1967), p. 55.

17. John T. Naughton, *The Poetics of Yves Bonnefoy* (Chicago: University of Chicago Press, 1984), p. 25.

18. See Sarah Lawall, "Yves Bonnefoy and Denis Roche: Art and the Art of Poetry," in *About French Poetry from Dada to Tel Quel*, ed. M. A. Caws (Detroit: Wayne State University Press, 1974), pp. 69–95.

19. Bonnefoy, *La Poésie française et le principe d'identité* (Paris: Maeght, 1967).

20. Jackson, *Yves Bonnefoy,* pp. 49–53.

21. See also Sarah Lawall and Mary Ann Caws, "A Style of Silence: Two Readings of Yves Bonnefoy's Poetry," *Contemporary Literature* 16, no. 2 (1975): 193–217.

22. But only hints at such regress: just as Bonnefoy's ambiguity is not the rational coordination of alternative readings described by William Empson in *Seven Types of Ambiguity* (1930), so it is not the "enigma text" of indefinable meanings and infinite regress studied by Marjorie Perloff in *The Poetics of Indeterminacy: Rimbaud to Cage* (Princeton, N.J.: Princeton University Press, 1981). It might be compared with what Hugh Silverman calls "hermeneutic semiology" in his "Phenomenology: From Hermeneutics to Deconstruction," *Research in Phenomenology* 14 (1984): 32. Finally, a semiotician of the type Bonnefoy decries would probably charge that the poet's strategies for evoking "presence" actually recuperate the idealist One by incorporating it in the bloody rebirth of a new poetic persona. At this point, it is not so much a matter of categorizing what Bonnefoy has done as of examining the literary strategies he has devised, and their corresponding aims.

CONTRIBUTORS

INDEX

Contributors

Kevin Brownlee is Professor of French at the University of Pennsylvania and author of *The Poetic Identity of Guillaume de Machaut* (1984).

Sylvia Huot is Associate Professor of French at Northern Illinois University and author of *From Song to Book* (1987).

George Joseph is Associate Professor of French at Hobart and William Smith Colleges and author of *Clément Marot* (1985).

Doranne Fenoaltea is Professor of French at the University of Florida, Gainesville. Her most recent book is *Du palais au jardin* (1990).

Catherine Ingold is President of the American University in Paris, and coeditor of the Saint-Amant section in *La Poésie française du premier 17e siècle: textes et contextes* (1986).

David Lee Rubin is Professor of French at the University of Virginia and editor of *Continuum* (1989–). His most recent book is *A Pact with Silence* (1991).

The late John Porter Houston was Professor of French at Indiana University and author of more than a dozen books on poetry and fiction in French and English from the Renaissance to the twentieth century.

Sandra Daniel, who has written extensively on nineteenth-century French literature, lives in Charleston, South Carolina.

Suzanne Nash is Professor of French at Princeton University. Her study *Paul Valéry's* Album de vers anciens: *A Past Transformed* was published in 1983.

Sarah Lawall is Professor of Comparative Literature and Adjunct Professor of French at the University of Massachusetts (Amherst). Since *Critics of Consciousness* (1968), she has published many essays on literary theory and modern French poetry.

Index